OLD WIVES'

AND OTHER WOMEN

Tania Modleski

OLD WIVES' TALES

AND OTHER WOMEN'S STORIES

NEW YORK UNIVERSITY PRESS
New York and London

NEW YORK UNIVERSITY PRESS
New York and London

© 1998 by Tania Modleski

Library of Congress Cataloging-in-Publication Data
Modleski, Tania, 1949–
Old wives' tales, and other women's stories / Tania Modleski.
p.   cm.
Includes bibliographical references (p.   ) and index.
Portions of some chapters have been previously published in
slightly different form.
ISBN 0-8147-5593-3 (acid-free paper)
1. American literature—20th century—History and
criticism—Theory, etc. 2. Feminism and literature—United
States—History—20th century. 3. Women and literature—United
States—History—20th century. 4. Feminism—United
States—History—20th century. 5. Feminist criticism—United
States. I. Title.
PS152 .M63 1998
810.9'00082—ddc21   98-25366
CIP

New York University Press books are printed on acid-free paper,
and their binding materials are chosen for strength and durability.

Manufactured in the United States of America

10 9 8 7 6 5 4 3 2 1

For Teresa McKenna

CONTENTS

ACKNOWLEDGMENTS

I would like to thank the National Endowment for the Humanities, which generously provided me with a grant that enabled me to write portions of this book.

I an indebted to many people for reading and commenting on the manuscript and to many others for inspiration and support. Thanks to Sophia Nardin, Jane Nardin, Teresa McKenna, Tania Coiner, Nadia Medina, Dana Polan, Patrice Petro, Hilary Schor, Devon Hodges, Maeera Shreiber, and Vincent Cheng.

I am grateful to Karin Quimby and Amy Garawitz for their valuable research assistance. Thanks also to Jennifer Morrow for research assistance and assistance in the preparation of the manuscript.

Finally, thanks to the students in my graduate seminar on women and genre for their enthusiasm and insights.

Portions of the following chapters have been published in slightly altered form:

"Breaking Silence, or an Old Wives' Tale: Sexual Harassment and the Legitimation Crisis," in *Discourse* 16.1 (Fall 1993): 109–25.

"Ax the Piano Player," in *The Psychoanalytic Review* 84.5 (October 1997): 727–42.

"My Life as a Romance Reader," in *Paradoxa* 3.1–2 (1997): 15–28.

"The White Negress and the Heavy Duty Dyke," in *Cross-Purposes: Lesbians, Feminists, and the Limits of Alliance.* Ed. Dana Heller (Bloomington: Indiana University Press, 1997), 64–82.

"A Woman's Gotta Do . . . What a Man's Gotta Do? Cross-Dressing in the Western," in *Signs* 22.3 (Spring 1997): 519–44.

"Doing Justice to the Subjects: The Work of Anna Deavere Smith," in *Female Subjects in Black and White*, ed. Elizabeth Abel, Barbara Christian, and Helene Moglen (Berkeley: University of California Press, 1997), 57–76.

INTRODUCTION

Feminist Criticism Today: Notes from Jurassic Park

❏

The initial impetus for this work came out of a long, brewing reaction to my previous book, which I had written, in part, to challenge some of the ideas that had gained currency within feminist theory and popular culture—ideas which had the effect of marginalizing women or effacing them entirely. Not to keep the reader guessing about my main argument, the cover illustration showed a family of four reading a book together, and the woman's face and body were whited out. Of course, the title of my book also said it all: *Feminism without Women*.

So when I began to conceive of my new project, I thought why not put women back into the picture? Maybe I could, figuratively, white out the man for a change, even the kids. Why not look at new work being produced by women in the cultural sphere? At first I conceived the project broadly, thinking I would write a book about women as cultural producers. Then I conceived it more narrowly, a book about women filmmakers. In the end, as I shall presently explain, neither of these topics exactly fit the contours of the book I ended up writing.

I

My previous book had denounced a phenomenon I had labeled "post-feminism." By that term I meant to designate a state of affairs in which feminism was presumed to have won the day and thus to have rendered feminist critique unnecessary. In thinking of a new project, I felt it would be interesting to look at a phenomenon I began to conceive of as "postfeminism in the good sense." I had in mind the kind of work by women artists that might challenge certain feminist orthodoxies but that in fact has been made possible by feminist politics itself. In other words, it seemed to me that women artists are now able to risk being labeled as politically incorrect because they can assume a certain level of feminist consciousness on the part of their audience, and, equally importantly, can be assured of a ready market for their work. Insofar as they expand women's turf, the explorations of these intrepid artists, I believe, have the potential to benefit us all.

What I began to fear about undertaking such a project, however, is that I would unwittingly be contributing to the misconceptions of revisionist histories of feminism and feminist cultural theory that minimize the boldness of earlier feminists, exaggerate their political and theoretical naiveté, and grant all the complexity to a new generation. I can identify the precise moment at which my worry was born, the moment I became aware that generational issues *were* at stake.

Sitting in on a discussion of current feminist literary criticism, I heard a woman some years my junior praise the work of another feminist scholar she judged to be on the cutting edge of a "second generation of feminist critics" (generations, it appears, can now span as little as five to eight years). She spoke with envy of the accomplishments of the second scholar, saying "A lot of us have been interested in looking at the work of seventies feminism, working with it and against it, but she does it better than anyone else."

And I'm sitting in the back of the room, thinking "Yoo hoo. I'm still here. Not a dinosaur. Not dead yet." I had thought that most of us "seventies feminists" had not been left behind but had constantly been involved in feminist debates, continually modifying and reassessing our positions. I had thought a lot of us were as up to date as many of our younger sisters. Why, if that was the case, would a new "generation" want to go back to the ideas of the seventies—as if they still existed in some pristine condition—in order to dispute them and complicate them when those ideas no longer hold sway even among the "older feminists" who have *themselves* disputed and complicated them? To put it succinctly, why would they want to fossilize us when we have evolved?

Not long after, I read a book of feminist literary criticism in which the feminist dinosaur actually made an appearance. In *The Erotics of Talk*, a study of some of the literary texts that have been canonized by feminist critics, Carla Kaplan, who explicitly places herself in the category of younger feminist, aims to complicate one of the dominant reading practices of seventies and early eighties literary criticism, in which the critic presumably reads literature for stories about herself (25). She links the critical enterprise of the so-called earlier literary feminists to the project of consciousness-raising, which, says Kaplan, sought to emphasize only the commonalities among women and repressed difference. Of consciousness-raising Kaplan writes: It "sometimes seems like a lumbering dinosaur, waddling off to be replaced by sleeker, more elegant, less sentimental paradigms, ones that don't rely on identification and essentialism, that recognize the mutability and contingency of identity, that better understand the built-in difficulties of audition and recognition" (156).

A lumbering, waddling dinosaur. Gosh. I hadn't realized our image had deteriorated that badly. Although Kaplan raises the specter of the dinosaur in the context of a criticism of "performativity" feminists like Judith Butler who have tended to regard consciousness-raising as a bankrupt practice and an utter failure, I still wish she hadn't put it quite that way. Such images have a performative power of their own and can't help but be a bit galling to the older, i.e. middle-aged, feminist.

Despite Kaplan's qualified defense of consciousness-raising in the final chapter of her book and depite the dazzling persuasiveness of her readings, what concerns me is that by focusing on one strand of feminist criticism she may end up confirming a newer generation's perception of earlier feminism as bland, monolithic, and wholly repressive. For, as I have discovered in the last few years at conferences and in graduate seminars, it seems to be more and more the prevailing view that the seventies and eighties feminism was hostile to all expressions of difference and intolerant of all but the most repressive affirmations of sisterhood. This view seems to have provoked an extreme reaction on the part of feminist literary critics who appear to be intent on uncovering evidence of, and thus in a way eliciting, what Helena Michie calls "sororophobia." In contrast to earlier feminists who supposedly sought only their own likeness, sororophobic critics emphasize difference, discord, and dissension, engaging in a hermeneutics of suspicion and viewing with distrust appeals to shared problems and agendas.

By now the sororophobia paradigm seems to be well entrenched. But for it to have established itself, it has been necessary for many contemporary feminists to ignore or downplay the heated debates that occurred among seventies and eighties feminists and feminist literary critics and to oversimplify many of their arguments and models. This has led to a paradoxical enterprise in which the sororophobic critic represses the differences at stake in two decades of feminist thought while taking it to task for itself engaging in such repression. Lest the uninformed reader be misled by such misrepresentations, I want briefly to review the history of debates that have characterized feminist literary criticism almost since its inception.[1]

If it is demonstrably true, as I would claim it is, that consciousness-raising clearly emanated from and addressed a more diverse group of women than current academic feminism can hope to reach, it is also true that seventies and eighties feminist literary criticism, which today is accused of tolerating only one paradigm—and a very repressive one at that—was characterized by a great deal more contentiousness and debate than is often supposed. One main source of conflict, of course, was over the role of continental philosophy in theorizing feminism. I recall, for example, a special issue of *diacritics*, published in 1982, on the topic. The issue centered on the French feminist challenge to certain forms of American feminism. It included an exchange between Peggy Kamuf, a Derridean scholar, and Nancy Miller, a "French-feminist" American critic, who debated the usefulness of the term "woman" and the advisability of instituting women's studies in the academy. At least three versions (or "paradigms," if you will) of feminism were in play in the debate: the so-called American feminist position (not represented by a debater in the *diacritics* issue), the French deconstructive position (Kamuf's), and the position (Miller's) which sought to bridge what seemed like a gulf between the two positions. (I remember that Miller invoked a conceit comparing feminism to shoes—with American feminists wearing the sensible kind, and French feminists, the stylish but impractical sort. Apparently, to the "younger feminists," we have outlived the relevance of Miller's conceit: today, regardless of where we stood in relation to continental philosophy, we all wear Dr. Scholl's.)

It cannot be stressed enough that virtually every attempt in the seventies and eighties to establish a prevailing paradigm was met with vociferous resistance. I recall that when Sandra Gilbert and Susan Gubar published their magisterial work *The Madwoman in the Attic,* Mary Jacobus criticized it in a review in *Signs* using criteria widely accepted today among feminist critics. Jacobus felt Gilbert and Gubar repressed the diversity of women's literature by always finding the same story, the story of the author's—and the reader's—resistance to patriarchal culture. I also recall a lecture given by Gilbert and Gubar at the University of Wisconsin at Milwaukee in which they attacked Jacques Lacan and Jacques Derrida, calling the latter Derridada and his feminist followers Derridaughters. Jane Gallop stood up in the audience and attacked the pair, who hastily assured her that she and they were not in fundamental disagreement. But Gallop refused to back down, insisting that in fact they really, really did disagree.

In addition, Gallop's brand of psychoanalysis, like that of film and literary theorist Jacqueline Rose, represented a challenge to the kind of psychoanalytic literary criticism that tended to seek out sameness. Most of this latter sort of criticism drew on the work of Nancy Chodorow whose aim had been to explain why women identify so strongly with their mothers and why they want to reproduce, as their mothers did. Chodorow's theory was applied to literature by critics interested in devising models of the sort of readings rejected by so many feminists today, readings that drew on the formation of the mother/daughter bond to explain the reader's identification with the heroine and with the author. But other feminists like Rose attacked Chodorow's brand of psychoanalysis and continually emphasized the failures of identification and the fractured nature of identity.

Furthermore, literary criticism by women of color began making itself felt from very early on. While some white feminists may have stubbornly refused to back down from an analysis that acknowledged only commonalities among women, the work of women of color gained ground rapidly among white feminist critics. *This Bridge Called My Back: Writings by Radical Women of Color*, edited by Gloria Anzaldua and Cherrie Moraga, was published in 1981. Its purpose was not merely to challenge white women's racism and not merely to insist on the differences between white women and women of color, but equally importantly to explore the bonds among diverse women of color. The project was to affirm similarities, while also acknowledging differences, impediments to mutual understanding, and prejudices. Around that time Biddy Martin and Chandra Mohanty wrote a highly influential article, "Feminist Politics," with a similar purpose. The effort to negotiate difference while theorizing a way to hold on to ties that bind women to one another—common experiences, similar backgrounds, and/or values and ideals—seems to me even today to be much more satisfying intellectually and politically than a model which forces us to choose between similarity or difference—and this, I would argue, is equally the case with the imaginary ties formed between a work of art or a literary work and its consumers. Some of the most exciting contemporary work by female artists is motivated by this double imperative, or so I argue in my discussion of Anna Deavere Smith in this volume.

The writings of critics like Martin and Mohanty seem to me to represent a high-water mark in feminist criticism and theory. Some of the complexity that characterizes such work has in my view drained out of the feminist critical enterprise. Therefore I choose, somewhat contrary to my original intention as I described it at the beginning of this introduction, to represent myself not as someone who is breaking, even partially, with the feminist past because of its alleged naiveté, but as someone who is continuing in its fine tradition. And indeed, as I look over the essays collected here in my book, I see that one of the threads running through them is a refusal to cede complexity to those feminisms that simplify or caricature the history of feminist literary and cultural theory, making themselves appear to have risen from the ashes of a tradition they themselves have torched.

Thus in the opening chapter on Anita Hill I begin by looking at the way one self-proclaimed proponent of postmodern feminism caricatures a tradition that arose out of consciousness-raising and that emphasizes the authority of experience. The writer mocks this feminist tradition, claiming it relies on a naive belief in the transparency of language, a faith in language's ability to directly transmit "authentic experience." I suggest that by focusing on the issue of narrative we avoid the extremes of, on the one hand, a feminism which despairs of communicating experience and, on the other, a feminism naively optimistic about the ability of language to name and change reality. Our experience of reality is never direct and immediate, but is given shape in part by the stories that circulate in a given culture. As most of the feminist commentators on the Thomas/Hill hearings pointed out, the narratives enabling Hill's detractors to discredit her accounts were manifold and threatened to swamp Hill's testimony, which many found incomprehensible. But Hill's story did get told, and in the end a lot of people judged it credible. Rosemary Bray points out that the narratives weren't entirely arrayed against Hill. There was in fact precedent for her account of her experience as a victim of sexual harassment. Bray situates Hill's testimony in a tradition of sentimental fiction, a genre with roots in the nineteenth century. Bray compares Hill to the nineteenth-century slave Harriet Jacobs, another victim of sexual harassment (on the part of her white master). According to Bray, Jacobs made use of the genre in order to communicate a tale she insists is true, incredible as she feared the story would be to her readers. As Bray's analysis leads us to understand, fiction lies at the heart of truth, but it doesn't for all that make the experience less true.

This brings me to the common thread uniting all the chapters. Each of them deals with genre. Genres, of course, consist of the often-told stories people in a given culture use to make sense of the world; such stories, as I

7

have said, mediate between us and "reality." For me, some of the crucial questions for a politically engaged feminist cultural criticism are how the stories that women tell get legitimated or discredited, and how feminism can help and has helped to change the stories and thereby change the conscious and unconscious fantasies that wed us psychically to particular versions of reality. The title of my book, *Old Wives' Tales*, is meant to flag these issues. In choosing it, I wanted to suggest that many of the stories told by women are always already discredited by the larger culture. On the one hand, feminism can help grant legitimacy to women's tales, and by circulating them can continue to alter our very experience of reality. On the other hand, feminism obviously ought not to affirm women's accounts simply because they *are* women's, for sometimes the stories women tell *qua* wives, like the ones invoked by Clarence Thomas's wife, are intended to discredit other women's stories and to shore up patriarchy. The double meaning intended by my title captures, I hope, the complexity of my relation to genre (to say nothing of the category of "woman") elucidated in the chapters that follow.

Thus by the time the reader finishes this book, I hope she finds it impossible to situate me in either of the camps that appear to be at war in feminism. These essays will, I hope, serve to document the struggle of one seventies, eighties, and nineties feminist—me—to hold onto some basic political beliefs and goals while remaining attuned to important cultural changes which women have wrought and from which they stand to benefit.

The struggle is most clearly in evidence in the two articles published here on romances. In the early eighties I and several other women published studies of romance that attempted to grapple with the complexities of these enormously popular novels and of their effect on readers. Most of us critics recognized that romances, like all forms of popular fiction, do in many ways endorse the status quo; at the same time, we all looked at them somewhat sympathetically in order to think about what they offered women that patriarchal culture denied them. Having continued to read romances over the years, I seized an opportunity to write an article about transformations in the genre since the late seventies. At the request of Kay Mussell, who was editing a special issue on romances for the journal *Paradoxa,* I wrote a personal piece in which I discussed my own relation to romantic fantasies over the years, looking at the conflicts and contradictions I, as a feminist, experienced in being so attracted to them. I talked about how my attitude toward romances has mellowed, in part because I have changed and in part because they seem to be changing as well.

When the *Paradoxa* issue was published, it turned out I was practically the only person among a host of critics and romance writers who *had any reservations whatsoever about the genre.* All the writers attacked the earlier studies as simplistic, as well as entirely negative in their evaluation of romances. They touted themselves as "cutting edge" authors and critics, who, as I put it in my rejoinder, had achieved the full flowering of feminist consciousness. I responded by pointing to some of the absurdities of the claims made on behalf of romances (e.g., "Reading and writing a romance may be the most subversive thing a woman can do when it comes to contesting patriarchal culture"). I felt it necessary to insist once again on a claim I would have thought was unimpeachable: that far too many romances continue to eroticize male dominance and that this is not such a good thing.

Now, it is true that I could have rewritten the essays so that I presented my ideas as a seamless whole, the final, definitive word on romances in the nineties. But I thought it important at least to try to demonstrate how the critic who wishes to stay relevant yet politically committed is continually shifting and responding to a changing world. This is one of the reasons several of these essays have a personal dimension. The last chapter in particular, dealing with the death of my mother (invoking the genre of the maternal melodrama), seeks to pit the certainty of our theories against the contradictoriness of our lives. The chapter presents my mother as a model of a woman who, despite all the forces physically weighing her down in her last years, struggled to keep moving. Utterly faithful daughter of the patriarchy that she was, she nevertheless inspires her feminist daughter to keep trying to be the peripatetic critic.

In many ways, of course, genre, with its conventions and the security provided by predictable endings, represents stasis and fixity and thus appears at odds with a project that seeks evidence of psychic and social transformations. Female genres, those genres which have traditionally appealed to women, are perhaps the most rigid of all. Romances tell the same courtship story over and over. Melodrama and the Gothic, only a little less predictable than romances in their plots, deal with people who are trapped in their world—hence the "claustral" nature of the genres, to use Peter Brooks's term. The maternal melodrama particularly, in demanding female self-sacrifice, requires women to relinquish their own plots so that others may have theirs. But precisely because such generic stories exert such a strong psychic hold on most of us, women who seek to change the stories and the feminist critics who try to detect those changes, often find themselves having to come to terms with them. So the first part of the book looks at transformations occurring in women's genres and looks at the way new realities, or new critiques of existing realities, are being articulated in forms familiar and pleasurable to masses of women.

Women artists are not, however, confining themselves to genres traditionally thought of as female. They are not staying in their appointed places, but are moving into male genres like minstrelsy (the blackface tradition of entertainment), the war film, and the Western—the genres I turn to in the second part of the book. Throughout the latter half of the book I look at how male fantasies have in fact shaped the lives of both men *and* women in this culture and how women artists are crossing borders and staking out territory declared off-limits by men and also, importantly, by some feminists. For to the extent that feminists have affirmed popular genres at all, they have tended to affirm only female ones like sentimental fiction or the woman's film. Many feminists would at one time have deplored the authorial "transvestism" I explore here, judging it to be a capitulation to a masculine system of values. In fact "transvestism" was a term of opprobrium in film theory during the seventies and eighties, and we used it to designate what we viewed as the altogether unfortunate plight of the female spectator forced to identify with a man in patriarchal cinema. New work on transvestism as a positive condition, however, enables us to rethink the issue—and Maggie Greenwald's film *The Ballad of Little Jo,* about a woman who cross-dressed in the West, provides a perfect occasion for such reflection.

Two essays present readings of work that can be situated in the largely (and justly) discredited blackface tradition of entertainment which throughout its history in nineteenth- and twentieth-century America has chiefly been a male preserve. In my chapters on Sandra Bernhard and Anna Deavere Smith, I ask what happens when *women* do themselves up, figuratively, in blackface or indeed in whiteface. Both essays make reference to a history of blackface in Jewish entertainment, showing how blacks have traditionally been made to represent a fixed pole at one end of the racial continuum, thereby enabling others a mobility denied to them. In the chapter on Smith I point out how the black woman in particular has been made to represent space (and how critics and reporters continue the tradition by referring to Smith as theater, as medium, rather than actor). Smith's work militates very strongly against this state of affairs, as the title of the series of her work—"On the Road"—clearly indicates.

The tug of the familiar, the pull of the strange and the new: this book takes it on faith that life itself is characterized by the desire for sameness and the desire for difference, as well as by longings which propel us forward in desire, fear, and hope and those which exert the magnetic force of a past invested with the same affects: the poignant memories of long ago, the horror of being trapped in the past, the hope born out of ancient dreams.

In many ways I have tried to be true to the past, yet committed to a future augured by so many propitious signs in the present, and I see these commitments as intertwined. So I look to the old stories for signs of renewal and change. Hence the emphasis on genre. And I look to the recent past where the latest dreams of a feminist future were born. I try (it is not always easy) to be receptive to voices which say the dreams sometimes weren't ambitious enough, inclusive enough. Some of those voices have spoken, though, without fully acknowledging the legacies of the past. Hence the quarrels with some current feminist theory and political agendas.

12

I don't know if there will be a sequel to these "Notes from Jurassic Park." I would like to believe that announcements of my extinction have been premature. But even if you think differently, could you ever really be sure? Remember what happens in the movies when you feel certain that the monsters have been put to death. Just when you think you're safe you find yourself in a darkened theater anticipating an entirely different sort of movie, and then during the previews of coming attractions you suddenly hear the ominous words:

"We're baaa-aack."

I

BREAKING SILENCE, OR AN OLD WIVES' TALE

Sexual Harassment and the Legitimation Crisis

❑

In an article on politics and the body published in a special issue of *differences* on postmodern feminist politics, the author Joan Cocks outlines, via a reading of Nietzsche, what she calls the "degeneration of radical politics" (152). Toward the end of the piece Cocks observes: "We find in segments of the population hyper-alert to the sexual harassment and abuse of women and children (a real enough harassment and abuse, to be sure), a suspicion of all socio-physical entanglements, a distaste for the confused opaque jostling in life in which, barring the grave offense, people must fend for themselves" (154). Written before the Thomas hearings, this statement, notwithstanding its parenthetical qualifier, will from a post-Thomas perspective, strike many feminists as itself symptomatic of a degeneration of radical feminist politics. Cocks joins up with men all across the land who have been deploring the fact that since Hill's allegations, they don't know where to draw the line anymore, that the most innocent forms of affectionate display in the work place are liable to be misconstrued, that the "confused opaque jostling in life" in which women "ought to fend for themselves" is now interpretable as sexual harassment and men are in constant danger of being victimized by sexually hyper-alert women. As to the question of what constitutes the "grave offense," Cocks gives no specifics; but we might note that one strategy in discrediting sexual harassment complaints is precisely to deny the gravity of almost *any* accusation. Definition is in fact precisely at issue: Who is authorized in a patriarchal society to make and enforce definitions of sexual abuse? And on what grounds and in whose interests are they made? These questions, precisely the questions, I would submit, for a feminist political theory, are entirely elided in the article.

Turning to Cocks's footnotes, where she lists some of the degenerates, we find the name of Catharine MacKinnon, whose work is sure to crop up in almost any discussion—and there are many such today—which deplores feminist theory's alleged hyper-alertness to women's sexual victimization. It will come as no surprise to most of my readers that Catharine MacKinnon is *persona non grata* in many academic feminist circles. Yet inasmuch as feminists were generally united in their misery over the Thomas hearing and its outcome, the time may be right for a rethinking of the feminist challenge mounted in some quarters to theorists and activists like MacKinnon who, it will be recalled, wrote her first book on sexual harassment in the work place and who was co-counsel in the Supreme Court case which made sexual harassment illegal for the first time in history. Given that the wife of Supreme Court Justice Clarence Thomas declared in an infamous *People Magazine* article that she feels Thomas "doesn't owe any of the groups who opposed him anything," we might expect MacKinnon's and feminism's victory in court to be short-lived and women having to fight this battle along with the abortion rights battle and the Affirmative Action battle all over again (108). Theorists need to be ready to prepare the ground for and reflect on feminist practice in the struggles that lie ahead.

In this chapter I want to examine in light of the Thomas hearings, contemporary feminists' attack on the belief in a shared "experience" (like that of sexual harassment) among women that cuts across race and class lines and hence can serve as a ground of feminist political action. Some feminists argue against the viability of this notion by appealing both to the way race and class divide women and to the fact that the language in which women's experiences are articulated cannot be trusted to render them accurately; some feminist legal scholars have turned to feminist literary theory to mount this latter challenge, and at the end of the chapter I want to turn to a brief consideration of the new alliance between law and literature to ascertain whether those of us in the humanities can join with feminists in legal studies to work for political change.

The belief in a commonality of "experience" among women, which once would have been sufficient grounds for feminist action around the Thomas/Hill episode, has frequently been assailed in certain quarters of feminist theory for being essentialist, as is the related belief that breaking silence and speaking about one's sexual experience can be liberating and lead to effective political action. "Within modernity, [the] voicing of women's experience acquires an inherently confessional cast," says Wendy Brown, writing in the same issue as Cocks and referring to Foucault's thesis that to speak about sex is to play directly into power.[1] Telling the truth about one's sex, in Foucault's formulation, is to relinquish sexuality to the authorities who use the knowledge gained about it for the purposes of social control. But for women, the paradoxes of speaking what they take to be the Truth about sex, especially when it concerns an act of sexual abuse perpetrated against them, are more excruciating than any encountered in Foucault. Catharine MacKinnon writes of one paradox in a way that will seem painfully accurate to those who were riveted to the television during the hearing. "One dimension of [the] problem involves whether a woman who has been violated through sex has any credibility. Credibility is difficult to separate from the definition of the injury, since an injury in which the victim is not believed to have been injured *because she has been injured* is not a real injury, legally speaking" (110). The state of affairs MacKinnon describes is a deconstructor's dream: woman is alienated from the truth about her experience in the very act of experiencing it. The sexually violated woman, it might be said, exemplifies the postmodern condition, personifying the crisis in legitimation and signifying on her discredited body what Nietzsche called, in a phrase much celebrated today, the untruth of truth.[2] (Incidentally, we might note that the defense in the Mike Tyson trial tried, unsuccessfully, to mobilize an argument which involved a double bind similar to the one described by MacKinnon, but from the male side. Through his attorney Tyson claimed—with considerable agreement expressed in public opinion polls—that his victim had no case because she allowed herself to be alone with him when it was generally known that Tyson was sexually aggressive with women. So, it would seem, a man cannot be a rapist if he is a rapist, and known to be such, just as a rape victim is often considered to be uninjured because she has been injured). In the face of the Kafkaesque nature of the legal system as women experience it, how do feminists who have witnessed a crisis in legitimation in women's accounts of their experience told in many mass cultural spectacles (not only the Thomas hearing but, for instance, the Kennedy-Smith rape trial) respond to a feminism which seems increasingly to be in complicity with the phantasmatic logic of patriarchal systems?

MacKinnon's solution to the problem is quite different from a certain vulgar Foucauldian position which would counsel silence; rather, she has attempted throughout the years to get women's voices heard and to develop "an account of the world from women's point of view"; in doing so she has frequently been condemned as essentialist. Wendy Brown, for example, taking a stand against MacKinnon's project, notes that women's words "cannot be anointed as Authentic or True since the experience they announce is linguistically contained, socially constructed, discursively mediated, and never just individually 'had'" (72). Brown is surely right to call into question a naiveté, where it does exist, about the ability of language to convey in a transparent way the truth about experience. But, just as surely, the task for a feminism skeptical about the "transparency" of language is not to celebrate, in Cocks's terminology, the "confused opacity" of life in which women who struggle to assign meaning to experiences of sexual violation are considered to be hysterically overreacting to men who are, after all, just jostling. If experience is socially constructed, as we are constantly reminded these days, how can women get to be social-construction workers in building their own truths (instead of always being the construction site)? If experiences are never simply "had" (although some, I would argue, come very close), how do women begin to discuss their experiences of *being* "had"?

There is a way to avoid the unproductive extremes of the transparency/opacity divide: we can look at the ways in which meaning and legitimation become loci of contestation, as various narratives which shape our understanding and experience of events circulate and get accredited or discredited in the process. This is a point made frequently by contributors to the volume on the Hill/Thomas controversy, *Race-ing Justice, En-gendering Power,* edited by Toni Morrison. Indeed, Christine Stansell in her essay, "White Feminists and Black Realities: The Politics of Authenticity," shows that prior to Hill's allegations, MacKinnon had actually spoken in favor of the Thomas nomination because, rather than seeing Thomas's story of growing up in poverty in the rural south as following "a more or less conventional narrative" (one which "turns upon the moment Thomas left his downtrodden mother to live with his grandfather"), she praised the judge's connection with "reality." Stansell quotes MacKinnon, "[Thomas] approaches issues from an actual experiential base rather than the kind of abstracted-from-life categories of legal analysis. . . . When he talks, he seems to start off with life experiences" (255). (It should be noted that MacKinnon's mistaken allegiance stemmed less from her problematic use of the term "life experiences" than from the logical fallacy of her thinking, which, starting from the notion that feminism draws on life experiences, concludes by assuming that anyone drawing on life experiences is feminist).

I would like to pursue the question of narrative and its relation to experience by focusing on a character who has not been much discussed in feminist analyses of the Hill/Thomas hearings: Virginia Thomas. My primary point of reference will be the extraordinary interview of her in *People Magazine,* on the cover of which we see Clarence Thomas, as one letter to the editor describes him, "grinning and hugging his wife like the latest television celebrity" (Stovall). The interview is entitled "Breaking Silence"—a title which exhibits the tendency of mass media to appropriate the words and slogans of the dominated group (here a slogan about the necessity *of*

17

speaking out) and to twist them to suit the interests of those in power. Virginia Thomas actually reveals that she herself has suffered from sexual harassment, but with the help of her husband got the problem solved "discreetly" (111). Thomas's revelation about her own experience places her in the company of a huge number of women, since, of course, during the hearings women continually testified to having been subjected to sexual harassment; what was disturbing about these revelations was that in this particular case the women "broke silence" only so as to place their experience in the service of a man charged with having harassed another woman. Indeed, Thomas's "breaking silence" was itself emphatically *not* connected to her experience of harassment but to the silence imposed on her during her husband's ordeal: "Forced to endure her husband's trial by fire, a wife speaks out at last" (108). Thomas wants to make a clear-cut distinction between her own experience of harassment and that allegedly experienced by Hill: "It wasn't verbal harassment, it was physical," she says, thereby invoking difference of experience to deny commonality with other women, a position which ironically allies her with certain anti-essentialist feminist theorists (111).

Apropos of "breaking silence," we may note in passing the double bind of a woman like Anita Hill in relation to the mass media. Punished during the proceedings by being subjected to the constant insinuation that she was telling these events to gain publicity for herself—i.e., to sell her story—she was then punished for *refusing* to tell her story for fame or a fee: "More than a dozen times in the past few weeks, *People* approached Anita Hill or her representatives for her account of her unwanted time in the spotlight, but she has declined to be interviewed" (108). Having absolved themselves of the responsibility to present both sides, *People* allows itself carte blanche (as it were) to publish the outraged wife's vilification of the wronged woman.

These accusations are shaped for us by being embedded in a narrative that has had an incalculably strong impact on the nation's psyche. Insisting again on difference between the women, Virginia Thomas says, "My case was also different because what she did was so obviously political, as opposed to trying to resolve the problem. And what's scary about her allegations is that they remind me of the movie *Fatal Attraction* or, in her case, what I call the fatal assistant. In my heart I always believed she was probably someone in love with my husband and never got what she wanted" (111). And so Anita Hill becomes in the "Virginia Thomas Story" the single woman so desperate for love and sex that she metamorphoses into a psychopath. There is, however, a strong irony here when we consider that, as in the film *Fatal Attraction*, it is the wife who kills off the other woman for the preservation of the family; only in Anita Hill's case it is a question of *character* assassination. Moreover, what Thomas fails to mention is that in the film, the husband *really did* become sexually involved with the woman.

The headline on the cover of the magazine trumpets the words, "How We Survived," suggesting that melodrama, not the suspense thriller, was the prevailing genre in the unfolding of the story. Thus, when Clarence Thomas finished his discussion of the trials and tribulations of growing up poor in the rural South, George Bush observed, "there wasn't a dry eye in the house." One of the Democratic senators who spoke on the day of the vote alluded to this remark, and invoked Richard Wright's determination in writing *Native Son* to construct a story that no one ("bankers daughters" is the group Wright invoked) could shed a tear over, a story that would deny middle-class whites the luxury of pathos. The senator continued, "At this point in time, Mr. President, America cannot afford the sentimentalization of black culture."

The first and most well-known melodrama of suffering black manhood, another narrative that has riveted America for well over a century, is, of course, *Uncle Tom's Cabin,* written by a white woman, Harriet Beecher Stowe (references to Uncle Thomas have indeed not been lacking in the alternative press). It is Stowe's story that Wright was writing against, countering with a more militant, angry version of black manhood than the one told by the white woman. In the context of the struggle between the sentimentalist and anti-sentimentalist versions of black America, Virginia Thomas's final remarks acquire a particularly sinister irony. Pictured with her husband reclining on the sofa and reading the *Bible* (it's really amazing that the photographer just happened by at that intimate moment), Virginia

19

Thomas says, "Even though I grew up in a comfortable, middle-class world, I've always hurt for black America and what white America did to blacks. But Clarence taught me to go beyond that—to treat all people the way you wanted to be treated" (116). Thus the black man who opposes affirmative action, and who was himself not above soliciting tears when they benefited him, teaches his white middle-class wife (the real-estate developer's daughter) to get beyond her compassion and thereby fulfills Wright's mission in the most perverse terms imaginable.

In this battle between the sentimentalists and the anti-sentimentalists as I have sketched it here, it will be noted that the women are white and the blacks are men—a state of affairs that of course characterized much of the mass cultural treatment of the Hill/Thomas controversy. For example, in an episode of the popular television program *Designing Women*, a program which featured a cast primarily composed of white women, several of the women engaged in a debate over the veracity of Anita Hill. The show's sympathies were clearly on the side of Hill: the final images showed George Bush reading a speech at the swearing-in ceremony and declaring that all "men" are created equal; several shots of various white men pronouncing verdicts against Hill were followed by a freeze frame of Anita Hill at the microphone, eyes cast downward. It was a very moving ending. Nevertheless, it is striking that the only regular cast member on this show other than the white women was a black male law student who in this episode objected to the judge's inadequate credentials. Here the black woman who was being talked *about* disappeared as a speaking subject, as a commentator on her own experience, so that implicitly race and gender became polarized.

In spite of the silence that surrounded them, African American women found other ways to articulate the complex interaction of issues of race and gender at work in the events surrounding the Thomas/Hill hearing. One of the earliest and most moving discussions of these events was written by Rosemary L. Bray in the *New York Times Magazine*. Speaking of the particular lack of credibility of black women's accounts of their experiences, Bray writes, "The signs and symbols that might have helped to place Hill were

20

long ago appropriated by officials of authentic (male) blackness, or by representatives of authentic (white) womanhood. Quite simply, a woman like Anita Hill couldn't possibly exist. And in that sense, she is in fine historical company" (95). Bray enters the lists in the battle of the narratives by invoking the slave narrative "Incidents in the Life of a Slave Girl," by Harriet Jacobs. This story, recently authenticated as a true story by Jean Fagan Yellin, was written in part because Jacobs could not interest Stowe in telling her account of her own slave experience. Bray remarks that this tale "would have made more instructive reading for the Senate Judiciary Committee than *The Exorcist*," which was invoked at one point in the Thomas/Hill hearing (95). Jacobs's narrative begins, "Reader, be assured this narrative is no fiction. I am aware that some of my adventures may seem incredible; but they are, nevertheless, strictly true" (1). Bray herself notes that this account, while "true," was nevertheless shaped by the conventions of sentimental fiction, the genre in which Stowe also wrote (95). Bray clearly is *not* then arguing for some immediacy of experience on the part of the writer, not relying on the naive assumption that one's experience can be communicated through language in such a way as to reveal the Authentic Truth. Rather, for Bray, the question is clearly one of credibility: whose story gets culturally legitimated and how? Whose stories are granted *no* relation to truth, and how are their authors discredited and relegated to the status of fantasists and hysterics?[3]

In view of the prominence of the category of hysteria in cases dealing with complaints of sexual abuse by women, it seems worth examining this term "hysteria" more closely. Postmodern theory has elevated hysteria to a paradoxical kind of truth status—the untruth of truth. Freud's thesis is that the hysteric's "original trauma" did not in fact always possess meaning at the outset, but only acquired it at a later time when other events or the acquisition of adult knowledge (e.g., of the sexual act) conferred retrospective meaning on the original event.[4] This Freudian insight is at the heart of the theory of "deferral" that functions so largely in postmodern and deconstructive thought. These theories draw on Freud to argue that there is no founding truth, only truth effects which are the result of iteration. What

21

interests me here about the concept of deferral, using the term in its more ordinary sense, is the extent to which it functions in women's responses to sexual harassment. Anita Hill was continually badgered for not having responded immediately to the insults dealt her by Thomas; she was considered guilty in large part because she deferred her complaint. Deferral is indeed extremely common in cases of harassment. "Barring the grave offense," where, for example, the boss throws you over the desk, holds a gun to your head, and rapes you, many offenses are not immediately registered as harassment by the victim; frequently the woman goes away confused about what happened and about what the incident really meant. Women often report checking with a confidante, whose role is to support her and help her understand that what happened was "really" offensive and demeaning and that she ought not to have to "fend for herself" in dealing with the matter.

Interestingly, then, the space of deferral is the space of women's hystericization, but it is also the space of feminist politics: it takes a second woman to help confer meaning on the first woman's experience, and this process greatly magnified *is* feminism (in fact, I have always maintained about women in patriarchy that "one is a hysteric; and two are a movement"). I hardly mean here to discredit the entire project of psychoanalysis, condemning it as nothing more than a patriarchal plot to consign women's experiences of real abuse to the category of fantasy. Indeed, psychoanalysis might prove useful in understanding not so much Anita Hill's fantasies, but Clarence Thomas's repression (assuming he did indeed forget everything that happened), to say nothing of his woman-hating (though psychoanalysis surely cannot provide a *sufficient* explanation for woman-hating). And, yes, Virginia, psychoanalysis can help to explain women's complicity in an oppressive system as well to understand the appeal, to women and men, of narratives like *Fatal Attraction*—the appeal, as a matter of fact, of much of the literary canon which from *Pamela* on eroticizes dominance, invests sexual harassment with its libidinal charge, and contributes to the confused opacity about sexuality experienced by women nurtured on fairy tales, television, and entertainment magazines, as well as the great tradition. As one, culturally legitimated, narrative about growing up male and female, psychoanalysis takes a place with many other narratives in shaping our understanding of experience. In any case, my ultimate point here is that feminism is not about uncovering original truths but about "changing the stories" and insisting on their credibility—a process that can only occur within a collectivity.

23

This conclusion—that feminism is about changing the stories and thus must connect with literary questions—is one that legal scholars like Patricia Williams and Drucilla Cornell are currently exploring. For example, in a version of the criticism we have already encountered of Catharine MacKinnon's supposed naiveté about language, Cornell in her book *Beyond Accommodation* criticizes MacKinnon for failing to recognize the importance of addressing what she calls "metaphors of the feminine" (147). MacKinnon, in Cornell's view, unwittingly validates male reality as the only reality (because, according to MacKinnon, men have the power to impose it on women) and thus is actually in complicity with the system she purports to be challenging. In particular, Cornell faults MacKinnon—referring to the latter's disagreement with the psychologist Carol Gilligan—for devaluing the feminine, which Gilligan's work tends to affirm. In turn, Cornell criticizes Gilligan for rooting her affirmation of the feminine entirely "in the way women are." Cornell prefers to emphasize with Luce Irigaray that women are always more than that which can be captured within representation—an excess that characterizes metaphor—literary language—itself and that Irigaray has famously said is revealed through the process of feminine *mimesis*. It is through literary language, Cornell contends, that new meanings will come into play. "To reach out involves the imagination, and with imagination, the refiguration of Woman. [This] kind of shift in the presentation of Woman is particularly important in legal discourse if the wrongs to women are to appear at all" (169).

While Cornell and MacKinnon share certain concerns, the emphases in their work place them in some respects at opposite poles. MacKinnon is wary of feminism's straying from an exclusive focus on women's oppression today, whereas Cornell insists on the utopian dimension of feminist discourse, since in Cornell's view, feminism needs an elsewhere from which to critique the present order as well as to imagine the possibilities for a world transformed along feminist lines. But Cornell, who in her own work does not seem to adopt the kind of feminine writing she advocates, never really discusses how feminists are to intervene in the legal system as it is today and so never suggests how we can make the wrongs to women, which her method purports to reveal, disappear. Part of the problem is her insufficient attention to the issue of the feminist collective which I have been arguing is crucial in the struggle to ratify the new meanings that feminism would put into play.

So the question becomes: how one can both address oneself to a legal system that is binding on women but has not heard the truth about the metaphorical nature of all language (clinging tenaciously to its faith in language's transparency) and at the same time not simply fall victim to a belief in the reality of the dominant group as the only reality. Patricia Williams's book *The Alchemy of Race and Rights* (the very title of which denotes transformative powers) seems to me a brilliant attempt to forge a language which points to a different future at the same time that it specifically and concretely addresses the wrongs historically and presently perpetrated against women and most particularly against blacks.

The Alchemy of Race and Rights is an amalgam of several genres of writing—autobiography, legal doctrine, anecdotes, critical theory, humor, and fiction. The book's many facets are appropriate to the complexity of its writer's cultural situation as a black female lawyer in a white man's world. Williams movingly discusses the contradictions of her position in American culture and reveals these to be at least as complicated as those expounded by MacKinnon. In the final chapter of the book, for example, Williams provides an account of her own history and ancestry that reveals the inadequacy of a model operating without recognition of the specific paradoxes of black women in relation to a law that doubly disinherits them. Williams's great-grandmother had been impregnated by a white lawyer named Miller who owned her; when Williams herself prepares to go to law school her mother reassures her, "The Millers were lawyers, so you have it in your blood" (216). Noting that the mother was implicitly advising her daughter not to look to her as a role model, Williams writes: "She hid the lonely, black, defiled-female part of herself and pushed me forward as the projection of a competent self—a cool rather than despairing self, a masculine rather than a feminine self" (217). Unable to claim her feminine heritage, Williams also reflects on the double-bind of a woman who inherits from an ancestral father the law that once made blacks into property: "Claiming for myself a heritage the weft of whose genesis is my own disinheritance is a profoundly troubling paradox" (217).

As we see from these quotations, Williams is not afraid to "risk essentialism." She speaks unabashedly of black selves and female selves as well as of black and female "ways of knowing" and insists on defending these ways against the imposition of male systems of thought. Like Cornell, Williams clearly feels that a repudiation of those traits traditionally assigned to women amounts to a kind of repudiation of women as they have historically inhabited their roles. In this respect both Cornell and Williams follow Gilligan's lead in affirming "the feminine." At one point Williams illustrates the importance of ratifying the experience of oppressed groups like blacks and women by recounting a story about a boy whose fear of big dogs is met by his parents' dismissive insistence that there is no difference between a wolfhound and a Pekinese. Williams says she used the story in the classroom to illustrate "a paradigm of thought by which children are taught not to see what they see; by which blacks are reassured that there is no real inequality in the world, just their own bad dreams; and by which women are taught not to experience what they experience, in deference to 'men's ways of knowing'" (13).

At the same time that she affirms "the feminine," Williams seems less averse than Cornell to adopting "men's ways of knowing" in order to contest the legal system from within.[5] Thus Williams continually uses the principles and language of contract law to expose the inequities of blacks and women in this system. ("Blacks have earned a place in this society," she

25

argues in a defense of affirmative action programs. "They deserve their inheritance as much as family wealth passed from parent to child over the generations is 'deserved inheritance'" [191].) In moving between black and female ways of knowing and white men's ways of knowing, Williams opens a space for whole *new* ways of knowing, which she gestures toward by using the literary language that Cornell calls for but does not herself employ: metaphors, allegories, fictional stories (which often read like folktales), etc. The voice that emerges is thus a profoundly personal one, designed not only to respond to the calls of feminist legal scholars to begin to formulate a reconstructed form of jurisprudence that would acknowledge the relational nature of human subjectivity, but also to reveal how "much of what is spoken in so-called objective unmediated voices is in fact mired in hidden subjectivities and unexamined claims that make property of others beyond the self, all the while denying such connections."[6]

For Williams the task is finally to reveal such connections and also to *forge* them in creating "a collective perspective or social positioning that would give rise to a claim for the legal interests of *groups*" (emphasis added). The story about the wolfhound, she says, is meant to show that

> in a historical moment when individual rights have become the basis for any remedy, too often group interests are defeated by, for example, finding the one four-year-old who has wrestled whole packs of wolfhounds fearlessly to the ground; using that individual experience to attack the validity of there ever being any generalizable four-year-old fear of wolfhounds; and then recasting the general group experience as a fragmented series of specific, isolated events rather than a pervasive social phenomenon. (13)

(I would note that although Williams seems to be speaking against opponents of affirmative action, she could easily be addressing those feminists who decry as essentialist any generalizable claims based on gender.) One performative accomplishment of Williams's style is that instead of proceeding in an abstract way to defend "group rights," Williams enacts a collective perspective, as it were, in part by staging many of the arguments as dialogic encounters: classroom situations, conversations with colleagues, anecdotes about her family, and so forth. As a member of two groups which have historically been "objects of property"—blacks and women—Williams becomes the voice of the goods when, to quote Irigaray, "the goods get together."

Operating at once from within male systems of knowledge and power and from the Irigarayan "elsewhere," Williams's writing is a kind of hybrid form fully adequate to the task which the case of Anita Hill, another African American lawyer, makes so urgent: the collective feminist enterprise of telling stories that are true to our shared experience, that contest the oppressiveness of much of this experience, and that put new meanings into play. But it also reminds us of the importance of our collective differences. Indeed, Williams's own family history makes some of these differences vividly apparent, helping us to see why feminism should be, *pace* MacKinnon, "modified"—certainly by terms like "African American." Indeed, Kimberle Crenshaw has forcefully shown how a feminism *unmodified* by race led white feminist supporters of Hill actually to undermine her authority: "White feminist acquiescence to the either/or frame worked directly to Thomas's advantage: with Hill . . . cast as simply a de-raced—that is, white—woman, Thomas was positioned to claim that he was the victim of racial discrimination with Hill as the perpetrator" (415).

I would like to end with a story drawing on the same version of history as that recounted by Williams, a history which is, after all, partly one of white female racism. This story, written as a response to the Virginia Thomas interview, was invoked by one of this nation's pre-eminent storytellers. In a letter to *People Magazine*, Alice Walker wrote, "Black women around the country are sharing a rich chuckle at Virginia Thomas's assertion that she believes 'Anita Hill was probably in love with [her] husband.' The mistress on the plantation used to say the same thing about her female slave every time she turned up pregnant by the master" (5). Virginia Thomas's story is, as Walker reminds us, an old story—an old *wives'* tale, so to speak—that functions to disavow the experience of the black woman so movingly depicted by Harriet Jacobs, whom Bray quotes:

My master began to whisper foul words in my ear. . . . The other slaves . . . knew too well the guilty practices under that roof; and they were aware that to speak of them was an offense that never went unpunished. . . . I longed for someone to confide in. . . . I dreaded the consequences of violent outbreak; and both pride and fear kept me silent.[7]

Women cannot afford to participate in the endless deferral of women's stories; they must instead become for each other the confidantes Jacobs lacked—engaging in their own confirmation process and granting legitimacy to each others' stories in their sameness but also in their differences.

PREFACE TO THE FOLLOWING THREE CHAPTERS

One of the stranger trends within feminist cultural studies has been the affirmation of works of high or popular art that feminists might at one time have deplored for their violence, especially their violence against women. Some time ago feminists began to question the notion that such works always and inevitably assign men to a sadistic role as protagonists and as spectators or readers. Thus began an effort to rehabilitate men by showing the extent to which many men preferred, often unconsciously, the masochistic role. The work which most extensively analyzes the phenomenon of male masochism with respect to popular movies is *Men, Women, and Chainsaws* by Carol Clover. Clover argues that films like *The Texas Chainsaw Massacre* invite an identification, whatever the sex of the viewer, with a persecuted heroine. But whereas the male viewer of a film like *The Texas Chainsaw Massacre* is judged to be subverting patriarchal authority by refusing phallic power, the female spectator is said to reaffirm this power since for women, as Kaja Silverman points out, the masochistic position is so close to the norm.

For some feminists the genre that has most disturbingly promoted female masochism is the romance. Years ago Germaine Greer denounced readers and protagonists of romance for "cherishing the chains of their bondage." Later Ann Douglas would argue that romances show women to be "magnetized by male sexuality and male brutality" (28). Feminist critics in the early eighties objected to the wholesale dismissal of the genre and proceeded to identify elements of protest against and resistance to female subordination in a male-dominated society. In the nineties these studies have been forgotten or been subjected to misreadings that drastically reduce their complexity. A few people continue to see romance and romantic fantasies as purely masochistic. The great majority of critics, however, now claim that romances, at least those being written today, have entirely repudiated "masochism"—and reveal a world in which equality between the sexes is a fait accompli.

In the next few chapters, I zigzag my way through the various positions being put forth about romances, attempting to create, in the end, a more nuanced understanding than is often revealed in current studies of the genre and of the transformations it has undergone over the past twenty years. In chapter 2, I look at Jane Campion's *The Piano*, and try to show how a work of high art indulges in romantic fantasy while simultaneously criticizing aspects of it. In chapter 3, "My Life as a Romance Reader," I show how writers of popular romance have been working to contest the eroticization of dominance that in the past seemed to be the core of romantic fantasy. In chapter 4, "My Life as a Romance Writer," I argue that the project is incomplete, and I quarrel with today's romance writers who, having become their own critics, proclaim themselves in their PR campaigns to have achieved the full flowering of feminist consciousness.

2

AXE THE PIANO PLAYER

❏

In her book *Men, Women, and Chainsaws,* Carol Clover, who finds much to affirm from a feminist viewpoint in the slasher films that appeal largely to teenaged boys, disparages Jane Campion's film *The Piano* in very telling terms: "Romance, in *The Piano,* is unimaginable outside the terrain of sado-masochism. The fact that it is inflected by Christianity and by feminism (of a sort), and that it is done up Masterpiece Theater-style [!] should not detract from its ecstatic investment in powerlessness and victimization" ("Ecstatic Mutilation," 22). Two double standards seem to be in play here, both of which I seek to nullify in this chapter: one privileging male (slasher) fantasies over female (romantic) ones and the other privileging popular (male) genres over art. For to maintain her position, Clover must deny Campion's formidable artistic gifts; in doing so she takes a place alongside numerous cultural critics who have reversed the high/low hierarchy that once prevailed in the academy, reducing high art to mere pretentiousness, while crediting popular genre with political subversiveness: "The only unconventional thing about [*The Piano*'s heroine Ada]," writes Clover, "is that she wandered into an art film and got taken seriously" (22).

In the pages that follow I want to affirm the artistry of Jane Campion and to follow her in her bold forays into what Clover dismisses as the "terrain of sadomasochism." As Campion explores the question of how women find space for their eroticism within the violent structures of patriarchy, she in the process reveals how the mother/daughter relationship is formed and deformed within these structures, and how violence—in particular (fantasies of) violence against the mother (as taboo a subject within feminism as outside of it)—becomes crucial to the separation of the daughter from her mother and to the daughter's emergence as a sexual being.

I want to begin by looking at a moment in the film where Campion self-consciously explores not only the issue of male violence against women, but of the *representation* of such violence and its effects on the real. In the scene in question, the people of the New Zealand village where *The Piano* takes place attend a pageant. The scene opens with a shot of little girls in angel wings being passed over the mud by a line of men outside the "theater." Flora (Anna Pacquin), the daughter of Ada (Holly Hunter), the film's protagonist, is one of the girls: she is indeed destined to be an angel of patriarchy, although she will muddy herself in the role (figure 2.1). (When she seals her mother's fate by deciding to take a message to her stepfather rather than to her mother's lover, she steps through the mud as she crosses from one set of boards leading down one path to a different set leading down another.) After the little girls sing the ballad "Barbara Allen," we witness a staging of the Bluebeard story. Behind a curtain, through which hang the heads of Bluebeard's former wives, the shadow of a man about to take an ax to his wife is seen, but as the woman begins to scream the Maoris in the audience, mistaking "art" for life, storm the stage to the great consternation of the rest of the audience.

While the attribution of such naiveté to the Maoris may be problematic, what interests me here is how the representation *does* become "reality" within the film. The first time we see the Bluebeard motif is in rehearsal: the minister, who is to play Bluebeard, is demonstrating the scene to the maid who will play the wife/victim. He has her hold out her hand and tries to get her to look at the shadows projected on the wall as the ax comes down

Figure 2.1. Holly Hunter (Ada) and Anna Pacquin (Flora) in Jane Campion's *The Piano*. © 1993 by Miramax Films.

on the hand. She, however, is riveted by the sight of the *actual* ax (though it is made of cardboard) and screams every time he attempts the blow. In this way the film foreshadows the confusion between real and represented violence that will mark the staging of the play, which itself foreshadows the horrifying mutilation of Ada's hand. Ada's husband, Stewart (Sam Neill), sips tea and benignly looks on during this rehearsal, although later he will enact the scene in earnest after learning of his wife's infidelity. Campion, who is surely aware of debates within feminism about the relation between representations of violence and actual violence and surely must know that the "sophisticated" feminist position is to insist upon the difference, seems to me to be inviting us to rethink this relation.[1] Insofar as Ada is physically mutilated, her finger chopped off (after she has symbolically mutilated herself by extracting a piano key from the instrument that serves as her voice and sending it to Baines [Harvey Keitel] as a token of her love), the film suggests that the violence at the heart of the socio-symbolic order, which may indeed be symbolic for men (castration is a fear but not generally a reality), is often literal for women.

Campion's statement about the relation of representation to reality is made all the more forcefully in that the play marks a decisive turning point in the film, the point at which its Bluebeard plot is actually set in motion. Watching the play, Ada sits beside her husband and Baines, who abruptly leaves when he sees the couple holding hands—a gesture Ada "stages" for his benefit. The camera shows a close-up of her wearing a small mysterious smile as Baines walks out of the hall. From now on, she will cease to be physically passive in her relationship with Baines and will become responsive and sometimes even take the initiative in lovemaking. As we shall see, however, there is a way in which this relationship too has overtones of the Bluebeard myth, especially in its evocation of the nineteenth-century female Gothic.

Before I even saw *The Piano,* a mythology seemed to have developed around it: according to various acquaintances of mine both in the United States and abroad, this was a film that women loved and men hated. To be specific, women were said to have found the film's central situation (the build-up of the relationship between Ada and Baines) erotic whereas men found it exploitative: after all, the heroine comes to love her sexual extortionist, the man who has prostituted her, by bargaining for her favors and allowing her to "earn back" the piano that was hers to begin with but that her husband had given to Baines in return for land. How, assuming the truth of the mythology, do we begin to understand women's particular investment in such a fantasy?

Let us be blunt and admit at the outset that the fantasy of being bought appeals to many women at a deep psychic level. It is no accident that Harlequin Romances frequently bear titles like *Bartered Bride.* Nor, I suppose, should it have been surprising to see some feminist critics actually praising *Indecent Proposal,* the popular film about a man who offers a married couple a million dollars to spend one night with the wife, as a "woman's film."[2] The difference between the reality and the fantasy, a cynic could say, may be nothing more than the price: talk shows airing after *Indecent Proposal* was released featured rich men who avowed they would never offer a million dollars for one night with a woman when she could be had for so much less. The female fantasy of women's enthrallment to men's economic power can be traced at least as far back as the nineteenth century. For example there is an erotically charged scene in *Jane Eyre* (a female re-vision of the Bluebeard story) in which Rochester withholds part of Jane's salary so that after visiting her dying aunt she will have to return to him for the remainder.

35

Indeed, Campion specifically refers to the nineteenth-century Gothic as a major influence on her work, although the text she most frequently invokes is *Wuthering Heights.* In an interview she compares the Brontës' moors with "the black sands of the west coast beaches around Auckland and New Plymouth [in New Zealand] and the very private, secretive and extraordinary world of the bush." She continues: "Other things seemed to click for me, too. For instance, the early and major colonization of New Zealand happened at about the same time as the Brontë sisters were writing" (Bilbrough 4). Campion never explains the significance of this connection, but recent feminist criticism has implicated Charlotte Brontë in the imperialist project, showing, for example, how the erotic liberation of Jane Eyre depends on an "othering" of the colonialized woman, depicted as a monster. Even today one of the favored chronotopes of romantic novels is the nineteenth-century plantation, and it is precisely the ownership of lands and peoples that gives the hero his appeal; as for the heroine, the erotic charge of being owned consists in the fetishization of the difference between herself and the other owned objects (e.g., slaves, servants)—of, we might say, her surplus value.

This extra value in both *Jane Eyre* and *The Piano* consists of something that in the nineteenth century might have been called "soul"—revealed in *Jane Eyre* by the pictures Jane sketches and in *The Piano* by the music Ada plays. We are to believe that Baines is enraptured by the heroine's strong will and passionate music, and that the "erotic barter" he proposes is a consequence of his captivation. It is unclear, in this light, what to make of the film's insistent linkage of the bargaining between Ada and Baines with the trading between the husband and the Maoris. An example of a parallel between the two kinds of barter occurs when Baines tells Ada to undo her dress so he can see her arms. He strokes them while she plays, and, interestingly, for the first and only time during the movie the music played is not "her own" (the purpose of the film's original score is to suggest that Ada's music is pure self-expression; at this moment, however, she plays Chopin). A cut reveals Stewart negotiating a land deal with the Maoris, and at one point he asks a companion how the Maoris even know the land is theirs. The question reverberates back to the previous scene, underscored by the music Ada plays: how do women know their *sexuality* is really theirs?

The film's linking of the colonial situation with Ada's plight seems destined to make rather contradictory points: The audience is invited to see both how women are property and how they are like native peoples in having their goods and services expropriated by white men. Such analogies, dubious as women of color have shown them to be, are undercut, however, by the differences registered in the film between the two situations.

First, Baines is unlike the average colonialist in that rather than cheating native peoples and luring/coercing them to accept white culture (the natives wearing top hats in *The Piano* emblematize colonial "mimicry"), he becomes part of *their* culture, signified by his scarification: he has gone native (figure 2.2). "His wildness," as one reviewer approvingly puts it, affords "others a glimpse of all that is brutal in their own natures: he lets them into the secret of themselves" (Lane 149). Needless to say this language traffics in very old stereotypes of tribal cultures as "primitive" and "savage." According to another reviewer, British society and Maori culture represent, respectively, "the civilized and the natural, the controlled and the passionate, the female and the male"—oppositions the reviewer credits "structural anthropology" with having first formulated. Campion, he says, has obviously studied the subject (Rothstein C19). If this is so, she must have failed the introductory course with its lesson that societies once dismissed as primitive are as complex as any other and that far from repre-

Figure 2.2. Harvey Keitel (Baines) in *The Piano*. ©1993 by Miramax Films.

senting nature, they may be studied in order to understand the very *rules* of culture.

Secondly, the film invites us to see Ada as progressively exempting herself from the status of property: from being an object of exchange (her father marries her off to a strange man; her piano is traded away by her husband), she enters directly into barter over the piano with her soon-to-be-lover Baines. Baines then lets her out of the deal. *Village Voice* reviewer Georgia Brown (who praised *Indecent Proposal* as a "woman's film") writes, "Baines is like the wise tamer in horse movies: patient, attuned to the animal, instinctively sensing when a direct move might be made. Then, wonder of wonders, he recognizes when a bargain exploits: 'The arrangement is making you a whore and me miserable'" ("Say Anything"). An arrangement that makes the woman into (something resembling) a horse before it makes her a whore would seem to me to be rather exploitative all along—to say nothing of the fact that it is the man, not the woman, who recognizes this exploitation when it *is* finally noticed. Brown's language reveals the extent to which the heroine *lacks* agency and is testimony to the fact that women continue to experience their dehumanization as erotic. It is true and important that the process of exchange between the two men, Baines and Stewart, is short-circuited when Baines tells Stewart he gave the piano back as a gift not to him but to his wife, and the effect of this remark is quite satisfying; even here, however, let us not exaggerate the heroine's control but remember that, as anthropologists and philosophers have long noted, the ability to confer gifts is a measure of the *donor's* power.

In regard to race, the film thus seems to want to have it both ways: on the one hand, to critique in liberal fashion both colonialism and the exchange of women by linking the two phenomena and on the other hand, to sustain a very old female fantasy which fetishizes these links (that is, which plays on a complex psychic avowal of sameness and difference). In any case, it is certainly clear that the parallels drawn by the film are not meant to reflect on white women and native peoples equally. Indeed, the lives of people of color, as is the case in the crassest of Hollywood films, are of no intrinsic interest; their main role is to *take* interest in the lives of white people—as when the Maori women counsel Baines to get a wife. "I already have a wife," Baines tells them. The image of the Maori woman who walks down the beach intoning a dirge-like melody as Ada and Baines go off at the end says it all.

To observe the presence of the popular romance fantasy in a work acclaimed as high art by the critical establishment is certainly not to deny entirely the work's ability to articulate (white) female desire and to contest patriarchal norms—although, as we have seen, this ability has been denied by at least one feminist critic, Carol Clover. It seems to me to reveal a great deal about the current state of feminist criticism that Clover, whose critical reputation in film studies rests on her affirmative analyses of films about crazed men who chase screaming young girls in order to slash them to bits with chainsaws (no mere finger amputation will satisfy *their* lust for butchery), stingingly rebukes *The Piano* for seeming to "love its horrors." Whereas a female critic like Georgia Brown revels in the most retrograde aspects of the film's fantasy, Clover reacts harshly to a film she regards as utterly complicitous with patriarchal violence against women. Overlooking the fact that in exploring the Bluebeard myth Campion actually investigates the relation between violence and its representation, Clover writes, "The underlying fantasy here—that violence is an expression of love, that blows are in their own way erotic compliments—comes awfully close to the one said to bind battered wives to their husbands" ("Ecstatic Mutilation," 21).

Since this is where I came in, having written my first book, *Loving with a Vengeance*, to show how women's fantasies did not simply reflect female masochism, I will refer the reader to the rather extensive literature on romance fantasies which argues that popular feminine narratives do testify to women's resistance to patriarchal norms and involve heroine and reader in a complex negotiation of the line between fantasy and reality.[3]

Interestingly, the women I talked to who were enraptured by *The Piano*'s eroticism referred in particular to the way the film resembles women's romances in building up slowly to the act of sex, depicting a kind of elaborate foreplay. Female spectators are also fond of pointing to the two scenes in which Ada, deprived of access to Baines, seeks out Stewart and strokes his body as he lies in bed, at the same time denying him access to her body. We might call these the film's most politically correct moments of eroticism—moments Campion singles out to show how they involve a reversal of standard gender roles. Here are her words from the Production Notes:

> Ada actually uses her husband Stewart as a sexual object—this is the outrageous morality of the movie—which seems very innocent but in fact has its power to be very surprising. I think many women have had the experience of feeling like a sexual object and that's exactly what happens to Stewart. The cliché of that situation is generally the other way around where men say things like 'Oh sex for its own sake.' But to see a woman actually doing it, especially a Victorian woman, is somehow shocking—and to see a man so vulnerable. It

becomes a relationship of power, the power of those that care and those that don't care. I'm very very interested in the brutal innocence of that.

It is true that this is a highly unusual moment in the history of cinema, for at this point Ada does seem to possess some sexual power. Of course, the episodes occur in the first place because her husband has locked her in the house and forbidden her to see Baines. Ada turns to Stewart partly to avoid an incestuous encounter with her daughter: lacking an outlet for her newly released sexual feelings Ada one night reaches out for Flora, with whom she sleeps, wakes up, realizes what is happening, and goes immediately to Stewart. This moment encapsulates one of the most remarkable achievements of the film: the way the eroticism of the central situation spreads out to suffuse the entire text, sexually charging the atmosphere and almost every aspect of the *mise en scène.* There is in the film a proliferation of fetishisms, voyeurisms, and other "perversions" (among them bestiality: as Stewart peeks in on Baines kneeling under the wires of Ada's hoop and performing cunnilingus while she stands in the middle of the room, the dog noisily laps at Stewart's hand. This audacious and humorous image might be compared to the highly sublimated and clichéd one of the horse invoked by Brown. I will return to the dog below.) In feminist film theory and criticism such perversions are always attributed to a male sexuality that operates at the expense of the feminine. But perhaps the very multiplicity of perversions marks the text as feminine. Take, for example, the film's fetishistic interest in clothes and materials—bed linens, shawls, stockings with holes in them, and of course Ada's dresses with their outlandish hoop skirts. These materials seem to have more to do with the kind of "sartorial augmentation" Emily Apter discusses in *Feminizing the Fetish* than with an originary lack in the female for which women's clothing serves as compensation—as "phallic cover-up" (97–98). There are no horrors beneath Ada's skirt, only treasures, and eventually almost everyone wants to be under it. For example, after Stewart sees Baines performing cunnilingus under Ada's hoop, we see Stewart lying under the floorboards of Baines's house, the better to spy on the two!

Of course this notion of fetishism depends upon woman's remaining the object rather than the subject of desire—hence perhaps Pauline Kael's denunciation of the film's "feminine smugness" (Espen 135). But given how rare it is for women to narcissistically value their own genitals, such "smugness" ought perhaps not to be so summarily dismissed. Nor must we neglect to point out how the film eroticizes the *male* body: when for example, it shows a close-up of Stewart's buttocks as Ada explores their contours or when we are presented with shots of a nude Baines, seen naked *before* Ada removes her clothes. Nevertheless, as the image of Ada gazing in the mirror and kissing herself indicates, this is a text that insofar as it identifies with Ada is for the most part about the desire to be desired.

But to what extent *does* the film identify with Ada? In her brief dismissal of *The Piano*, Pauline Kael clinches her discussion of the film's "feminine smugness" by observing: "This movie congratulates its heroine for any damn thing she does" (Espen 135). Most of the film's commentators seem at least implicitly to agree, and they praise or condemn the film according to whether they feel the heroine deserves such congratulations. The reviewer in the *Nation* asserts: "The difference between admiring *The Piano* with reservations and believing in it wholeheartedly comes down to one's willingness to identify with the heroine" (Klawans 706). The reviewer concludes by explaining why he, for one, has reservations, despite his willingness to "adopt the point of view of female protagonists" and of piano players: "So my failure to plunge into the being of the piano player in this new movie very likely reflects some shortcoming in the production [but of course; where else could the problem lie given such critical open-mindedness?]—perhaps Jane Campion's insistence that I should, I must, I *will* identify with Holly Hunter" (706). Campion's own remarks in the production notes would seem in general to support the view that the film endorses Hunter's character almost without reservation; she speaks of the film's spirit of "pure romanticism," countered only by an emphasis on "historical authenticity."

By focusing exclusively on the film's romanticism, however, the critics and even the director herself actually simplify a more complex film. Take, for instance, Campion's statement that the film involves "a triangle situation" in which there operate "powerful notions of jealousy for men—and for the woman perhaps" (Bilbrough 8). Such a remark is typical in the way it erases one particular character from the story. For, are there not two female protagonists and *two* triangles in the film? and is not the story of the *daughter*'s jealousy as compelling as (or even more compelling than) the story of the men's jealousy? Why is the daughter's story, despite the ritual critical nods to the astonishing power of Anna Pacquin's performance, continually written out?

Perhaps we can find a clue in a bit of contextual information: Campion's dedication of the film to her mother.[4] In response to a question about the significance of this dedication Campion says, "For a long time she has been a very strong advocate for this type of story. She always held up to my sister and myself the role of the martyr. She believes in love and its redemptive power. She is extremely romantic, which is something that both of us recoiled against, but her flame is still there" (Bilbrough 11). Although Campion is reluctant to recognize it, I would argue that *resistance* to the flame is "still there" as well and that the film is as remarkable as it is because it not only delivers up the [mother's] romantic fantasy but registers a powerful and angry critique of it from the daughter's point of view.[5] It is hardly surprising that the daughter and the mother should be so at odds in the text of a film created by a woman whose early work marked her as the poet laureate of the dysfunctional family (or perhaps it is more accurate to say that this early work was about the family *as* dysfunctional).

In the course of the film Flora, whose role as child seems to have been to some extent usurped by her mother, goes from being her mother's interpreter to being the mouthpiece of patriarchy. Thus, for example, after Stewart locks Ada in the house to prevent her from continuing her affair with Baines, Flora, who had initially sworn she would never call Stewart "Papa," scolds Ada for going to see Baines: "You shouldn't have gone up there, should you? I don't like it, nor does Papa." Flora's allegiance to patriarchy seems to develop as a response to her mother's exclusion of her, absorbed as Ada is by her love affair. Two rather extraordinary images mark the beginning and end of the process: on the beach the night they arrive Flora and Ada camp out in a makeshift tent fashioned out of one of Ada's skirts; the light from within makes the tent glow like a Chinese lantern, as one reviewer observes (Klawans 704). Later, of course, the place under Ada's skirt will be taken by Baines who kneels under the hoop while Stewart looks on. Flora, locked out and left to her own devices all the time, becomes enraged by her mother's apparent rejection of her. At one point when Ada refuses to allow Flora to accompany her to Baines's house, the child is nearly beside herself with fury and sputters incoherent curses, and when Stewart asks her where her mother has gone, she screams, "To hell."

43

Ada's sexual awakening seems to release her daughter's sexuality. After Flora witnesses the primal scene between her mother and Baines she starts humping the trees and teaches the Maori children to do the same; catching her in the act, her stepfather shames her and forces her to wash the tree trunks. The film is especially acute in its rendering of the psycho-sexual dynamics of a young girl's evolving sexuality when it shows how this sexuality evolves around the mother's exclusion of the daughter. During the time she is shut out by her mother and Baines, Flora enacts a sadistic game with the dog in which she pokes at it with a stick, and then strokes and soothes and cares for it in its consequent suffering. Freud analyzed a similar kind of activity in the play engaged in by young girls with dolls during what he called their "phallic" phase. According to Freud, this play is not related to the child's desire to be a mother but rather involves the girl's doing to the doll (presumably a pet would serve as well) what she would like to do with the mother—and what she experiences her mother as having done to her. Such play is a way of symbolically gaining mastery over one's powerlessness and making it sexually pleasurable ("Female Sexuality," 205–6).

The Piano seems to me unique in the way it frankly and unsentimentally depicts a young girl's developing sexuality— without in the least making the child into an erotic object, a pretty baby, for the spectator. Certainly the clarity with which the *mother* is presented as the primary object of the female child's active, "phallic" sexuality—a sexuality far removed from the romanticized polymorphously perverse pre-Oedipal fusion celebrated by so many feminists—is, as far as I am aware, unprecedented in film.[6]

44

I will refrain from following Freud into the further reaches of his thinking about female sexuality in order to avoid having to defend his theory of castration, according to which the girl turns away from her mother upon discovering her own and her mother's "lack." Suffice it to say that in *The Piano*, the "castration" of the mother is, ironically, brought about by the daughter, when instead of delivering to Baines the love note her mother has written on a piano key, she takes it to her stepfather. After Stewart chops off Ada's finger, he instructs Flora to carry it to Baines, who rather brutally tries to force the hysterical child to tell him what has happened. Finally, one of the Maori women intervenes, protesting, "she's just a little girl"—something everyone, including the film's spectators, are inclined to forget. Recalling Campion's description of her mother as a martyr ("She always held up to my sister and myself the role of the martyr.[7] She believes in love and its redemptive power"), we might be led to see a criticism here of Ada for her total investment in the ideology of romantic love.

Soon after this, Ada telepathically signals to Stewart her desire for Baines to take her away from New Zealand. Baines, Ada, and Flora leave together on a boat manned by Maoris. Ada orders the piano thrown overboard and arranges for the rope to carry her along with it, but after being dragged down into the sea, she changes her mind, unties herself, and resurfaces. "What a surprise," Ada's childlike voice-over comments, expressing our sentiments exactly. The happy ending—in which Ada begins to learn language, gets a job teaching piano, and lives contentedly with her lover—has, of course, been controversial; many commentators flatly refuse to believe in it and consider it to be the film's chief weakness. The film itself seems partly to undermine the narrative's conclusion through its final image: Ada at the bottom of the sea, her dress ballooned around her, anchored down by her piano.

To understand the ambivalence expressed in these alternative endings, we might turn one final time to Campion's discussion of her mother and consider the remainder of her answer to the question about the film's dedication which I here quote:

> I also think she has had a powerful struggle with life and death all   **45**
> through her later life and the courage with which she has encoun-
> tered this, and the depth it has drawn from me and the rest of the
> family, I am grateful for. It is not always comfortable, but that
> depth has been expanding and I guess I love her very much and I'm
> proud to dedicate the film to her. (Bilbrough 11)

Campion's symbolic staging of a mother's disappearance and return (a mother's "struggle with life and death") recalls Flora's response to her mother's withdrawal and the game the little girl plays of maiming the dog and then reviving it.[8] Campion's own avowed indecision about how to end the film reflects as well what must be seen as a larger feminist ambivalence with respect to the romance genre—an ambivalence that stems partly from our experience of art and partly from our experience of life. On the one hand, the film counters the tendency throughout the history of Western art to punish the adulterous woman. On the other hand, it defies our skepticism about the viability of the conventional happy ending, overriding our sense of the *unhappiness* created by current gender arrangements and their accommodation of male violence against women.

Most troubling of all, however, is the way this particular ending negates the horror the daughter has experienced, obliterating the girl's pain. The great tragedy for women in Western culture, Adrienne Rich has said, is the loss of the mother to the daughter and the daughter to the mother (237). Not only is there a severing of erotic ties but also a repression of the fact that the two share a common fate. ("I only clipped your wing," says Stewart piteously to Ada after hacking off her finger; we are, I think, meant to see a parallel with Flora and her angel wings.) The breathtaking accomplishment of *The Piano* is that it goes so far in poignantly depicting the tragedy Rich describes. Finally, though, the film draws back from its own bleakness, promoting the mother's story *over* the daughter's and subjecting the latter to a kind of repression. Instead of restoring the faith of mother and daughter in one another, the film puts its faith in a man: a man who once said he already had a wife, although such a person is never alluded to again. Which might leave us wondering if the ghost of Bluebeard has been exorcised from the film after all.

3

MY LIFE AS A ROMANCE READER

❏

This chapter was originally written at the invitation of Kay Mussell who was editing a special issue of the journal *Paradoxa* on romances. Mussell asked me to contribute a piece updating my thoughts about the genre. When the invitation came, I was in the middle of writing a memoir in which I had found myself trying to understand my own addiction to romances from the time I was a very young girl. When I originally wrote about romances in the late seventies I was attempting, just as I am now, to understand my attraction to the genre, but back then I focused on the object of the attraction, the texts themselves, whereas now I am focusing on the subject who was attracted, myself.

Because romances have been central to my fantasy life since I was a preteen, I was stunned that in the first version of her book *Reading the Romance* Janice Radway contended that textual critics like me have no way of knowing that we read romances the way romance readers read them. My response to Radway is a matter of public record, and she herself has modified her original position, so there is no need to belabor the point that in our culture *all* women imbibe romance fantasies from a variety of sources. That Radway's analysis of the appeal of romances ended up confirming many of my own arguments seemed to me to support my faith in myself as a representative romance reader. Yet the fact that Radway so vigorously denied any similarity in our arguments infuriated me and caught me up in a paradox: her vehement insistence on the differences between us undermined my belief in the bonds of women, in the fantasy of a shared identity.

So, if I challenged Radway by insisting on a certain sameness among women, she in effect challenged me with the fact of difference, and part of that challenge will be taken up in this chapter.

The move to personal criticism in the academy has in part been motivated, at least among politically committed critics, by the acknowledgment of difference and by the challenges a generation of critics has mounted to essentialist modes of thinking—thinking that posits commonality among members of a group based on shared experiences of oppression. The autobiographical critic declares that if she cannot speak for others she can at least speak for herself. Even a critic like Teresa de Lauretis in her magisterial book *The Practice of Love,* an ambitious attempt to revise psychoanalytic theory to account for lesbian subjectivity, feels the need every so often to remind the reader that she is delineating and explaining her own fantasies which may be very different from the fantasies of her readers. As this example suggests, such "personal criticism" does not relinquish the hope of illuminating the experiences of others, but is informed by an awareness of the problematic nature of speaking for these others, as well as the provisional nature of any conclusions drawn in the process.

In these comments, then, I want to discuss my life as the "romance reader" Radway was so confident I was not. This life was by no means over after I wrote *Loving with a Vengeance.* For I have continued to find romances extraordinarily appealing, having failed to exorcise my attraction by writing about it. Since publishing *Loving with a Vengeance* I have for the most part read for pleasure (if pleasure it be), and my efforts to "keep up with the field" have been fitful at best. Whereas romances in the seventies were required to adhere to strict rules, variations on the basic formula have proliferated, and I have become keenly aware that some variations are far more seductive to me than others. But if such an awareness makes me cautious about speaking on behalf of womankind and claiming to be representative, perhaps I can at least aim to shed a bit of light on the relation of public to private fantasy, a distinction that de Lauretis insists is necessary to counter a tendency within cultural studies to conflate the two.[1]

49

In what follows I will be relating a story in which my personal history intersects with the histories of romance and of feminism. It is a story that takes place at what may well have proven to be a brief moment in time, a time when the educational system allowed for some class mobility, in my particular case enabling a romance reader to become a romance critic and a university professor.

If I kiss you, I won't be answerable for the consequences.

This is the line (I've read it a thousand times in romances) that Germaine Greer singles out to mock in her witty denunciation of romances in *The Female Eunuch*.[2] But Greer never actually looks at the literal meaning of the words, which, removed from their context, are chilling. A man is threatening sexual assault and absolving himself in advance from all responsibility. The myth that men are unable to control their sexual drive beyond a certain point and that women lead men on—and so deserve what they get—by accepting romantic or sexual overtures from them is a myth that has all too often proved lethal to women. One of the main points of my analysis of romances is that the novels take the actual situation of women in our society, a situation in which the rape of women is a distressingly common if not routine event, and put it into a context that is soothing and flattering to women, allowing female readers to interpret instances of male brutality, even rape, not as expressions of rage and hostility, but of overwhelming desire and love.

But the line has special resonance for me given my family history. My mother's relation to my father was an abject one. She rendered herself entirely submissive to his authority, waiting for him to make decisions even about the smallest matters—such as which night he would take her to do the grocery shopping. My mother might express to me a wish that he would decide to go on a particular night, but when I would irritably suggest that she communicate her desire to him, she would say simply, "It's up to your father." My mother, and hence my brother and I, were terrified of my father's black moods, moods in which he would maintain a surly silence, occasionally broken by bursts of temper. We were also subjected to bouts of ridicule which would often seem to come from nowhere (I remember in particular his sneering at me for my "lack of common sense").

My mother adopted a policy of total appeasement at these times. Just out of my father's earshot she would command me in a whisper to apologize to my father, even when she conceded that I had done nothing wrong.

"But why, Ma?" I would plead, "I didn't *do* anything."

"I know, but would it kill you to try to make peace? Your father gets upset sometimes, he can't help it, that's just his way."

"But, Ma, it's my way not to apologize, what about *my* way?"

And so I grew up in a household in which the man was never held to be "answerable for the consequences" of his erratic behavior. Rather, we children (and my mother) were forced to assume all responsibility.

The guilt that my mother constantly made me bear resulted in a bizarre psychic episode in my adolescent life. I became convinced that I had committed the one sin against the Holy Spirit that can never be forgiven, a reference to which I had come across in the Bible. For some reason it struck me with absolute certainty that this sin consisted of picturing God naked, and of course once I got that in my mind, I couldn't get it out again. So for a year or so I went about my life certain of my own damnation. Years later, having long since lapsed as a Catholic, I realized that in a sense I had not been wrong about the gravity of my sin, for I had violated the cardinal rule of patriarchy, famously articulated by Jacques Lacan: the Phallus must remain veiled.

Given the extremely stern and forbidding guise patriarchy assumed in my early life, it is no wonder that I elaborated compensatory fantasies that eroticized the dreadful phallic imaginings which had colonized my mind. So after discovering the novels of Emily Loring and then later Harlequin romances, I spent years spinning romantic tales in my head. The narratives were full of male bronco busters and pert, saucy young women, and in a typical episode the tempestuous heroine, riding bareback on an untamed stallion, would gallop away from the hero, furious because he had been laughing at her lack of common sense. He would catch up with her, though, since his stallion was a little bit faster and his horsemanship just a little more skilled than hers. Driven crazy by the prospect of the harm that might have befallen her as a result of her reckless riding, he would yank her unceremoniously off her horse and crush her to him with a punishing kiss that left both of them panting.

I see now how these fantasies related to the treatment I and my mother experienced at the hands of my father, who as I said not infrequently mocked us and whose moods were unpredictable and hence confusing: in Harlequin terms such changeful behavior was a manifestation of the hero's vain struggle against succumbing to the heroine's attractions. "Punishing kisses" and their equivalent were staples I drew on frequently from the generic repertoire, for they enabled me to eroticize the burden of blame I constantly bore. Of course, the generalized sense of guilt I carried around marked me as very much a daughter of the times. It is easy to forget how much blame in the fifties and early sixties was heaped upon women. "Momism" was the term for the phenomenon of the overbearing woman who sucked the life out of her children. Women's frigidity, or their nymphomania, or their ball-busting, cock-teasing ways were blamed for all manner of social evils which were said to arise from the emasculation of the American male.

51

Eventually feminism came along and I believe literally saved many of us by telling us that we were not always "answerable" for the problems of the world in general and the behavior of individual men in particular. For me personally, feminism gave me the absolution I never got from Catholicism. But by then my fantasy life was irrevocably shaped, and the Harlequin romance was at its core.

"Who is that man?" Elizabeth Cady Stanton said into the bullhorn. "Can someone stop that man? He's absconding with one of my women!"
—Violet Fire, *by Brenda Joyce*[3]

While the fictively named town of Smithton, where Radway conducted her ethnographic study of romance readers, seemed to her as distant as a third-world country, my own small town in rural upstate New York could not have been all that different from the land of romance readers Radway encountered with such a sense of strangeness. My mother, who didn't believe in buying books ("we have libraries," she said—a view I thought at the time was benighted, but have since come to agree with), would get bags of paperbacks from the local elementary school teacher when the latter was finished reading them, and among these would be many Harlequins, which my mother and I would both read. But while my mother read many kinds of popular novels I only read the Harlequins, and even my mother, an ex-factory worker, a maid who cleaned hotel rooms, worried about the little addict being fostered in her midst and tried unsuccessfully to get me to vary my reading fare.

(Ethnographers of romance have pointed out that women readers sometimes refer to their reading habits as "addiction," and they go on to deplore the use of this term which they see as reinforcing society's devaluation of women's popular culture. Yet why are we to consider only the positive things the women say about their tastes and experiences as truth, which we are unwilling to modify by interpreting, and yet write off the negative feelings as social conditioning? Surely *all* aspects of romance connect to the social in the final instance, which is why we study it.

Believe me: I was an addict.)

English was my best subject in high school, so I planned to major in it when I went to college at SUNY-Albany (after all, awaiting me there were the novels of the Brontës and Jane Austen—plenty of halfway decent substitutes for Harlequins). My main reason for going to college was to get away from my hometown, but obtaining my mother's consent was not easy. "If it was your brother, I could see it. He'll have to support a family. But you're just going to get married. All you need is something to fall back on. Why not be a beautician or a secretary?" For a year the constant refrain, "beautician or a secretary, beautician or a secretary," would accompany the ever-increasing clatter of dishes that my mother would wash and throw into the drainer, while I dried and put them away and slammed the cupboard doors harder and harder as the argument progressed.

Little did my mother realize how Harlequin romances in some ways disinclined me toward marriage, just as critics for two centuries had feared would happen to women when their expectations about romance, derived from pulp novels, clashed with the cold reality of male/female relations in life. But males would have been damned by us young romance readers even if they had tried to enact the romance fantasy: I was always at some level aware that if a boy said something to me like "I won't be answerable for the consequences," I would consider him the biggest creep on earth.

In college, as I began acquiring cultural capital and rising out of my station in life, I put away my Harlequins. Then of course feminism burst on the scene, and along with Germaine Greer and other feminist writers we laughed at our old selves, our old trashy dreams, and got on with the business of loving each other and anticipating the revolution.

But loving each other was not simple. I think I'm by no means alone in having experienced this period as one of great confusion with respect to sex and romance. We embraced the concept of the woman-identified-woman, a term that referred to the primacy of women's emotional bonds over male/female ones and that enabled us to contemplate lesbianism as a "choice." At the same time, romance, as the Harlequin fixations of so many women attest, was so massively structured as heterosexual that the switch in erotic attachment from male to female seemed drastic and perilous; at least it did for me. Added to this was the burden of guilt (always guilt) I carried around: I couldn't understand how when one loved women so devotedly and deeply, one couldn't just "naturally" go the last step and surrender one's body to them. I fell in love with a woman who lived far away, but I was frightened of my own feelings, so I added an emotional distance to the geographical distance between us, and endured an abiding regret over my decision.

During this time I earned an M.A. at Albany and spent three years in the early seventies as an instructor at Old Dominion University in Norfolk, Virginia, where because the requirements for English literature had been dropped, the panicked faculty, desperate to hold onto its students, allowed us instructors who had been hired on "terminal contracts" to propose and teach a number of hot new courses that it nevertheless looked down on: The City in Literature, Sports in Literature, Madness and Literature, Afro-American Literature, and, of course, Women and Literature. Needless to say, while we did not directly deal with popular culture in those years, we certainly opened the gates fairly wide for the approaching barbarians.

Then, on a fluke, I was accepted at Stanford. The program I entered was called Modern Thought and Literature, and the man who had founded the program, Albert Guerard, had gone away on an extended sabbatical. The students, who, unlike the conservative faculty, were interested in Marxism, feminism, and poststructuralism, had gained control of the program, and for a while no one noticed who was in charge. The students were the ones responsible for admitting me, and so of course I felt like a fraud in relation to my professors, many of whom disdained my background. When he returned from his sabbatical, for example, Guerard made no effort to disguise the fact that he was scandalized by my having gotten into the program, which he had intended to be the preserve of Ivy League students.*

Nevertheless it must be said that the poor opinion some of my professors had of me because of my background, although it was very painful, was undoubtedly a factor in my decision to write about popular culture in my dissertation. Such a "low" topic seemed appropriate for one of my low status, and really I felt I had very little to lose. (The conflation of me with my "low" subject was unwittingly confirmed soon after *Loving with a Vengeance* was published. The review in the *Library Journal* had said that with the appearance of my book, romances and other forms of women's popular culture could no longer be regarded as trivial. My mother sent a copy of the review and a photo of me to our hometown newspaper, which published a short article on the book, and under the photo of me placed the caption, "Tania Modleski . . . no longer trivial." After all, I thought, that is why you want your accomplishments written up in your hometown paper.)

While I was still casting about for a dissertation topic, a classmate in a casual conversation told me that his sister read Harlequins, and that they had become very sexy, that the heroines actually had sex with the heroes. I couldn't believe it, for despite all the mauling and panting going on in the stories, I had thought the genre absolutely required the heroine's chastity. I took a look at some of the new Harlequins and that's how I came to resume my career as a romance reader. I was startled to realize that all those years of higher education and all those years of dedicated feminism hadn't lessened the attraction of the romances for me. I became consumed with the desire to figure out why I, a fervent feminist, had not shed these fantasies with all the rest of the false consciousness I had let go. So, although popu-

55

---

* I have one memory that captures this man perfectly for me. I was enrolled in a seminar with him, which I subsequently dropped, and we were reading Conrad's *The Secret Sharer*. To drive home the moral of the story about a man who discovers his double is a murderer, Guerard told us about a friend of his who had started out with the same advantages he, Guerard, had had, had attended the same illustrious university, had achieved the same grade point average, and yet had ended up teaching at Kansas State (or some such place). "There but for the grade of God go I," Guerard shuddered.

lar culture had never been studied or written about at Stanford, and although I had to go far afield to find a professor (Jean Franco in Spanish and Portuguese) who was willing to direct a popular culture dissertation, and although most of the female professors were advising women to write "safe" dissertations and then write feminist books after they got tenure, I decided it was time to look seriously at the culture out of which I had emerged and which I had never, it had turned out, entirely left behind.

"Rape is out," a romance writer told me after my book was published. She said it as if she were announcing a style trend. Apparently in some of the "bodice rippers," as the longer, racier historical romances were called then, the heroine was sometimes subjected to rape by a villain before being rescued by the hero, who of course always has dibs in the rape department.

The woman, whose *nom de plume* was Serita Stevens, and I were appearing together on a Chicago radio talk show. It was actually a horrifying experience in some ways. Stevens had been told by her publisher to promote her book, so every sentence she uttered contained four or five mentions of the title, and the talk show host was so annoyed, he stormed off the set. Nevertheless, the experience was also instructive. I found I wanted to argue with Stevens, to show her how the novels eroticized dominance, whether or not they featured an actual rape. At the same time, the male talk show host and the call-in listeners were so condescending to the novels and the female readers, I spent most of my time defending them. The dilemma was inherent in the task I had set for myself in writing the book: on the one hand, my purpose had been to show how the novels reinforce conservative notions of women's place; but, on the other hand, I had wanted to redeem the readers from critical opprobrium, to challenge the sexual double standard that reigned in popular culture criticism, and to demonstrate that romances not only spoke meaningfully to women's fears, desires, and hopes, but also contained elements of protest against female subjugation. The experience with Stevens showed me how difficult it is to treat texts as ambivalent, contradictory phenomena, a lesson I would learn many times over. For, in the years to come critics who wanted to be considered the first to defend romances would build a case against me by quoting only the negative parts of my analysis and then come charging in to rescue readers from my calumny.

There is no doubt, however, that I was very invested in my take on the novels and that I was particularly resistant to critics who slighted or ignored the tendency of romances to eroticize male power. I believed I had discovered the formula, and regarded all developments, like the one cited by Serita Stevens, as examples of what the philosopher and culture critic T. W. Adorno called "pseudo-individualization." Adorno applied this word to "standardized" mass cultural texts in comparing them to mass-assembled products like cars. For example, the fins on a certain model of Cadillac provided its owner with the illusion of possessing something different from his neighbors' cars, yet this model was essentially the same as many other automobiles.[4]

So, when people said to me, well, romances now sometimes foreground the heroine's career, I would say, sure, but the career is always secondary (which I still believe to be the case). And when people said, "rape is out," or suggested that the formula no longer required the hero to be all powerful, I was skeptical that real change had occurred. And over the years I found many, many novels which supported my position. To take a particularly striking example, in Brenda Joyce's *Violet Fire* from which I quoted at the beginning of the previous section, the heroine is a suffragist in the 1870s who goes down South to teach black children. Over the course of the novel she gets the hero to become more sympathetic to her causes, and by the end he's even telling her, somewhat anachronistically, that he never wanted to stand in the way of her "career." Throughout the novel the heroine is constantly in danger of being raped by Klansmen, but on every occasion she is rescued by the hero, who then overpowers her himself:

> "You need a thrashing," he said, his face inches from hers. "A real thrashing, the kind that will teach you some sense."

"Let me go," she ground out angrily, pushing against the steel wall of his chest. But he didn't budge.

"Then you need a protector," he said more levelly. "Face it, Grace, you need me."

"You are the most arrogant, conceited man I've ever had the misfortune to meet."

"You are the most unreasonable, lunatic woman . . ." he growled, then leaned forward, pinning her with his body, finding her mouth with his.

Beneath his onslaught, Grace froze. She tried to resist, she truly did. But it was hopeless. Her mouth softened, parting gently, and her body began a slow melting. She raised her hands and hesitantly put them on his shoulders. A deep, guttural cry of triumph escaped Rathe.

He didn't move his hands from the wall on either side of her neck, keeping her imprisoned with his big body. He pulled at her lush lower lip with his teeth, then licked the seam of her lips insistently. "Open for me, Grace," he breathed. (172)

An epilogue tells us that Grace continues her crusading after marriage, but her husband comes to the suffrage meetings she attends and rescues her each time trouble begins! ("Daddy has to rescue Mommy," he tells their daughter when a brawl breaks out.) If ever there was a novel that demonstrated the truth of Susan Brownmiller's thesis (in *Against Our Will*) that all men benefit from a system in which some men rape women, this is it. Moreover, it shows with exemplary clarity how a plot that pays lip service to feminism may be reinforcing woman's bondage on a deeper level.

Diversity may be more apparent than real even in the African American novels (or, as the *Romantic Times* euphemistically calls them, the "multicultural romances") that have appeared in recent years—a fact revealed in the very name of some of the authors like "Eboni Snoe."[5] In Snoe's *The Passion Ruby* the heroine Sienna is described thus: "Like Aunt Jessi's hair, her own curled into tight, spongy ringlets when washed, and both their skin tones were more a mellow brown than yellow. Sienna's petite frame was curvy but slim, her facial features a balanced design of large, almond shaped eyes, a small nose, and lips that were neither too wide nor too thin (6)." While the novel includes a few superficial details that signify African Americanness and black pride (not only the mellow brown skin of the heroine, but the dreadlocks the hero wears, his occasional references to the "hood" he grew up in, the heroine's addressing another woman as "girlfriend"), there are many more ways in which African American identity is disavowed (as in the description of the heroine's features, which stresses what she is not—in this case, "Negroid"). The novel not only takes few liberties with the formula as it has been developed by white women, its exoticism and stereotyping make its racial politics troubling. The villainess of the piece (who at one point "flaunts her chocolate breasts" as she leans over the hero) turns out to be a priestess of a cult religion in Martinique who derives her power by stealing men's sexual energy:

59

> As if guided by her pronouncement, a sexual frenzy began, creating a collage of undulating, moving body parts. It was shocking to see, for the men were no more than tools, the women controlling the entire act. Again and again they were forced into orgasm by the voracious females, until their bodies and their mouths cried out in agony for release. . . . The men had been turned into mere vessels of unwilling energy, the women into sexual vultures. (298)

This evil, sexually predatory black woman is significantly given the most feminist speech in the novel just before she is vanquished by the heroine:

> "This world is a man's world. Since time immemorial, a woman's value has been determined by her youth and her beauty, not what's in her head, not what's in her heart. . . ." She raised her eyes to the crowd. "I did not make the rules, I simply obeyed them, found ways around them." (305)

However, other African American romance novelists, like the enormously popular Beverly Jenkins who writes for Avon, are reworking the rape conventions in important ways. Jenkins's *Indigo* is a historical romance set in slavery times. (Given the master-slave psychosexual dynamic that lies at the core of so many romances, a novel with such a setting and such a protagonist must be of particular interest to students of the genre.) At one point in the novel, the heroine is threatened with rape by one of the white slave catchers. The introduction of the historical reality of the rape of black women by white men introduces a frank political dimension into the fantasy, thereby undercutting its erotic potential.

On the other hand, *Indigo* does incorporate an erotic fantasy of male power. The hero Galen, a fabulously wealthy Creole, is brought wounded to the house of the heroine, Hester, a poor, but literate, dark-skinned ex-slave who is a conductor on the Underground Railroad. Throughout the novel he showers her with gifts, including crates of hams and crates of flimsy nighties; and ultimately he elevates her to his social position by marrying her. For some characters the marriage presents a problem, and the novel boldly explores issues of class and skin color among African Americans. At the same time the romance plot's elaborate playing out of the fantasy of male potency works to displace many of the social, political, and, especially, economic issues of slavery. When Hester winds up in jail for helping fugitive slaves, for example, Galen "redeems" her by theatrically presenting the sheriff with a bag of real gold (here one might recall Jean-Joseph Goux's equation of the gold standard with the phallus to see how the slippage between the political economy of slavery and female erotic fantasy is effected), and at the end of the book he buys Hester's mother out of slavery and presents her to Hester as a Christmas present: "She looked over at her husband sleeping at her side. Through him all blessings flowed. Who else would be so extravagant as to give someone their mother for Christmas?" (356).

Indigo, far more than Jenkins's other novels, is a Cinderella story. Jenkins has said that she uses the romance as a vehicle for presenting history lessons to people who wouldn't ordinarily read history books. She remarks, "People are so busy fanning themselves from the love story when they close the book they don't realize they've gotten all that history."[6] If it is true that in *Indigo*, the romance alleviates the pain of reading history, it is also true that the romance transforms the pain of history itself and serves as an elaborate compensatory fantasy for it. (In view of the novel's partial rerouting of the historical suffering of African Americans into erotic fantasy, it is interesting to note that the secret passages in the heroine's house which have been designed to allow slaves to elude slave catchers become the means for the hero [shades of Mr. B—— in *Pamela*] to sneak into the heroine's bedroom at night.)

61

Somewhere in my continuing search for romance novels which contained the right mix for me, I noticed I was discarding a lot of half-read novels that neither fit the formula as I understood it nor suited my desires and fantasies. Eventually it dawned on me that the elements of the formula that most disturbed me were the very same ones I desired for my reading pleasure, and that I had very complicated stakes indeed in maintaining my position.

This became clearest to me when a young friend of mine, an extremely talented writer whose pseudonym is Caitlin Clark, decided to write a romance, thinking that she could perhaps make enough money to support herself as a writer. Caitlin herself had not been a romance reader, but she embarked on a program of research, and filled me in as she went along on what she was discovering. I read drafts of her romance, and served as "consultant." After reading the first draft, I was amazed to hear myself saying things like, "you haven't made her vulnerable enough," or "you should have humiliated her more here." And I even prodded her in my marginal notes to make the hero more phallic. When she described the hero's house as "small, cozy, and very, very masculine," I joked, "How can something be small and yet very, very masculine?" When she had him driving a Mazda Miata, I found a review in *Consumer Reports* which noted that tall drivers are apt to feel cramped in the Miata's interior; I thought the car needed to be bigger, more powerful, and more expensive, and suggested a Jaguar. The compromise car turned out to be a black Mustang (which the author contrasted to the white horse the heroine always pictured her lover to be riding, an image which was brought back at the end to make a political point.

"I would have ridden in on a white horse to claim you," the hero says, "but I figured you're probably for animal rights." "I am," Summer whispered, "but if you treated the horse well . . .").

Yet at the same time that I, the feminist critic, was plumping for a more phallic hero, for, let me just say it, a more sado-masochistic scenario, I was secretly delighted that a woman could fantasize a hero who drove around in a tiny car and lived in a tiny house. And I was thrilled to see how Caitlin was reworking other important conventions. Not only did she invent a female friend who was loyal to the heroine as well as smart, witty, and beautiful, but she complicated a typical romance scenario in which the hero becomes embittered toward women because of a great wrong done him by a woman from his past. The hero blames his ex-wife, a.k.a. the "evil other woman," for the fact that their baby was stillborn (he suspects her to have been drinking and taking drugs during her pregnancy even though he has no proof that she had done so). The heroine, however, mentally demurs, "her rational side" telling her that the hero "wasn't completely innocent. He had gotten into the mess because of a lust he couldn't or wouldn't control." And she makes the hero consider the wife's point of view: "Have you ever considered that the relationship must have been difficult for her, too? . . . Difficult to be the wife of a man who married her out of a sense of obligation and didn't love her. Difficult to lose her baby." While the hero initially resists ("She trapped me," he stubbornly maintains) he later concedes the point and even hints that perhaps he should have allowed his wife to contemplate abortion: "I denied her a say in her own future even though I didn't love her, never had and never would." Here then was a man being held "answerable for the consequences" of his actions.

This encounter with author and text enabled me actually to experience the way fantasies are constructed and how they can be changed, and the effect was rather liberating. Caitlin took me up on some of my suggestions and resisted others, and the result felt like a kind of "compromise fantasy" (by which I do not mean to claim much credit for the work). The process also made me appreciate some other novels that hadn't quite suited my fantasies or that somehow managed to work for me despite the liberties taken with the conventions. In one that Caitlin lent me, a Harlequin entitled *Fortune's Cookie* by Nancy Martin which she used as a model, the hero has misgivings about having had sex with the heroine so he slinks away from her bed in the morning while she is still asleep. Formerly in these novels the heroine would retreat into hurt silence when she is rejected, perhaps setting in motion what I identify in *Loving with a Vengeance* as a revenge fantasy: the heroine runs away and in doing so makes the hero aware of how desperately he loves her, at which point he comes to her and confesses his love. In *Fortune's Cookie*, however, the heroine storms up to the man's desk at the office where they both work as newspaper reporters and angrily confronts him.

63

I recall another novel that reworks the formula even more extensively. In *Lady Dangerous* by Suzanne Robinson the eroticization of dominance is not absent, but is made problematic. The hero is an English lord who for a period of time had been a gunslinger in America. The man is practically a schizophrenic, since his cowboy persona comes upon him unpredictably. When he is in this altered state he tends to sling the heroine over his shoulder to take her off and have his way with her, but his attempts to ravish the heroine are thwarted each time by the appearance of his butler, who reminds him of his manners. It turns out that the hero had been raped by an uncle, and he must be made to see the connection between his uncle's behavior toward him, and his own toward the heroine. The author also stresses how the hero's possessiveness of the heroine—a quality that is usually so thrilling in romantic fantasy and so terribly damaging in real life—is motivated by a great deal of fear, much of it stemming from his childhood experiences.

So, it seems, some women are in fact boldly lifting the veil on the phallus and are finding mortal men standing behind it, somewhat sheepish, perhaps, at having been exposed, but maybe a little relieved as well.

Times change and romances are changing (a few of them; not enough of them). And I? Am I stuck in a time warp, clinging to my fantasy and to my analysis of it, a fixed entity amidst the change?

Earlier I mentioned a woman who had been in my life years ago and whom I left behind because I could not sort out my feelings. Years later this woman came back into my life temporarily. By this time, lesbian feminists had for quite a while been pointing out that in seeing lesbianism as a political choice feminism in its earlier days had too often tended to occlude one aspect of sexual relations: desire, or passion. I discovered how potent a factor the missing element can be when I met this woman again and took up with her where we had left off (just like in the old "Second Chance at Love" romance series.) After this experience, I continued to look for the same fantasy elements I had always wanted in romances, but I read the novels differently. And this different kind of reading was enabled by a development in the formula that I never anticipated. It had seemed to me absolutely crucial that in order to promote the reader's identification with the heroine the stories be told exclusively from the heroine's point of view, albeit in the third person. The Harlequin Company had at one time made this a requirement in the guidelines it issued to prospective writers. Now, however, authors are free to move back and forth between the hero's and heroine's point of view. So after my encounter with the woman from my past, as I read the lovemaking scenes I found myself identifying with the lover of woman as well as the woman herself and vicariously experiencing the touch, taste, and smell of a woman's body. To illustrate how easily the novels lend themselves to cross-gender readings, take the following passage from Elizabeth Lowell's *Only Love,* change the names and the masculine pronouns, and you have . . . lesbian sex:

> At first Shannon didn't understand. Then Whip [!] bent and nuzzled the tender skin of her inner thighs. His tongue flicked out just as his lips brushed over her softest skin. Shannon gasped Whip's name as she understood.
>
> "You told me whatever I wanted, however I wanted it," Whip said, nuzzling her. "Right now, this is how I want it."
>
> Shannon's breath came in with a ripping sound as Whip caressed her lovingly. He smiled, repeated the intimate touch and felt her response all hot and sleek around him. The scent of her pleasure was a primitive perfume, telling Whip what he already knew. The virgin widow was his—whatever he wanted, however he wanted it. (343)

My experience thus confirmed what I was told by my gay graduate students, when we were discussing the romances I had assigned in a seminar on genre I was teaching: that the romances were as erotically pleasurable for them as they apparently are for straight women. In fact both the lesbian and the gay man in the class found the novels I had asked them to read (all by Elizabeth Lowell, whose writings are very steamy) to be more erotic than most of the explicitly gay and lesbian romances they had read.

Which suggests that ethnographies ought perhaps to be conducted in the Castro District as well as "Smithton" . . .

65

It was in fact a gay male writer who once said to me, "we're so accustomed to talking about the fluidity of desire but the real issue is the fixity of desire." My own story seems to illustrate the point, certainly as regards my fantasy life, which has been utterly intractable. Yet, the fantasies that have appealed to me have remained more static than my life, and as my life has changed, I have found myself assuming a different relation to the fantasies. In turn, the life changes have made me aware of the limits of my own analysis of mass-produced fantasies for women and have given me insight into some of the transformations that have been occurring in the genre itself.

I do have reservations about the genre, as is no doubt clear. Yet I stand by my statement at the conclusion of my discussion of romances in *Loving with a Vengeance,* and would say that even with the most retrograde romances one should not condemn the novels so much as "the conditions which have made them necessary." Recalling the words of the villainess quoted earlier, "This world is a man's world. . . . I did not make the rules," I want to end this chapter as I did my earlier work, by repudiating the kinds of analyses that make romances largely "answerable" for, rather than the consequence of and response to, an unjust system.

4

MY LIFE AS A ROMANCE WRITER

❏

The thought of living his life without her left him with an emptiness noth-
ing would ever fill, not even football.
    —*Susan Elizabeth Phillips,* Nobody's Baby but Mine *(341)*

The previous essay was published, as I have said, in a special issue of the
journal *Paradoxa* on romances. Its editor, Kay Mussell, had assured me that
a piece of personal criticism would be appropriate for the issue, since many
of the contributors would be writing from their own experience.

    But when I received the volume and read through it, I felt as if I were
hanging out to dry. There I was confessing to having sado-masochistic
fantasies while the other contributors, many of them authors of romances,
were writing self-serving defenses of the genre, representing it as the full
flowering of feminist consciousness: "'Reading and writing a romance
may be among the most subversive acts a woman can engage in when it
comes to challenging patriarchal culture,'" writes one critic (62).[*] While

---

[*] Right up there, I guess, with struggling for effective sexual harassment policies, working
at rape crisis centers, and protecting abortion clinics.

I was exposing myself and making myself vulnerable to my readers as I wrestled with contradictions in the genre, in myself, and in my relation with the genre, these women admitted to nothing but the achievement of a fully developed, *absolutely unconflicted* feminist sensibility. As I wrote the article, I confess (but why do I keep confessing when nobody else is?), I was feeling expansive, tolerant. I basked in my ability to perceive the changes in the genre and especially at my own ability to change (to some extent) with the genre and the times. But after reading the other articles I regretted having lent myself to this postfeminist celebration, and felt the need to respond.* Although this chapter, published in a later issue of *Paradoxa*, might strike some readers as overly pessimistic, it should be considered along with the previous chapter for a balanced assessment of the genre. Together the chapters, I hope, will support what I have always maintained about popular culture—the importance of seeing both pro-gressive *and* regressive elements in popular texts. If this particular essay emphasizes the negative it is in order to counter the insane optimism of the majority of the articles, which bear out Meaghan Morris's view about the banality of cultural studies today.

In the *Paradoxa* issue, the writers lump together older critics of romance, including me, Kay Mussell, Ann Snitow, and even Janice Radway, who

---

* Do I exaggerate when I label the articles postfeminist? Here is a fairly characteristic re-mark: "the most subversive message in romance [is] that women can get what they want (and what women want certainly isn't limited to heterosexual relationships—there's no rule that says we have to be literal when interpreting romances), and come through the gender wars with their sexualities, intellects, and emotions intact" (71–72). Obviously if women *can* get everything they want and not be damaged by a society which oppresses them on the basis of their gender, then feminism is moot. Beyond this I am intrigued by the possibili-ties opened up by the permission to dispense with the literal. Presumably we are entitled to see the hulky football player heroes of Susan Elizabeth Phillips's romances as figures for les-bians. Fair enough up to a point; I myself, conscientiously following a "rule" of literary crit-icism, showed how a (limited) lesbian reading is possible now that point of view is no longer restricted to the heroine. But can we see the union of man and woman as figures for any-thing at all? Can we, for example, say that the marriage at the end of a given romance stands for the heroine's winning a bowling tournament? Apparently even in the realm of interpre-tation women can have it all.

although she attacked numerous critics for their negativity about romances, is now herself viewed as being too critical of romances. Hoisted on her own petard, I think to myself at first. Yet ironically I started feeling defensive on her behalf as well as my own—now I think of her and me in terms of "us." The writers in the special issue tend to talk about all us eighties critics with the same or even a greater degree of vitriol than they express toward patriarchy, and indeed, they tend to see us older critics as in league with patriarchy insofar as we employ "academic discourse" and insofar as we each, for whatever reason and however partially, view romances in a negative light. For example, borrowing a trope from the work of people of color without finding it necessary to discuss the romances of women of color or to talk about the problematic way people of color figure in white romances, one author asserts that the romance writer is a "trickster" and as trickster mounts "a deliberate, systematic challenge to both the limitations posed by traditional patriarchy and those perceived by academic feminism" (59). Further, writes this romance author and Berkeley Ph.D. student, past studies "such as Radway's, Mussell's and Modleski's . . . were products of academic cultures rooted in the politics of feminism, literary criticism, and academic careers. They are not bad scholarship according to the dictates of the academy, but they are productions of institutional cultures that both teach and reward reductionism [sic] (59)." I leave it to the reader to judge how successfully this writer's prose as exemplified here has avoided the horrors of the academic discourse she deplores.

As to the substance of the remarks, let us put aside the fact that in the seventies we were advised, as I said in my previous chapter, that writing about feminism and writing about popular culture would be career-busting activities (to say nothing of writing about them both together). And let us agree for the sake of discussion that romance plots can teach us about feminism less "reductively" than the popular culture studies of those of us who have been incorporating the work of de Beauvoir, Marx, Freud, Irigaray, Benjamin, Adorno, and de Lauretis. Let us, in short, think not about how romances can be understood by critics, but about how critics can be comprehended by romances.

So how is this for a romance plot? The female authors of "past studies" assume the role of the older women, the scheming adventuresses, who disdain the heroines—the younger critics—for their lack of sophistication (to wit: their unwillingness or inability to adopt "academic discourse"). We aim to take away their men, and that is why we look skeptically at the heterosexual courtship plot that is at the heart of the genre. We conceive a diabolical plan to insinuate ourselves into the men's world, the academy; we pretend to be interested in the men and their concerns and we adopt their lingo not because we really care about them (we are cold and selfish), but because we want the (institutional) rewards they have the wherewithal to bestow on us. In the end, though, the heroines will prevail. The men will see that these spunky little tricksters are the ones who are really on their side, and though of course the heroines seek no rewards, they will reap them.

69

Many of the contributors to *Paradoxa*, as I have said, are romance writers themselves and are using the occasion of the special issue to write elaborate apologias for the work they do.* Jennifer Crusie Smith, also a romance writer and academic, has written an article in which she quotes her own novels, and analyzes them as feminist, praising herself in particular for her use of humor. A blurb from her article appears in "The Romance Writers'

---

* A lengthy interview with prolific romance writer Jayne Ann Krentz affords her the opportunity to list her grievances against romance critics. The past studies were seriously flawed, she maintains, in contrast to the work of the "cutting edge" [i.e., totally uncritical] work of scholars like those writing in the *Paradoxa* issue (55). One of the things that disturbs her is that earlier critics of romance, in her view, tended to treat all romances as if they were the same story. Krentz's complaint takes on an irony when one turns to the romance novel database on the Web and looks at readers' reactions to her work. Here are some samples: "Although I've read every Jayne Ann Krentz novel and have enjoyed them all, I feel like I've read the same novel over and over again." "I feel that she recycles and regurgitates all of her material over and over. She needs to apply her great skills in writing towards new situations and original characters." "I have read either five or six of Krentz's books and I'm just tired of the predictability in every single one. This book followed the same exact pattern and I definitely felt cheated after reading it. I'm through with this author." Even those who like her work mention the predictability factor: "While it is true that her novels all seem to follow the same pattern, it is a pattern I find extremely enjoyable."

Report" along with an ad endorsing the journal. In the article, Smith argues that romances "help get [women's] reality on the page" (89). Relying on a socio-biological study by Helen Fisher claiming that ancestral women "who paid attention to what their kids were wearing and to the decor of their environment survived and passed on their genes," Smith argues that women's tendency, so pronounced in romance novels, to read the world anxiously for clues about their loved ones, their habit of "watching to see if those around them were comfortable" is part of "the nurturing that is also an aspect of our anthropological inheritance" (86–87). I don't believe that any feminist analysis has failed to notice that romances reflect certain realities of women's existence—though to be sure we did not always see the potential of socio-biology to confirm our insights. In the old days we called this tendency of romances "reinforcing the status quo." We used to think it was a problem. At the same time we tried to be careful not to denigrate the women who inhabited a reality that in great measure had been imposed on them. Further, many of us also saw in romances certain utopian elements that spoke to women's desire for a *different* reality.

Smith writes that romance fiction shows the reader "a woman like herself who struggles to attain" her goals ("control over her own life," "children," "vocational fulfillment, "great sex," and "a faithful loving partner") and who "wins, not because she's beautiful or young or lucky, but because she works for them." Forget feminism; stick with the Protestant work ethic, and it's possible to have it all.

In her book *The Erotics of Talk*, Carla Kaplan chides earlier feminist critics of romance for supposedly confusing symbolic revenge (in the form of a rebellious heroine) with real revenge (195n). It seems to me that this criticism is more appropriately leveled at the new generation of romance scholars, who, unsupported by a feminist movement, have now completely collapsed the registers of the symbolic and the real. When the earlier studies were undertaken, they were written with the idea that the information romance criticism would yield could help us in our efforts not just to effect "transformations in the romance genre," as the subtitle of the *Paradoxa* issue has it, but to change the world. We wanted a better place for women and we sought female empowerment *in* the world, not just in books. Now the very notion of female empowerment has been reduced to gobbledygook and announced as a fait accompli. "The actions [the heroines of romance take] are realistic, and because of that they have an empowering effect on their readers," writes Smith. She supports her point by quoting author Susan Elizabeth Phillips, "one of the biggest names in romance today," who says that reading romance novels gave her a "fantasy of command and control . . . a fantasy of empowerment." This, says Smith, "is a beauty of a fantasy, especially since it's not fantasy at all." Phillips is "one of the most empowered women I know. The romance fiction she read simply reminded her of her own capabilities, thereby reinforcing her own experience of reality" (85). In other words (I think), the fantasy of female empowerment reaffirms the *reality* of female empowerment. Normally of course, we do not have fantasies of possessing something that is already ours. I cannot imagine, for example, having a fantasy of being a university professor, nor do I need to be reminded that I am one in reality. What is in the nature of female power that makes women prone to forget they have it—and hence to require the aid of mnemonic devices in the form of romances?*

Since Smith singles her out for high praise (as do other contributors), let us look at how female empowerment works in the romantic fiction of Susan Elizabeth Phillips, a true *auteur* whose semi-comical work I myself confess to enjoying enormously. Phillips's latest novels have all featured heroes who are football players, on the verge of retiring (or in one case already retired and acting as a football coach). What is the fantasy of empowerment offered by Phillips? It is, as my epigraph suggests, the belief that women are more important to men than football. In the first of the trilogy of football books (*It Had to Be You*), for example, the heroine inherits a pro-football team which is coached by the hero. Toward the end of the book the hero avers that he would never throw a game for anyone, not even the heroine. Of course, the heroine gets into danger. She is kidnapped and as ransom the villain requires the hero to throw a championship game. Naturally the hero

---

* "Oh yeah, I remember now; I possess the power to time-travel back to the middle ages."

prepares to comply with the demand, but the heroine gets herself free in enough time for the game to be won.

According to readers whose comments I came across on the Internet, Phillips's novels have indeed had empowering effects on their lives. One of the readers says she was laughing so much reading one of them that her husband actually *looked up from the football game he was watching* to see what was so funny. Call me old-fashioned, but beyond celebrating such micropolitical triumphs I would want to inquire more closely into the relation between a fantasy of empowerment in which women are chosen over football and a reality in which, as the title of one book has it, "the stronger women get, the more men love football." The reality I refer to is, moreover, one in which men in groups (whether in sports or the military) often pose a serious sexual danger to women. In this respect it is striking that at the beginning of two of Phillips's novels, the heroine is together with several members of the football team and finds herself in the position of having to do a striptease, the very ineptness of which turns the hero on and sets into motion the machinery of the marriage plot.

But don't try this at home, folks. One of the writers in the *Paradoxa* issue maintains that romance novels can have a direct impact on women's lives, and she cites an instance in which one of her novels, about the recovery of an abused wife, caused a reader to go to work at a battered woman's shelter. I can only hope to God that none of Phillips's readers will be moved, on seeing the positive effects of the heroines' bold initiatives, to go strip before a gang of professional football players.

Of course, unlike Smith many of the contributors recognize that for the most part romances are not "realistic" but function as "myth" or fantasy.* Still these contributors wind up making similar extravagant claims. In an article on romance novels as "women's myth" the authors write:

---

* Jayne Ann Krentz in the *Paradoxa* interview says that academic criticism has "often criticized popular fiction—romance fiction in particular—because it is not realistic. But that is a ludicrous criticism which completely misses the point. It is not the task of popular fiction to be realistic" (52).

Women have appropriated an apparently normative story line to create a vision which is not normative at all—that men should become
responsive to and responsible for their emotions. Thus, romance
novels do not reflect, as some authors would suggest, that women
are content with or blinded by patriarchy. They simply take on an
issue which has received relatively little attention in the women's
movement—the place of emotion in a rational society. (230)

Now, this is not exactly news. *All* of the studies published in the early to
mid-eighties went to great lengths to show how the novels revealed
women's discontent with patriarchy. All talked about how part of the satisfaction of reading a romance comes from the fact that the heroine triumphs, as they say, "on her own terms." But these terms have, in fact, been
spelled out in large measure within and by a patriarchal order that has *assigned* women to the affective realm. So when the authors baldly claim that
the novels "are quite revolutionary" (230) we are entitled to be a bit skeptical, to insist on some qualifications to the claim. Who, we may well ask,
is reading these novels? Are men reading them and learning about the importance of "emotion in a rational society"? Are women translating this
revolutionary message into their daily lives, confronting men on their bi-
ases against emotion and hence bringing about the "revolution" proclaimed
on the pages of *Paradoxa*? And even if this is so, even if women are manag-
ing during half time to make the case for emotions to their husbands, what
kind of emotion is celebrated in the novels? Are not the emotions stirred up
by this fiction overwhelmingly if not exclusively those having to do with
romantic yearning (with the fantasy being that men have those yearnings
too)? Do such emotions encompass, say, compassion for Rwandan
refugees?*

So is reality actually being altered by romances, or are romances for the
most part affirming the importance of a "reality" (the life of the emotions)

---

* As for the claim that the women's movement has paid relatively little attention to the emotions, I suggest that the authors time-travel forward into the second half of the twentieth
century and read some of the classic feminist texts by Rich, Gilligan, et al.

that men will continue to denigrate at the same time they require women to inhabit it?

Please note: I am not saying it *is* the role of fiction, popular or otherwise, to overthrow patriarchy (and that is why it is ludicrous to call it "revolutionary"). For many of us scholars of popular culture, popular fiction (like television, movies, and rock-and-roll) mediates between the individual and society. We turned to the insights of political theory, psychoanalysis, and reader response theories in order to begin to understand the complexity of the mediation process. It is true, and I for one am proud of it, that we were guided by a feminist agenda. We had hoped our work would begin a sophisticated conversation among women committed to feminism. Needless to say the romance issue of *Paradoxa* was sorely disappointing, given the dismal anti-intellectualism of many of the essays.

So to the *Paradoxa* contributors who say romance is reality—or reflects reality, or impacts directly on reality—and to the other contributors who say romance is fantasy, I argue that the significance of romance lies in a complex relation of the one to the other and that feminist scholarship helps play a role in furthering our understanding of this relation.

In the case of the work of a Susan Elizabeth Phillips, a feminist scholar might appreciate, as I myself do immensely, her attention to older women's sexuality in her subplots, her mockery of men for some of their macho ways, and the ribbing they get for, say, desiring only very young women. I think these aspects of her novels can help to bolster female self-esteem and get women to turn a more cynical eye on some aspects of male attitudes and behavior. But a feminist scholar looking at the work of Phillips and at her use of humor is obliged to consider the work in the context of theories of humor and of a tradition of women's humor, which some scholars believe serves a conservative function in providing an outlet for women's anger against men. Insofar as women adopt an amused boys-will-be-boys distance from male behavior, they may very well be contenting themselves with an illusion of superiority that substitutes for real power.

Finally, a feminist analysis must, I think, keep reckoning with the way dominance continues to be eroticized in many romances, including the work of Phillips. (Note that I do not say *all* romances eroticize violence; indeed one of the main points of "My Life as a Romance Reader" was to discuss how I became aware of changes occurring in this regard.) So I find myself back to the point I so recently bragged about having transcended: feeling the need to caution against overoptimism in this key area.

Before returning to Phillips, I can't resist quoting from the work of an extremely popular romance writer, Linda Howard, in order to show just how far away romances can get from the "equality" between the sexes proclaimed by the *Paradoxa* articles. These passages from *Heart of Fire* seem to me far more shocking than the ones I quoted in my earlier essay. The first quotation seems particularly apt in that, like Smith's analysis, it too relies on a socio-biological explanation for sexual difference:

> So she sat there, letting her weight rest against him, letting his heat protect her from the chill, and against her will she was swamped by primitive female satisfaction. Women had felt the same way thousands of years before, sitting in firelit caves and leaning against their rock-hard, muscled mates, men who used their strength to keep their families fed, to guard them, to stand between them and danger. [Note how the women authors drawing on socio-biology neglect to mention the part about men spreading their seed thinly across the population.] Her field might be archaeology rather than anthropology, but she was well aware of the seductiveness of his strength. A few hundred years of civilization couldn't override instincts developed over years that numbered in the millennia. In a flash she saw how easy it was for the dominant male in a group to have his pick of the females. His very dominance made him *their* prime choice. (76)

I skip to the end, lest the reader think that the hero softens up somewhat or that the heroine moves beyond the cave man fantasy. The following quotations are from a scene in which the heroine has run away from the hero, and he finds her conveniently lying in bed somewhere:

> She had never seen that expression in his eyes before, so savagely intent that she shivered in primal alarm. . . . With two paces he was at

the side of the bed. His big muscular frame seemed to blot out the rest of the room. Her breath came in quick, shallow pants as she raised her hands to protect herself, knowing the gesture was useless. . . . Shock reverberated through her with the realization of what he was going to do. He pushed her legs apart, opening her to him, and stared down for a moment at her exposed female flesh. . . . Silently he unbuttoned his pants and opened them, freeing his erection. (293)

Then he "enters her":

She was stunned, disoriented. She felt the overwhelming possessiveness of his lovemaking and was keenly aware of the claim he was staking. He was refusing to let her go. . . . When she climaxed, when he pounded into her with his own release, it was with those fierce blue eyes holding hers, forcing her to accept that she was his. (294)

Before romance writers and critics rush to denounce me for looking down on the readers of romance who enjoy this stuff, let me assure them, once again, that I enjoy it myself. And before I am told that I cannot generalize from my experience, that I am the only pervert in the crowd, I wish to point out that the novel I have quoted from was a best seller, and I only bought one copy.

Even novels like Suzanne Robinson's *Lady Dangerous* which I cited in "My Life as a Romance Reader" cannot be said to have freed themselves from the erotics of domination. Precisely in order to criticize S&M dynamics, the novel continually evokes them, and doubtless on more than one occasion the reader experiences a delicious *frisson* when the man hauls the woman off to ravish her, even if he is thwarted in his intentions at the last minute. Certainly these dynamics are also present in the work of everyone's current favorite, Susan Elizabeth Phillips, for all her work's playfulness—a fact brought home to me when I loaned one of her novels to Caitlin Clark. I thought that because she herself is an excellent comic writer she could learn something from Phillips about the comic possibilities of the genre. She found the first part of *Nobody's Baby but Mine* very funny, but she did

76

not find the rest of it amusing. She was disturbed by the hero's propensity to physically restrain the heroine—carry her off, pin her down, lock her up, and so forth. A small woman who is also beautiful, she herself has had enough experiences with men trying to assert physical domination that she could not enjoy the novel.

Alas, however, no one is listening to the dour critics anymore, and indeed the *Paradoxa* contributors who counsel women to learn about feminism by reading romances rather than studying critical texts were heralding a moment whose time has come. At a major conference on romances being held this year at Bowling Green University, the keynote speaker is not a scholar, as one might expect at a university conference, but a romance writer—none other than . . . Susan Elizabeth Phillips. I can see that there is nothing left for me to do if I wish to carry on being a feminist critic but to become a romance writer myself. So I will write a romance, and then I will analyze it, quoting liberally to show what a feminist I am and what a great humorist, and then wait for the marketers to blurb me in order to sell my books and to sell copies of the journal in which my discussion of myself appears.

Truth to tell, I have already begun my romance. In fact I think I'll quote from it here. First, you have to know that my novel is about a female reporter who decides to go undercover to research the life of prostitutes. She meets a man who is working undercover to bust a major drug dealer. They have sex a couple of times. The first time he is selfish, and acts somewhat rough (because of course he can't stand the idea of all those other men who have had her). Then he discovers she is a virgin, and he is furious at himself. She gives him a tongue lashing saying she will never forgive him. Her anger comes not from the fact that he took her virginity (which she had allowed to happen), but that he treated a woman badly. The fact that he thought she was a prostitute was no excuse; after all he had put himself in the role of the john.

But the second time they have sex, he has come to realize his love for her, and he decides to show her how women can have sexual pleasure as well as men (since for whores it's always about the man's pleasure). Here's part of the sex scene, which has to do with the man's desire to perform oral sex on her:

> She turned her face into his neck and said in a small voice, "No, I just can't." "Yes, you can," he softly insisted. She couldn't see him smile. "A deal is a deal. If you go back on it, what will happen to that code of honor you prostitutes are so proud of?" [He still believes she is a prostitute, and mistakenly thinks he himself has initiated her into the life.] She didn't know of any code, but she didn't want to give herself away, so she just shook her head.

He teases her sexually and forces her to admit that she wants it, and afterwards she is overcome by embarrassment which he finds tremendously appealing.

Now, my novel is feminist for all sorts of reasons. First, it is forcing the man to say that he loves and wants to marry the woman despite the fact that he believes her to be a prostitute. So it challenges the sexual double standard "with a vengeance" (as a critic once put it). Second, as we see from the above scene, the attention is on female sexual pleasure rather than male sexual pleasure (not that the man doesn't ultimately have an orgasm too—just like in Phillips's novel where the football game that the hero is prepared to lose for the sake of the heroine is won after all). Third, it makes a strong case for women as sex workers, and it redeems from societal scorn all sorts of marginal types: transvestites, transsexuals, even lesbians, who we're told in *Paradoxa* can be "secondary characters" today, such is the incredible political progress we romance novelists have made.

So please don't tell me that this novel is just an excuse for the sex scenes, which play on women's psychic investment in a double standard that allows for, even demands, male sexual experience while preferring women to possess virginal innocence. That would be implying that this investment partly undermines the socially progressive messages I sneak in throughout the novel. Don't question me about the fact that a disproportionate number of beautiful virgins in their twenties and thirties populate romance fiction at the end of the twentieth century. It's not fair pointing to Susan Elizabeth Phillips's novels in which one of the heroines is a 30-year-old virgin and another one, having been raped years earlier (rape must be back "in"), hasn't made love in fifteen years—her lack of experience, given how gorgeous she is, is such a turn on for reader and hero alike. It's beside the point to talk about how the physical power of the men is constantly stressed in Phillips's novels and in mine, as is the readiness of the heroes to use their physical superiority over the heroine in titillating ways.

Don't try to tell me that writing a piece of genre fiction involves compromise (like much of life) in which the writer must adhere to traditional codes and conventions at the same time that she works bit by bit to change these conventions, thereby accommodating—and creating—different fantasies and greater aspirations. In short, don't tell me that my gains have been more modest than I want to believe. And please don't take away from me the biggest fantasy of all: that when I am sitting at my computer composing my stories or soaking in a bubble bath reading a steamy romance novel, I am in the very process of making the revolution.

5

THE WHITE NEGRESS AND THE
HEAVY-DUTY DYKE

❏

The following chapter had already been written when I was asked to submit something for a collection of essays called *Cross-Purposes: Lesbianism, Feminism, and the Limits of Alliance.* I reshaped the material to respond to the implicit question of the book, or rather, I expanded the question and then answered it in my essay. The question that I (and other contributors, as well, notably Sue Ellen Case) posed concerned the advisability of severing bonds between a queer lesbian (or "postmodern" lesbian) position and a lesbian feminist position as it has evolved from the seventies to the present. Because that polemic is, I think, an important one, I am including the reshaped version here.

In the early part of the century Virginia Woolf, writing in *A Room of One's Own,* praised women for their lack of colonialist ambition, remarking that a British woman could pass "even a very fine negress on the street without wishing to make an Englishwoman of her" (52). Recent feminist theory, much of it emanating from women of color, has challenged such self-con-gratulatory views, revealing the sometimes colonialist ambitions of femi-nism itself. All too often, it has been suggested, a white woman cannot en-counter a black woman without wishing to make a certain kind of *feminist* out of her—a white, middle-class kind, that is.

In this essay I would like to consider the converse of the situation Woolf depicts. Much theoretical attention is currently being devoted to the study of racial mimicry in general and blackface in particular, and for the most part this writing has tended to assume that blackface, the fantasy of be-coming black, is a masculinist one. This suggestion has been explicitly ad-vanced by Suzanne Moore and remains implicit in Eric Lott's work on min-strelsy and the blackface tradition—a tradition which, as Lott and others have argued, continues to this day "without the blackface." Lott writes, "Our typical focus on the way 'blackness' in the popular imagination has been produced out of white cultural expropriation and travesty misses how necessary this process is to the making of white American manhood. The latter simply could not exist without a racial Other against which it defines itself and which to a very great extent it takes up into itself as one of its own constituent elements" (476). But the question which seems pertinent to feminist theory today is how white *womanhood* might have been created out of white cultural expropriation and travesty of blackness. In other words, in what situations might we find a white woman wishing to make "a very fine negress" out of *herself?*

81

The first part of my title, "The White Negress," is, of course, taken from Norman Mailer's mid-century essay, "The White Negro," which celebrated the white hipster's identification with the image of the sex-ually potent black man. Mailer's essay provided a literary apologia for the cultural thievery and plagiarism of black culture that functioned, and would long after the writing of the essay continue to function, as a kind of "open secret" in American society. In this essay I want to look at Sandra Bernhard's film *Without* You *I'm Nothing,* which brings the

White Negro into the nineties and makes him a woman (or at least dresses him in drag).

Before doing so, however, I want to make clear that there is certainly historical precedent for white female blackface. In the 1930s there was Mae West whose musical numbers in films like *She Done Him Wrong* are directly taken from the tradition of black female blues performers, as the very title of one of West's songs, "Easy Rider," suggests (Ivanov). Hazel Carby has written about how black women used this music to register protest against their oppression and to express desires of their own ("It Just Be's Dat Way Sometime"). Given that one of Mae West's projects was to redefine norms of femininity to accommodate the possibility of female sexual desire, it is important to recognize how this white woman's rebellious reconstruction of womanhood depended, in part, on a masquerade of black femininity—a masquerade, needless to say, that had nothing to do with cross-racial solidarity. For while West incorporated aspects of blackness in her performance numbers in the films, the narratives tended to be as racist as most films from that day to this one. In *She Done Him Wrong,* for example, West frequently uses her black maid as the butt of her jokes, and at one particularly telling moment the maid replies to West's command for her to hurry up by calling, "I'se comin', I'se comin'" to which West responds, "Yeah, you'se comin', and your head is bendin' low. Well, get here before winter." This kind of dialogue alerts us to the film's double movement of expropriation in which the white woman not only mines and mimes the black woman's musical tradition, but also, by invoking the lyrics of Stephen Foster's "Old Black Joe"—a staple of minstrel shows—situates the "real" black woman within the minstrel tradition, itself a white travesty of black art and culture. That in the song these words are spoken by a dying black *man* further dissociates black women from their own sexuality so as to secure it for the white woman.[1]

While West's blackface was unacknowledged by her and unremarked (at least officially) by audiences, Bernhard is highly self-aware and parodistic—quintessentially postmodern—in her adoption of "blackface" (figure 5.1). The very title of her film *Without* You *I'm Nothing* (most people omit

Figure 5.1. Sandra Bernhard impersonating Nina Simone in *Without You I'm Nothing*. © The Academy of Motion Picture Arts and Sciences.

the emphasis on the word "you" when pronouncing the title) suggests quite clearly the postmodern awareness that the other is constitutive of the self, even though whites may believe the reverse to be the case—that the (white) "self" is prior to the (black) "other": "Without *me* . . . ," Sandra at one point starts to say to the film's diegetic African American audience, stumbling over the title line. The film spoofs the belief in the originary (white) self in a variety of ways—for example when Bernhard's cigar-smoking female manager, who addresses the camera directly, tells us that Sandra "doesn't have any influences.[2] She doesn't need any. And if you want my opinion, they've *all* stolen from her: Donna Summers, Tina Turner, Whoopi Goldberg, Nina Simone. And I have even seen traces of Sandra in Diana Ross." The camera cuts to Sandra on stage impersonating the "cross-over" artist Diana Ross, relating a story about crossing the country on a late-night flight from New York to LA to visit a depressed friend (who turns out to be Warren Beatty), interspersing the account with verses from Ross's hit songs. (Earlier Sandra had impersonated Nina Simone, insinuating a mocking tone of self-pity into the angry lyrics, "I'm awfully bitter these days/My parents were slaves.") In myriad parodic ways the film shows "whiteness" to be derivative and phantasmatic, caught up in the impossible dialectics of desire in which the wish to assimilate the other coexists with the self-cancelling need for the other's recognition. The film's ending makes it very clear that one cannot have it both ways: As Sandra, vulnerable and alone, stands nearly naked on the stage and stares out into the audience, the one remaining spectator, the ethereally beautiful, nameless black woman who drifts through the film appears at first to be writing the name "Sandra Bernhard" on the table and thus providing the token of the recognition Bernhard seeks, but is then shown to have written a sort of curse: "Fuck Sandra Bernhard."

This curse, apparently meant by the filmmakers to reveal a black female subjectivity that exists outside white appropriations of it and that exhibits nothing but contempt for those who engage in such appropriations, marks perhaps the single greatest failure on the part of the film to comprehend the position of the African American in relation to white American culture. For the fact is, African Americans often do not have the luxury of complete rejection of mainstream, dominant culture, but must conduct ongoing negotiations with it. One can point, for example, to bell hooks's discussion of the film in her book *Black Looks* which, while it reveals deep ambivalence toward the project, gives the film a highly nuanced reading that is the result of numerous conversations hooks had with "folks from various locations" as well as with students: "After weeks of debating with one another about the distinction between cultural appropriation and cultural appreciation, students . . . were convinced that something radical was happening, that these issues were 'coming out in the open'" (39).

"Fuck Sandra Bernhard" is in fact a sentiment most likely to have been uttered by some of Bernhard's formerly most ardent supporters in the white lesbian community. In an article published in *Outweek* expressing great disappointment over Bernhard's failure to come out clearly as a lesbian, or even to take a public stance unequivocally supporting lesbianism, Sarah Pettit strongly criticizes the fact that in bringing her stand-up performance to film Bernhard came to focus more on race relations than on relations between women which had been featured more prominently in her stage show. Pettit claims that in the early version of the show Bernhard revealed herself to be "a female artist clearly drawn to other women for inspiration and sustenance," but in the film this "dykeyness" has disappeared (39). In a rejoinder to Pettit that explicitly aims to identify the film's "challenge to a certain formulation of lesbian (feminist) identity," Jean Walton trenchantly responds to Pettit's criticism, arguing that Bernhard's numerous impersonations of black women performed before a bored and/or annoyed black (diegetic) audience underscore the dubiousness of an ideal that posits being "drawn to other women for inspiration and sustenance" when it is considered in the context of a whole history of white culture's appropriation of African American culture (249).[3]

Although both essays make many valuable points, when they are considered alongside one another they reveal a familiar squaring off of positions. The queer, deconstructive, or postmodern critic (Walton uses the term "postmodern," but "queer" seems to me an equally apt term) faults the lesbian feminist for focusing too much on sameness or commonality among women: thus Walton criticizes Pettit for implying a "definition of lesbianism that relies for its stability on one's all-encompassing solidarity with women, on one's identification with them as a political group, on a demonstration of supportiveness of them, and indeed, almost an embracing of them in a kind of unconditional love" (248). For her part, the queer critic, Walton, claims the moral and political high ground, priding herself on respecting the differences among women supposedly ignored by most lesbian feminists. Bernhard, in constantly changing "her own 'identity' to construct a persona," becomes for Walton the anti-essentialist heroine who is capable of showing us how racial identity is "as much a matter of drag as of skin color" (249, 252). Yet this view simplifies in its turn, for it seriously underestimates the extent to which skin color condemns a large segment of our population to a fixed position within dominant systems of representation and impedes certain people's ability to alter their "identities" and construct other "personae."

Indeed, this line of (white) feminist thought, for all the lip service it often pays to the multiplicity of identities and positionalities, may neglect to see how it sometimes requires the black woman to signify little more than difference itself, which the critic may then assert in order to differentiate herself from "white lesbian feminism," which in turn is viewed as monolithic. It thus may share in common with a great deal of American thought the tendency to see racial and ethnic difference in terms of a black/white binary. In this regard it is perhaps not surprising to see how small a role the issue of Bernhard's Jewishness plays in analyses of Bernhard's racial masquerades. At most, Jewishness in the film is referred to more or less in passing as "one of the positions from which Sandra speaks"—as if this position, particularly in its relation to the issue of blackface, did not possess a history and a tradition outside the text and a weight and an insistence within it that makes it more than one in a plethora of possible identities from which postmodern woman is invited to select (Walton 255). A whole history of popular entertainment positions Jews on a sliding continuum between the fixed poles of black and white and thus enables a certain free play of identity but inhibits others.

In a fascinating article on the film *The Jazz Singer*, Michael Rogin observes how "the jazz singer rises by putting on the mask of a group that must remain immobile, unassimilable, and fixed at the bottom" (437). (I myself made a similar point in *Feminism without Women* where I had also considered how the black woman in a film like *Crossing Delancey*—a film written and directed by Jewish women about a young Jewish woman living in Manhattan and distancing herself from her roots—comes to represent embodiment and sexuality and thus allows the heroine a more sublimated relation to romance.) Drawing on Irving Howe, Rogin points out that Jews "had almost entirely taken over blackface entertainment by the early twentieth century," especially in music (he refers as well to Jewish song writers who "turned to black-derived music to create the uniquely American, melting pot sound of the jazz age"), and he speculates that such "'musical miscegenation' produces the excitement of racial contact without its sexual dangers" (440).[4] Rogin stops short of the logical conclusion of this line of reasoning, but other analysts of the phenomenon of blackface like Kobena Mercer and Eric Lott allow us to see that since the "miscegenation" most often involved two *male* artists, the sexual excitement must have had a homoerotic dimension as well.

In what follows I want to extend this line of inquiry to account for Bernhard's blackface and to suggest that for all Bernhard's apparent sexual daring, "blackface" enables her to distance herself not only from interracial lesbian sexuality but, especially, white lesbian sexuality (and, it follows, from lesbian identity). It is not accidental, I would argue, that on the one occasion on which she "speaks" about lesbian relations in the film she is in "blackface," singing "Me and Mrs. Jones." I will, then, be taking a position which is in direct opposition to several of the film's commentators who assert that the "dykeyness" which Pettit claims is lost from the film version of Bernhard's show asserts itself in Sandra's relation to black women (39). To the extent that "dykeyness" is present, I maintain, it is disavowed, and in a manner not altogether unlike the way hom(m)osexuality has been disavowed in much male art and culture.

As was the case with the jazz singer, assuming blackface allows Sandra to explore her identity along a racial continuum, in which the Jew as outsider stands somewhere between the white Christian and the African American. For example, early in the film, following Sandra's Nina Simone impersonation, the black man at the microphone in the Parisian Lounge where Sandra supposedly is performing lauds her and calls her "our very own Sarah Bernhardt." This misrecognition—a reversal of the tendency of whites to misname blacks—invokes the turn-of-the-century performer whose Jewishness and "degeneracy" Bernhard seems to be playing on. The man at the mike then introduces the next performer: Shoshana, a Madonna-wanna-be who comes out on stage dressed in a sexy costume and does an extremely awkward striptease. The camera then cuts to a shot of the nameless black woman, who is walking across the screen with Watts Towers in the background. In the next sequence Bernhard attempts to lead an unresponsive, primarily African American audience in some Israeli folk songs; she then segues into a brief comic autobiographical sketch which features a fantasy of growing up in an upper-middle-class Christian household. Her name would be Babe, Bernhard fantasizes, her brother's Chip, and they would sing Christmas carols in harmony on Christmas Eve. The fantasy ends with a little talk by the mother, who says, "And may all your Christmases be white," whereupon the camera cuts to three children singing in the snow, one of whom is a black boy.[5] Another cut shows the black woman standing in front of a Jewish market reading *Kabbalah and Criticism.* The wish invoked here (parodically, to be sure) seems to be that if the Jewish woman cannot assimilate herself to the dominant culture (mocked as shallow anyhow), perhaps she can assimilate *her* other, the dominant culture's more extremely marked other, to her own culture and traditions.

A similar wish appears to be present in the next sequence, which begins with Sandra as a black lounge singer (whose piano player is Jewish: "you know how well we people get along") performing the number "Me and Mrs. Jones." This number is followed by one more appearance of Shoshana and then a shot of the black woman listening to rap music and clipping a lock of her hair—a shot that is the mirror image of an earlier one of Sandra performing the same act, also in front of a mirror. Again, then, the pathetically failed identification with the white feminine ideal, Madonna (whose Christian name is Christian indeed), appears to invite a compensatory fantasy of the other's identification with the self.

89

The film's fixation on Madonna is revealed in a variety of ways. Madonna is central to the Diana Ross number (figure 5.2), for example, since the friend whom Sandra-as-Diana flies across country to cheer up is Warren Beatty, Madonna's love interest at the time. This kind of quadrangulation of identities and desires is familiar to queer theorists when it involves men as the primary subjects and objects.[6] Indeed it has become commonplace in cultural studies to see a homoerotic component in these "geometric" relationships in which women function as objects between men, and no doubt something of this sort is at stake in the relations among Bernhard, Beatty, Madonna, and Ross. Certainly it is tempting to read into the film's erotics the flirtation that developed between Bernhard and Madonna around the time of the film's release, with both women fanning speculation about the nature of their relationship but never satisfying the public's curiosity. Yet, what of Bernhard's relation to the black woman? To what extent does Bernhard make explicit the hidden homoerotic aspects of minstrelsy by revealing the white woman's desire for the black woman and to what extent is Bernhard simply involved in the erotics of disavowal characteristic of minstrelsy?

Perhaps the fact that most critics have declined comment on the erotic dimension of Sandra's cross-racial impersonations indicates that political correctness is not to be found in this aspect of the film. Queer critics looking for less guilty pleasures than those which are so obviously shot through with relations of domination have turned to the figure of the nameless black woman in order to locate interracial lesbian desire. They point in particular to the final performance number in which Sandra, dressed in stars-and-stripes' patterned G-string and pasties, sings Prince's *Little Red Corvette,* and then waits for a response from the woman who, it turns out, is the one remaining audience member. To posit such a desire would be to

Figure 5.2. Sandra Bernhard impersonating Diana Ross. © The Academy of Motion Picture Arts and Sciences.

posit a way for lesbian desire to move, exogamously as it were, across racial, communal, and psychic borders—out of white lesbian feminism, out of the space of the (white) woman-identified woman, out of the problematics of identification/appropriation/assimilation.

But I confess I do not see how the film may be said even here to signify explicitly Sandra's desire for the nameless woman, if only because we assume until the last moment that Sandra is performing before the entire audience. We aren't even aware until the end that the black woman has in fact been *in* the audience, and her presence comes as a surprise since she has nowhere previously occupied the same space with Sandra. Sandra's expectation of applause, moreover, seems to me to bespeak not a recognition of/desire for the other in her difference, but a longing for the other's recognition of the success of the white woman's racial masquerade.

Lauren Berlant and Elizabeth Freeman express disappointment about Bernhard's failure in the end to resolve her "feminine and sexual identities into a lesbian love narrative" (!) and actually label Sandra's final performance "lesophobic." They write:

> The film imagines a kind of liberal pluralistic space for Bernhard's cross-margin, cross-fashion fantasy of women, but shows how lesophobic that fantasy can be, insofar as it requires aesthetic distance— the straightness of the white-woman-identified woman—as a condition of national, racial, *and* sexual filiation. Her desire for acceptance from the black-woman-in-the audience perpetuates the historic burden black women in cinema have borne to represent embodiment, desire, and the dignity of suffering on behalf of white women, who are too frightened to strip themselves of the privileges of white heterospectacle. (173)

Interestingly, "lesophobia" may be seen to surface in the film at the precise moment when Bernhard explicitly deals with gay male *homo*phobia. In a narrative accompanying Sylvester's song, "I Feel Real," which she relates in the second person, a straight man finds himself in a gay disco where he is brought by a friend and where he soon finds himself caught up in a homosexual encounter with a black man. As the story comes to a climax, the camera circles around the scantily clad black men who serve as Sandra's back-up singers in the number and positions itself for a moment in back of a leather-clad black man who stands behind Sandra, subliminally suggesting her identification with the disavowing subject. When the scene ends, there is a cut to a curious shot of several white female bodies in a steaming shower; in the foreground of the image, the women pose erotically for the camera as they wash themselves and each other, while behind them, the figure of the black woman, wrapped in a white towel, walks across the frame, constituting a strikingly chaste and austere presence in the midst of what by comparison seems a sodden and undignified tangle of bodies. Not only does this scene suggest a "lesophobic" parallel to the disavowal of gayness the sequence has just registered; it enlists the black woman as agent of this disavowal and it problematically situates her, in contrast to the sexualized black man in the disco, outside of erotic desire. We might at this point be entitled to ask how far we are from Mae West and the double movement of expropriation of the black female performer's sexuality I noted in her work; if in stealing this sexuality West had relegated the actual black woman to the position of the debased servant in the narrative, Bernhard turns the coin over and makes the anonymous black woman in the film an exemplar of uplift: in contrast to the sexy black songstresses Bernhard portrays, the black woman has achieved class mobility in white society (at the outset she is playing Bach on the piano; later we see her as a scientist in a lab). This represents a marked and very important shift from a film like *The Jazz Singer,* which, as we have seen, depended on blacks' immobility; in Bernhard's postmodern version of minstrelsy African Americans engage in a kind of whiteface (as when they perform a classical ballet in the background while Sandra sings Prince's "Little Red Corvette"). Yet in reproducing and assigning to Sandra's psyche the very split experienced historically by black women in relation to representations of their sexuality (as Hazel Carby writes, "Racist sexual ideologies proclaimed the black woman to be a rampant sexual being, and in response, black women writers either focused on defending their morality or displaced sexuality onto another terrain"), the film may be said to engage in the ultimate form of female blackface (*Reconstructing*, 174).

Against Walton and most other critics who see the nameless woman as the object of Sandra's sexual desire, I am arguing that this woman, as opposed to the sexualized females Sandra impersonates, signifies the white lesbian's desire to desire exogamously[7] and is presented as a kind of fantasized way out of the dilemmas of embodiment (the awkwardness of a Shoshana), as well as dilemmas of (Jewish and white lesbian) identity. In this regard the black woman in *Without You I'm Nothing* might seem to function altogether differently from that famously described by Valerie Smith, who has argued that the African American woman, in keeping with historical constructions of women of color associating them "with the body and therefore with animal passions and slave labor," serves as a means for white feminist theorists to consider "the material ground of their enterprise." Yet is it not the case that, however self-consciously and parodistically, the African American woman is still "emptied of her own significance in order to become a sign in another's"? Is she not still being used to reveal "something of the content of [white women's] own subject positions," although it is true that in this case she signifies a *refusal* of some of these positions (45)?[8] And is there not an analogue here to the practice of some deconstructive, queer white theorists who invoke black/white racial difference as the most privileged of a supposedly endless array of differences, which, once posited, allows them not only to repudiate an identification with white lesbian feminism but to look away from the material realities of bodies and circumstances that limit the play of identity?

Discussing *The Jazz Singer*, Rogin observes that the Jew in blackface may by evoking "an imagined alternative communal identity" free himself "from the pull of his inherited Jewish, communal identicalness" and become "a unique and therefore representative American" (440). While *Without You I'm Nothing* reveals a desire on the part of the white (Jewish) subject to imagine (her)self as part of an "alternative [i.e., African American] communal identity," to transcend the "communal identicalness" of Jewishness and, in Bernhard's case, white lesbian feminism, and to become uniquely and representatively American, it emphasizes the arrogance and impossibility of these goals (after all, Sandra's "alternative community" is out the door by the time she finishes her final number). In the preface to the striptease Sandra, wrapped in the flag, delivers the "Without *you* I'm nothing" speech to the diegetic black audience, and in an exaggeratedly lyrical voice she speaks yearningly of her desire to get out of the main highways into the byways where she can be at one with the people:

> I wanted to walk through the Midwest early in the morning and watch all the farmers on their way to work in the amber fields of grain in Nebraska, to pick strawberries next to my Chicano brothers and sisters underneath the hot California sun, to watch the morning light shining off the body of the Lady of the Harbor onto all the Korean grocers as they stock their salad bars. These were the sounds, sights, and smells that I wanted to incorporate into my world view.

Needless to say the Whitmanesque ideal of the artist communing with (and containing) the multitudes with whom he mingles in his travels across the nation is thoroughly deflated: "I never wanted to depend on Triple A," Sandra confides. Of course, the subversion of the notion of the American artist as representative is, it must be noted, especially easy to achieve via a *woman* artist. For when have women ever been able to sustain the remotest illusion of themselves as representative?

But this parody of the imperial American artist/subject marks a striking contrast to the number which comes right before it—a number which is uncharacteristically serious and which situates an "alternative communal identity" in the gay male disco subculture of the seventies. Sandra, in (counter) drag as the black gay male drag disco artist, Sylvester, performs a moving hom/femage to the late singer's memory and provides us with a glimpse of a vision that is, for once in the movie, not simply invoked in order to be parodied. In the number "Do You Want To Funk?" and its preface Sandra/Sylvester offers up a kind poetic incantation extolling "the beat," which is said to span place and time and connect us all to one another throughout the world. This entire sequence begins, once again, with Sandra as Jew, in black wearing a veil and chanting. She goes on to claim her "roots" in the culture of the seventies: "Of all the decades we've exploited— and we've exploited them all—the seventies remain the least understood, yet the most central to my aesthetic and philosophy." Here then, at last, Sandra posits a kind of community and an identity founded in a certain gay male subculture.

It seems very clear, then, that the Sandra of the film is hardly the straight white-woman-identified woman that Berlant and Freeman see, but a queer gay-male-identified one. That Bernhard's alliance with gay men, which she quite openly declares in the film as well as in talk shows and interviews, tacitly colludes in the social and cultural erasure of the lesbian feminist becomes clear when we remember that the seventies which Sandra says were so central to her "aesthetic and philosophy" were not just the era of gay male discos but *also* the decade of the lesbian feminist.[9] But the lesbian feminist is a figure Bernhard not only distances herself from, as in the film, but continually baits whenever she gets a chance to do so. For example, in an interview which was published in the *Advocate* and is often cited by Bernhard's queer supporters as evidence that she is "out," Bernhard actually admits that she could envision herself living with a woman partner for the rest of her life, although, she hesitates, "two women can't have babies, . . . can they?" The interviewer responds:

Well, they can, but they need to get some sperm from somewhere.

SANDRA: Oh, don't print that, because then they'll really come after me: "She doesn't even want to get sperm from men!" But I'm not antimen, so there's no point of even talking about it really.

INTERVIEWER: There's a big difference between being against men and preferring woman. Most women have better things to do than obsess about how much they hate men.

SANDRA: Right on! Jesus, The *Advocate* was smart to send you. I was so afraid that they were going to send in some heavy-duty dyke who was just going to fry my ass. (72)

Sandra assumes agreement between herself and the interviewer, but to me their emphases seem very different. Whereas the interviewer wants to assert the positivity of affirming and loving women, Bernhard wants to ward off the image of the man-hating dyke—an image that has, of course, long been used as a bogey to scare rebellious women.

96

Sandra's grounds for hesitating about living with a same-sex partner are surprising, to say the least. For all the acclaim given Bernhard as an exemplary postmodern artist who lays bare the performative nature of gender (and race) by continually "reproducing" herself into a seemingly endless variety of identities, she here hedges against lesbian identity by invoking woman's role in *heterosexual* reproduction. One can ask who is the greater essentialist—Bernhard who appeals to male/female biological functions in thinking about what kind of social arrangement she will enter into or Pettit, who in taking Bernhard to task for conversations like the above in which Bernhard affirms lesbians with one hand and slaps them with the other, asserts that Sandra plays "with the boundaries of our existence *for her work and for her own private gain.* Lesbianism is not an essentialism that blocks out the world; it is quite persistently a way of life for many women very much in the world, often in truly painful and violent ways" (42, emphasis in original). What this passage suggests to me, although Pettit herself doesn't make the connection, is that in her public persona "Sandra" appropriates lesbianism in a way that is analogous to the filmic Sandra's appropriation of African Americanness. Whereas the film is aware of many of the problems of such appropriation when it comes to blackface, the Sandra of the talk-show circuit seems entirely insensitive to its effects on lesbian community.

If we needed more evidence that Bernhard's fame has been achieved to a certain extent at the expense of lesbian feminism, which is thereby threatened with renewed invisibility (to the extent that it has ever been visible), we can turn to some curious details behind Bernhard's assumption of a role on *Roseanne*, playing a woman who came out as gay (and then qualified her declaration some episodes later by saying she was bisexual). According to a book by Geraldine Barr, Roseanne's lesbian-feminist sister who claims to have collaborated with Roseanne until the latter married Tom Arnold and got rid of her, in the sisters' original plan Roseanne's TV sister Jackie, the fictional surrogate of Geraldine herself, was slated to be a lesbian and eventually to have her own spin-off show. (Instead, it was Tom Arnold who got his own spin-off program, the atrocious *Jackie Thomas Show*—a title that even appropriated the TV sister's given name.) Ironically, then, Bernhard who so anxiously disavows lesbian sisterhood came to replace the (surrogate) lesbian sister of Roseanne Barr Arnold.

According to Barr, Jackie's lesbianism was supposed to be revealed gradually and would therefore never be a major issue or problem. Barr's ambition to produce a television show about a woman like herself whose lesbianism *would be only one component of a complex identity* gives the lie to those who see the lesbianism which emerged from the women's movement as a monolithic construction. In her biography/autobiography *My Sister Roseanne* (whose original splendid title *Behind Barrs* was dropped), Barr acknowledges her roots in seventies feminism and details her dream of building a sisterhood that would speak from, to, and about the women whose lives have been unacknowledged in the history of Hollywood entertainment. As a lesbian working-class Jew who grew up among Mormons in Utah, Barr herself occupies a site of so many intersecting differences that she would seem to be a postmodern feminist's dream, were it not for the fact that so many of her differences are unassimilable to postmodernism's favorite categories (its canonized differences, as a friend of mine put it) and that *she gives these categories positive content* rather than mining them strictly for their potential to subvert other categories.

Contrasting Bernhard to Barr on their relation to regional identities, for instance, we could note that Bernhard's assumption of such identities is meant to debunk the possibility of authenticity in a postmodern commodity culture—as when she sings a duet of the Hank Williams song "I'm So Lonesome I Could Cry" in front of a facade of a barn that opens onto a scene of New York City. By contrast, Barr actually believed in the possibility of bringing to the arena of mass entertainment the perspectives of actual working-class Moms who live in trailer parks in the Midwest and West. Even more striking, perhaps, is the difference between Bernhard and Barr in their attitudes toward their Jewish identities. While Jewishness for Bernhard is (in the film) a vehicle for negotiating her relation to other identities, for Barr Jewishness came to be not only something to be struggled against because of its patriarchal structures and laws but something which possessed positive meaning for her and inflected her evolving definition of lesbian sisterhood. For instance, she and Roseanne intended to give the name *Beshert* to their production company, which they planned to use to "help empower working class women through the arts" (Barr says she saw the obligations entailed by worldly success "in spiritual terms where, if you take vast sums from the universe, you must return vast sums in kind" [G. Barr 177]). "*Beshert*," Barr explains, is a Yiddish "word that means that an event or a relationship is preordained. . . .[if] you meet someone, fall in love, and instinctively know that the other person is perfect for you . . . a perfect soul mate, that is *beshert*. . . . Rosey and I were sisters preordained to be Sisters" (216).

The point of this brief comparison is not to dole out political (or spiritual) correctness awards, but to inform (or remind) readers that lesbian feminists consciously faced many of the issues that "queer" feminists sometimes claim to have discovered and, moreover, that it had hope and vision and risked self-affirmation even as it struggled with differences and fought against oppression. It had humor too, and its humor was a major weapon in the fight against oppression. To take one example that bears repeating in light of Bernhard's fear of being perceived as a man-hating dyke, we might consider the famous Roseanne joke that Barr says came out of her and Roseanne's discussions at the "Woman to Woman Bookstore in Denver," where, in the sisters' early days before Hollywood, straight and lesbian women of many colors congregated and hashed out differences: "They say lesbians hate men. How can they? They don't have to fuck them" (134).

I am certainly not arguing that lesbian feminism is exempt from the charge of appropriating others' differences and engaging in its own forms of blackface. In an important article published a few years ago, "Homelands of the Mind: Jewish Feminism and Identity Politics," Jenny Bourne traces the "coming out" process of Jewish lesbian feminists like Elly Bulkin to the black lesbian feminist statement of the Combahee River Collective. "The most profound and potentially the most radical politics," the Collective had written, "come directly out of our own identity as opposed to working to end somebody else's oppression" (2). According to Bourne, feminists like Bulkin seized upon this statement as a rationalization for their coming out as lesbians and then as Jews and to claim "commonality" with African American women in their "experiences of oppression" (12). Yet the process didn't always work that way. Geraldine Barr, for example, learned from women of color to reject the arguments of liberal white women when they argued, "We must concentrate on our similarities and celebrate our differences" (107). For Barr and the women of color she encountered on her journey to "Sisterhood," differences were the source of tension, and liberal feminism was at fault because it "rarely touched black women, rarely touched Hispanic women, rarely touched women who were raised in poverty" (110).

Roseanne seemed to share her sister's values and goals—so much so that in her first book, *Roseanne: My Life as a Woman,* she wrote in her dedication to her sister: "Where do you end and where do I begin?" Such words in retrospect seem ominous. For as this chapter is meant to demonstrate, the boundaries and borders that exist between people and between the categories in which they seem to fit must be acknowledged and respected. When Tom Arnold entered the picture, Roseanne figured out the answer to her question, which turned out to be not at all rhetorical. "Sisterhood is dead," she announced just when Geraldine Barr, having voluntarily taken a back seat to Roseanne who as a straight woman and a mother was judged to be in the best position to speak for the majority of women, was about to realize her ambitions to become a producer and launch her own projects. In this case at least, the decision about "the limits of alliance" seems pretty much to have been made *for* the lesbian feminist. But now what? Where should she go? The queer "deconstructor" of identity, having "allied" herself with the straight feminist and become more than a little phobic, would prefer to have nothing to do with her. Perhaps these new "allies" need not worry about her fate: since she "can't have babies," maybe she and her kind will just die out. Then queers and straight feminists will never have to recognize the extent to which the heavy-duty dyke has given birth to *them*, the extent to which her commitment to the representation of women in the variety of their differences might in truth lead them to say, "Without *you* I'm nothing."

6

DOING JUSTICE TO THE SUBJECTS

The Work of Anna Deavere Smith

❏

In *Fires in the Mirror,* her smash hit one-woman show performed at New York's Public Theater in the summer of 1992, African American performer, Anna Deavere Smith, plays the parts of twenty-nine people whom she interviewed about the Crown Heights riots that occurred in Brooklyn the previous year. She invited people who were directly involved in the Crown Heights events to discuss their experiences, and asked others—people like Angela Davis and Ntzoake Shange—to reflect more generally on issues of racial identity. Although Smith excerpted the remarks of her subjects, she aimed to reproduce their speech with complete fidelity, repeating their words verbatim and even including slips of speech and stammerings. Later Smith designed a similar show, *Twilight: Los Angeles 1992,* about the Rodney King beating incident and the turmoil which ensued. This piece was first performed at the Mark Taper Forum in Los Angeles. It was then revised for a run at the New York Public Theater and revised again for Broadway's Court Theater. Both of these theatrical pieces not only concern public events but have *become* major public events, often uncannily producing and reproducing the politics reflected in the works and revealing with exceptional clarity that socially engaged criticism must understand how the media and other institutions shape interpretation. Before proceeding to a discussion of Smith's work itself, therefore, I want to analyze the responses of the critics to Smith's performances. In what follows I will be focusing more on *Fires in the Mirror* than on *Twilight*, since as a more reflexive text that aims to account for the complex processes of identity formation, *Fires in the Mirror* clues us into the theoretical and political issues at stake in Smith's work as a whole. Smith's performances are part of an ongoing series of pieces entitled *On the Road: A Search for American Character*. Typically Smith has constructed her plays as follows: having been invited to come into a specific community to interview people about a controversial event, usually one involving racial conflict, and sometimes gender antagonism as well, she records interviews with the people involved, memorizes their words, and then "performs" them on stage. The interviewees are then invited to attend the performance. In her earlier work audience awareness that the interviewees were present had a very unsettling effect, particularly because audiences often responded in ways that seem to have been unanticipated by the subjects—for example, bursting into laughter over something said with great earnestness or passion.[1] In the earlier work too, audiences often knew the people whom Smith impersonated, but as the work has gained international attention, it has inevitably changed, so that the "communities" being investigated have been major metropolises and the events have been of cataclysmic proportions; the people being portrayed would thus most likely be unknown to audience members, or known only through media representations.

In some ways, Smith's work marks her as an exemplary postmodern artist. She problematizes the authority of the speaking subject, foregrounding the split between the way people consciously present themselves and the way they appear. Other postmodern aspects of Smith's art include the reliance on quotation and allegory (by including the observations of critics and theorists, the work may be said to contain an interpretation of itself) and the site-specific nature of the performances.[2] Indeed, as regards this latter aspect, Smith is a pioneer and the theater owes her a great debt on this account alone, for while site-specificity is common in the visual arts, it has hitherto not characterized contemporary theatrical practice. Yet its postmodernism notwithstanding, there seems to be something about the work that induces even sophisticated poststructuralist critics to lapse into older critical vocabularies in analyzing it. For example, Barbara Johnson, while insisting on the craft involved in putting the piece together, can nevertheless speak of the way "'Fires in the Mirror' holds its mirror up to America" (10). Certain questions thus inevitably arise about the work's relation to theoretical issues concerning art and representation: Does this almost "purely" mimetic art, hailed by so many critics in the main-stream press as presenting "the true words of real people," testify to a naive belief in the myth of presence, or to the belief in language's function to mime or mirror a pre-given reality, or to the belief in the artist's representativity, her ability to speak for, or in this case *as*, the subaltern? These are questions with both metaphysical and political dimensions, which we might sum up in a single question: In light of the demands of black America for justice ("no justice, no peace") during the political strife in Crown Heights and in Los Angeles, can Smith's representations ever (as we say of photographs with especially fair likenesses) hope to do "justice" to their subjects?

Certainly, the overwhelmingly white male critical establishment has pictured Smith in terms that evoke the very emblem of liberal justice, the woman with the scales, and have continually pronounced her to be "fair," "impartial," "balanced." Frank Rich wrote of *Fires in the Mirror,* "Her show is a self-contained example of what one person can accomplish, at the very least, in disseminating accurate, unbiased inside reportage." The highest praise in journalistic commentaries thus came in the narcissistic form of praise for Smith's skills as a *journalist*, praise which in an ironic kind of postmodern reciprocity offset the press's earlier characterization of the riot-torn Crown Heights, with its angry inhabitants and "outside agitators" commandeering the airwaves, as "theater" (Klein 28). Smith herself has sometimes seemed to acquiesce in the assessment of her work as uncommitted to a particular viewpoint. In a *Newsweek* review, Smith discusses with Jack

Kroll her reluctance to drop from *Twilight*'s final script Stanley Sheinbaum's account (figure 6.1) of how his attempt to talk to gang members
aroused the fury of the police: "'Stanley said, "F— you! I'll talk to whoever
I like. Why do I have to be on one side?"' Smith says: 'It broke my heart to
lose that, because it helps me to make the point of why do *I* have to be one
one side?"' ("Fire," 63). And, of course, this passage helps Kroll to make the
point of why does *he* have to be on one side (when even the black female author isn't)? Thus by mimicking the mimic, the media reviewers avoid having to deal with the political issues at the heart of Smith's work.

104

From the view that truth lies "in the balance" of the opposite sides of
what Jean-François Lyotard calls the postmodern agon, it is but a step to
declaring that the struggles (between blacks and Jews, blacks and Koreans,
blacks and whites, etc.) are meaningless in their own terms. Observe the
contortions of thought in the following remarks of a *New York Times* discussion of *Fires in the Mirror*:

> With the rioting in Los Angeles fresh in our minds, the obvious re-
> mark to make about "Fires in the Mirror" is that it couldn't be more
> timely. Yet the timelessness of the piece is what impressed me. Put
> the specifics aside and you have a view of people so at odds with one
> another that human nature itself seems to be to blame. We are stub-
> born creatures, claiming right for ourselves and wrong for the other
> guy, and that stubbornness repeatedly dooms us to violence.
> Nonetheless, we advance a thousand and one reasons, grand and piti-
> ful, to explain why giving an inch just isn't possible (D. Richards
> H5).

And so, a work which started out scrupulously to reproduce the specifics of
people's opinions, utterances, and mannerisms and to locate itself in the
time and place of the struggle it documents ends by being acclaimed in
terms that evacuate all politics, "set aside" all specifics.

Doubtless this move is facilitated by the fact that the work in question
is a one-person show and specifically a one-*woman* show—and even more
specifically, a one-woman show by an African American. Because Smith

Figure 6.1. Anna Deavere Smith as Stanley K. Sheinbaum in *Twilight: Los Angeles, 1992.*
© Jay Thompson.

plays all the parts herself, her body seems for many of the reviewers to contain—in various senses of the word—the conflicts she acts out, emblematizing our national motto, "In Many One." Indeed, Kroll's review of *Fires in the Mirror* begins by quoting Whitman, "I am large, I contain multitudes" ("A Woman"). (John Lahr, in the *New Yorker,* also compares Smith to Whitman, to the disadvantage of the latter: "Whitman's great poem, of course, invoked the voices of America but celebrated only himself" [90]). Yet surely there are significant *differences* between the self-description of a white man who says he "contains multitudes" (or even who says he's large) and the designation of a black woman as a container of the teeming multitudes. Does not this line when it is applied to an African American woman conjure up the notion of the black woman as the archetype of the maternal, as, in the words of one reviewer, "a vessel of empathy for people caught in some of life's inexplicable situations"? (Clines C9).

The view that female actors are "vessels of empathy" is not new. Diderot in his writings on the theater consigned women to the category of "passive mimesis," evoked by "*pity* or sympathy, compassion, the first and most primitive moral and social aptitude." As opposed to the male actor whose work involves "active, virile, formative, properly artistic . . . mimesis," women according to Diderot "alienate, split or alter themselves . . . only in passion and passivity, in the state of being possessed or being inhabited" (Lacoue-Labarthe 263).[3] In this regard, we might note the tendency of reviewers to use language about Smith that conjures up the image of her as a kind of spiritual medium: "A Seance with History" blares the headline of one review (D. Wright). This image, needless to say, is doubly fraught when used to describe a black woman.

As medium, the woman's body actually becomes co-extensive with the theater itself. Jack Kroll, at the conclusion of his review of *Twilight,* quotes Rodney King's aunt, who says she has learned about love from watching Smith's show, and then observes, "That's a lot of power for theater to have ("Fire," 63). The name of this theater is Anna Deavere Smith." The association of the female body with the space of theater, some have argued, goes very far back in Western thought. Luce Irigaray, for example, argues that Plato's cave is actually a figure for the female body, the womb. The cave, we remember, is a kind of theater, a deceptive shadow world where men are transfixed by images projected on a wall, images that are mere copies of the material world, itself a copy of the ideal world that the mind of the philosopher strives to apprehend. The magicians who project these images are like the artists whom Plato would banish from the just society for keeping men enthralled with the world of seductive imitations. For the philosopher, then, art and the feminine must be left behind.

Irigaray condemns the Platonic idealism the parable is meant to illustrate, the philosophical tendency to impose sameness and identity on all things, making them into more or less good copies of Truth: "No two ways about it, a form, even if it be a shadow, must be sired by, standardized against *one* face, *one* presence, *one* measure: that of Truth" (*Speculum*, 292). The operation by which everything in this world is made into a reflection of the ideal is metaphor: "the 'like,' the 'as if' of that masculine representation dominated by truth, light, resemblance, identity" (265).[4] Here we encounter the familiar terrain of humanism, so vividly illustrated in the passage I quoted from the *New York Times* article: racial difference is subsumed by human nature so that racial conflict is attributable to human beings' *natural* tendency to be "at odds" with one another. "A thousand and one reasons" for racial animosity, a thousand and one grievances, are reduced to one cause, one motive: the stubbornness of man as a species.

As I have said, Smith's work, in immersing itself in the details of specific racial conflicts, hardly endorses the humanist approach of the *Times* writer. It insists on our confronting the pervasiveness of racism while at the same time showing how strict adherence to racial identity impedes our understanding of one another, and it offers by way of example the possibility of crossing racial boundaries to put oneself in someone else's "skin." Smith's approach vividly illustrates the practice Irigaray counsels women and other "inferior species" to adopt in order to avoid the obliteration of human differences that occurs in the process of creating metaphoric equivalences: the practice of *mimesis*. Drucilla Cornell defines this practice:

> *Mimesis*, understood as a non-violent ethical relation to what is Other, and not as a mode of artistic representation that supposedly . . . mirrors . . . the real in art, is an expression of Adornian non-identity in which the subject does not seek to identify or categorize the object, but rather to let the object be in its difference. [*Mimesis*] identifies with, rather than identifying as. (148)

Now, this description of "mimetic identification" applies almost uncannily to Smith's performance, which involves, more literally than almost any other conceivable performance, an "identification with" the other. Smith's work thus seems to represent a challenge to racial essentialisms ("identifying as" an African American, as a Latino, etc.) and to affirm the specificity and uniqueness of the human subject. Her performances indeed approach the state of what Philippe Lacoue-Labarthe has called "absolute vicariousness . . . the very lapse of essence" (116).

We can begin to understand the breadth of the praise Smith's work has received, both from the mainstream press and from postmodern critical quarters—camps that might be expected to be "at odds" with one another. On the one hand, the work seems to evoke a humanist fantasy of the kind anatomized by Irigaray, whereby the maternal body becomes the ground of representation. For some, the body in Smith's performance seems to present a welcome image of plenitude and wholeness in a society that has been rent asunder by contending elements. Hence, the frequency with which Smith's work is seen as contributing to the "healing" of a racially divided America, despite her frequent disclaimers to the contrary. Smith's body becomes a utopian image of the body politic, and her work is affirmed in the name of the nation: *E Pluribus Unum*. Thus John Lahr concludes his review in the *New Yorker,* "'Twilight' goes some way toward reclaiming for the stage its crucial role as a leader in defining and acting out that ongoing experiment called the United States" (94). Yet one might counter this remark with Gayatri Spivak's trenchant observation that "women can be ventriloquists, but they have an immense *histor-ical* potential of *not* being (allowed to remain) nationalists; of knowing in their gendering, that nation and identity are commodities in the strictest sense: something made for exchange. And that they are the medium of that exchange" (803). In this country black women have had to bear the greatest burden as mediums of exchange, their bodies frequently becoming the site for the playing out of racial and sexual tension. Anita Hill is only one recent example of such a woman, pressed into the service of the collective national psyche.

On the other hand, Smith's work seems to play into a *post*humanist fantasy of the sort Cornell indulges, a fantasy that also grounds itself in the maternal body but that explicitly opposes, as Spivak suggests we must oppose, the concept of identity: the maternal body, says Cornell, is "a 'subject of heterogeneity' in which the One is tied to the Other and, therefore, is not truly One. [The] 'maternal body' presents us with an image of love through non-identity" (185). But if the metaphoric process condemned by Irigaray obliterates the *object* by appropriating it, mimetic identification as Cornell defines it endangers the *subject*, who "loses control" in being "taken over" by the other (149). Such language powerfully returns us to the image of the black female medium.

And indeed, Cornell recognizes that *mimesis* is based on certain stereotypes associated with femininity, but argues that for this very reason it should be adopted as a means of turning "subordination into affirmation" (148). However, for anyone to notice the difference (between mere subordination and subordination-turned-into-affirmation) such a move would seem to entail a self-consciousness about gender and to involve a certain acceptance of identity politics—affirming oneself *as* a woman, in Smith's case, as a black woman. In this regard, we might recall John Lahr's implicit praise of Smith's subordination of herself to her subjects: "Whitman's great poem . . . invoked the voices of America but celebrated only himself"; and we might reply: But isn't it *time* the black woman celebrated herself? Unfortunately, the celebration of black womanhood (*as* black womanhood) is the least developed aspect of Smith's work.

In any case, I hope it is obvious by now that what the rhetoric of the actress as medium obscures is the extent to which Smith has been *subject* to media-tion—in part, ironically enough, through the very process of the media's granting her a priveleged contact with the "real" (rather than focusing on her artistry). This insistence on the real further obscures the extent to which at its most sophisticated the work functions as a complex commentary on the impossibility of accessing the real through language and representation: the author, in this regard, is no passive medium but a complex mediator. One brilliant moment in the play, for example, has Smith portraying Jewish writer Letty Cottin Pogrebin, who is represented as speaking on the phone (to Smith). Pogrebin has apparently been invited to speak about her uncle Isaac's experience of the Holocaust, and she says, "Well, it's hard for me to do that because I think there's a tendency to make hay with the Holocaust, to push all the buttons. And I mean this story about my uncle Isaac—makes *me* cry and it's going to make your audience cry and I'm beginning to worry that we're trotting out our Holocaust stories too regularly and that we're going to inure each other to the truth of them" (59). Pogrebin decides, then, to read from her own book an account of Isaac, "the designated survivor" of the Holocaust whose mission was to "stay alive and tell the story": staying alive meant passing as an Aryan and, among other atrocities he had to perform, being required to shove his own wife and children into the gas chamber. Later Isaac told his account, which Pogrebin heard "translated from his Yiddish" by her mother, to dozens of agencies and community leaders, and after "speaking the unspeakable" for months "when he finished telling everything he knew, he died" (61–62).

It might be said that the story of Isaac as told by Pogrebin illustrates what Shoshana Felman, analyzing the testimonial accounts of Holocaust survivors, calls "the crisis of witnessing": the conflict between the necessity of telling all and the impossibility of "speaking the unspeakable"—to say nothing of the *obscenity* of our desire to *hear* the unspeakable (to "make hay with the Holocaust").[5] This conflict is self-consciously reflected in Smith's own rendering of Pogrebin's story, which is characteristically reproduced with what appears to be absolute fidelity, but is also delivered over the phone, a device which, along with the book from which Pogrebin reads and the mother's English translation of Isaac's Yiddish, provides one more layer of mediation between us and the horror experienced by Isaac.

Indeed, all of Smith's work in her "On the Road" series may be said to negotiate this conflict and to oscillate with great artistry between the desire to capture the real and the awareness of the difficulties and even dangers of attempting to do so. Perhaps, however, the decision in *Fires in the Mirror* to end with Gavin Cato's father mourning the death of his son tips the balance rather too far in one direction, so that the tears shed on stage seem to offer a guarantee of the real—of raw human emotion—and to provide the cathartic comfort which Pogrebin wanted to avoid, thus lending some support to the humanist position that the politics of the event can be peeled away to manifest the authentic human tragedy underneath.

Yet even here, Cato's parting line (the final line of the play) in which, scorning the supposed power of the Jews to prevent his speaking out, he says "No there's nothing to hide, you can repeat every word I say," contains a reflexive turn that invites us to ponder the meaning of the strategy of repetition governing the work as a whole, rather than allowing us to rest in the illusion of transparency (139). It is to this issue and to a consideration of the function of repetition in art created for a multicultural society that I now turn.

Recently, theorists of colonialist discourse have been developing a line of thought analogous to Irigaray's. Homi Bhabha's work in particular addresses itself to the question of mimesis, or what he calls "mimicry." Both Irigaray and Bhabha are attempting to understand how people who have had an alien language and culture imposed on them (by men, by whites, by colonizers) can use language in such a way as to signal that their speech emanates from an "elsewhere"—a place outside the master discourse. In an article of particular interest for discussing Smith's work, Bhabha looks at the question of repetition through an analysis of the poem "Names" by Derek Walcott. The poem begins, "My race began as the sea began / with no nouns, and with no horizon / with pebbles under my tongue, / with a different fix on the stars." Walcott's poem goes on to tell of the colonial encounter, of the way the colonialist went about naming places in the new land after those in his home land, applying "belittling diminutives" to them: "then, little Versailles meant plans for the pigsty, names for the sour apples / and green grapes / of their exile. . ."). But the African, who seemed to acquiesce in these names, "repeated, and changed them" (Bhabha 51–52).

112

Analyzing this poem for the light it sheds on the question of identity politics, Bhabha sees two versions of language being articulated in it: the imperialist project of naming, which rests on the presupposition of the ability of language to "mirror a pre-given reality," and another process on the part of the African who "in repeating the lessons of the masters, changes their inflections" (53). Bhabha seizes on the transformative potential of repetition as it is poetically affirmed by Walcott to point to "another destiny of culture as a site—one based not simply on subversion and transgression, but on the prefiguration of a kind of solidarity between ethnicities that meet in the tryst of colonial history" (51).

What Bhabha's analysis does not really bring out in Walcott's poem, however, is the *triple* notion of mimeticism at work in it. First, as Bhabha notes, is the view of language as mirroring reality. On a second level, though, there is the imitative naming practiced by the colonist, who is exiled from, and envious of those who are privileged in, his own country—and no doubt envious as well of the new culture in which he is an alien: hence, the "sour apples" and "green grapes," denoting the envy that leads him to apply "belittling diminutives" to the country he now inhabits. And finally, at a third level, there is the transformative potential of the mimicry practiced by the colonized people: "Listen, my children, say: *moubain*: the hogplum,/ *cerise*: the wild cherry,/ *baie-la*: the bay,/ with the fresh green voices they were once themselves/ in the way the wind bends/ our natural inflections" (52). In the poem the color green marks the shift in levels of repetition, from the second meaning to the third: from suggesting the envy at the heart of mimetic rivalry, the "green" as it recurs in the phrase "fresh green voices" comes to signify a culture no less "natural" or "authentic" and certainly no less creative than any other, despite having passed through a colonial culture that has commanded its subjects to "mimic" its alien language and customs. As we shall see, Smith's work brilliantly oscillates between these two modes of repetition: repetition in the form of mimetic rivalry, rooted in envy and anger, and repetition as a transformative process, yielding complex surprises and illustrating how repetition is always repetition with a difference. Moreover, by mimicking not just members of the dominant culture, but various ethnic groups as well, Smith does indeed prefigure, to quote Bhabha again, "a solidarity between ethnicities that meet in the tryst of colonialist history."

In our own society, minstrelsy as a popular, peculiarly American form of entertainment has historically been a principle means by which the dominant culture "belittled" African American culture through mimicry (and recent analyses like those of Eric Lott have shown how envy and desire are components of the attraction minstrelsy held for so many whites). Smith's work, which involves figuratively adopting whiteface, blackface, brownface, and so forth, can be interestingly situated within the tradition of minstrelsy because it plays so close to the edges of caricature, sometimes pulling back in time and sometimes not. Indeed, to the extent that reviewers criticized the show their reservations had to do with their feelings that it too frequently fell into caricature (Wood). These reviewers neglected to see the dynamism of Smith's portrayals, the ceaseless volatility of the process whereby types dissolve into individuals and individuals crystallize into types. In Smith's acting style, her emphasis on individual speech mannerisms (accents and the like) continually threatens to topple her impersonations over into caricature. Just when people are presented as most like themselves, they suddenly seem like "types," our laughter as suddenly seems to border on ridicule, and we find ourselves confronting our own racism. On the other hand, a laugh, a subtle gesture, a certain vocal inflection will give us a glimmer of an individual behind the type (e.g., the black nationalist Leonard Jeffries's wry tone of voice which seems to mock his own infamous megalomania when he remarks that there might not have been a *Roots* without him—since he found the lost manuscript in the Philadelphia airport). Here we see the dual aspect of mimicry: its aggressive aspect, so obvious in minstrelsy, which reduces people to stereotypes and robs them of their complexity, and the utopian aspect Bhabha assigns to the mimicry—the promise of solidarity embedded in Smith's artistic practice of identifying with an "other" whose differences are scrupulously observed and preserved: imitation as theft and imitation as the sincerest form of flattery.

Smith not only *practices* mimicry in such a way as to prefigure solidarity between ethnicities, but her text also contains a complex commentary on how mimetic processes function—always unstably—in the constitution of identity. In a section on "Hair" in *Fires in the Mirror,* for example, Al Sharpton defends his hair style against those who see it as imitating the hair of white people (figure 6.2). He angrily insists that he wears his hair like James Brown because Brown was a kind of surrogate father to him, and not because he wants to look like whites. "I mean in the fifties it was a slick. It was acting like white folks. But today people don't wear their hair like that. James and I the only ones out there doing that. So it's certainlih [*sic*] not a reaction to whites. It's me and James's thing" (Smith *Fires*, 22).[6] Bhabha's thesis is strikingly illustrated by this example: while Sharpton might appear to be caught in that "inauthentic repetition" to which the dominant culture appears to doom the subordinate one, in actuality he is engaged in an intra-racial play of male mimetic desire. This play not only remains in a resistant relation to white culture but, insofar as it attests to a tension between individual and group identity, links him to members of other subordinate groups, other ethnicities within our society who also struggle with questions of authenticity and inauthenticity—like the Lubavitcher woman who immediately follows Sharpton and speaks of her ambivalence about wearing wigs. At odds with their respective groups over the question of adopting the customs and styles which signal their difference from the dominant culture, the militant black minister and the Lubavitcher woman appear for a moment to have more in common with each other than with members of their own groups.

Figure 6.2. Anna Deavere Smith portrays nineteen characters including the Reverend Al Sharpton (pictured) in *Fires in the Mirror*. © Adger Cowans.

In his book *Typography: Mimesis, Philosophy, Politics* Philippe Lacoue-Labarthe has written that "every culture . . . is built violently upon the ground—and the threat—of a *generalized* state of competition," of violent "mimetic rivalry" (102). While this may be true, what it neglects is the way subordinate cultures have been forced into particularly virulent forms of mimetic rivalry *with each other* through divide and conquer strategies practiced by the dominant group. At no time in American history has the virulence reached greater heights than it sometimes has in the relation between blacks and Jews. On the other hand, solidarity between ethnic groups has probably never been stronger between any other two groups. Seeing a history of shared oppression, blacks and Jews have worked in civil rights coalitions together, although such solidarity has sometimes broken down into rivalry when it appears to one group that the other is receiving preferential treatment: one of the most obvious examples of this is the break between blacks and some Jews over the question of affirmative action. Many Jews have opposed affirmative action programs on the grounds that they themselves have managed to achieve their successes without such programs and that their own gains would be eroded as African Americans progress.

Crown Heights, where during the riots warring factions continually accused each other of receiving preferential treatment, is a perfect site for the study of the relations between blacks and Jews, for understanding the mimetic rivalry that has driven these two groups apart and the forces that have contributed or might contribute to drawing them together.

During the middle part of the century, when Caribbean immigrants began moving into middle-class Jewish neighborhoods as the latter were moving out to Queens and the suburbs, blacks aspiring to the status of property owners began to "imitate the Jew," as Mary Helen Washington puts it in an afterward to Paule Marshall's novel *Brown Girl, Brownstones,* a novel set in Brooklyn during this period (312). The Lubavitchers, however, halted the process of upward mobility, of white flight from Brooklyn as blacks moved in. In 1969 the Grand Rebbe, Joseph Schneerson, ordered the Lubavitchers to remain in Crown Heights and, according to one Lubavitcher, to "'make linkages' and establish a relationship with their new neighbors" (Noel 38). Whatever the original intention, however, the Lubavitch community, which has acquired a great deal of political power over the years, has grown to the point where, as some commentators have remarked, they "steadily harass" their black neighbors to sell their property (Logan 105). "Nothing's wrong with that," one rabbi says about pressuring blacks to sell their homes at a profit, "That's the American business market" (Noel 39).

The rabbi's remark interestingly allies him with the mother in Paule Marshall's novel. To be sure the latter, in her obsession with becoming a property holder in Brooklyn, with Crown Heights as her ultimate goal, is more brutally direct in her defense of the American way: commenting on the inevitability of mimetic rivalry the mother asserts, "power, is a thing that don really have nothing to do with color": "Take when we had to scrub the Jew floor. He wasn't misusing us so much because our skin was black but because we cun do better. And I din hate him. All the time I was down on his floor I was saying to myself: 'Lord, lemme do better than this. Lemme rise!'" And she maintains, "people got a right to claw their way to the top and those on top got a right to scuffle to stay there." And though the world "won't always be white," people of color once they get on top "might not be so nice either 'cause power is a thing that don make you nice" (224–25).

Selina, the novel's heroine, resists this philosophy, dimly envisioning another truth and going off on her own at the end of the novel to seek it out. Embracing the condition of exile, Selina as a doubly displaced person (from Barbados, from Brooklyn), may be said to embody the kind of "diasporic consciousness" theorized by Daniel Boyarin and Jonathan Boyarin. The Boyarins, like Smith in *Fires in the Mirror* and like so many thinkers addressing questions of race and ethnicity today, set out to think through the problems of integration and difference, and in particular they ask how Jews may hold on to "ethnic, cultural specificity but in a context of deeply felt and enacted human solidarity" (720). They argue that at certain moments in Jewish history when Jews and Jewish identity have been endangered, a certain insularity has helped preserve group identity; at such times it might have been necessary for Jews "to undertake the education, feeding, providing for the sick, and the caring for Jewish prisoners, to the virtual exclusion of others" (and here one can't help recall the ambulance that was widely said to have abandoned the dying Gavin Cato—in reality, the police had ordered the ambulance to leave with the Jewish driver, for the crowd was angry and city ambulances were coming on the scene; but the fact that people were all too ready to believe the worst attests to the widespread perception of Jews as chiefly concerned with "their own") (712). However, the Boyarins maintain, under conditions of Jewish hegemony, where Jews claim sole right to the land, diasporic consciousness—"a consciousness of a Jewish collective as one sharing space with others, devoid of exclusivist and dominating power"—is the only way of achieving "a species-wide care without eradicating cultural difference" (713).

"Race and space," the Boyarins write, "together form a deadly discourse" (714). They point out that Abraham, the father of Jewry, was "deterritorialized" when he was told to leave his own land for the Promised Land, and they call for a "prophetic discourse" which evinces "preference for 'exile' over rootedness in the Land" (718). This is not to deny the importance of attachment to the land, they say, but it is to recognize the attachment others have to it as well. (The final image of Selina in *Brown Girl, Brownstones,* who as she leaves Brooklyn throws back one of the two bangles worn by girls in Barbados, suggests this attachment to two places at the very moment of exile). In stressing "deterritorialization" and rejecting myths of autochthony, the Boyarins align themselves with many leaders in the African American community, who increasingly question notions of black "authenticity" as the grounds of political practice, stressing instead the "political and ethical dimensions of blackness" and what Cornell West, using the same term as the Boyarins, calls the "prophetic nature" of a discourse based on new and different coalitions (26).

Within Smith's text, Angela Davis similarly calls for a rejection of a politics grounded exclusively in race, which she claims is too static a concept; instead of remaining anchored in a single community, she recommends using the "rope" of the anchor to move across communities. Smith's mimetic practice, which consists of juxtaposing voices from these various communities, works to realize in aesthetic form the movement across borders, signifying a refusal to stay in place or to be fixed. Thus the very premise of Smith's performances is diasporic consciousness.[7] Further, *Fires in the Mirror* suggests that what blacks and Jews have in common is the condition of diaspora; their common ground is their "groundlessness." Ironically, this condition has been the source of intense mimetic rivalry between the two groups, particularly over the question of whose experience in the diaspora has been worse. Thus in Smith's text Conrad Mohammed argues that slavery was infinitely more brutal than the Holocaust.

Obviously there is a danger in invoking diasporic consciousness to avoid the understanding that people in the here and now live unequally in the diaspora, and that such inequalities—for example, Jews having more political power in Crown Heights than blacks—need to be worked out. Yet insofar as it disputes the validity of claims to original rights *and* original wrongs, diasporic consciousness marks a shift from mimetic rivalry to solidarity—a shift, again, that is inherent in the very concept of Smith's work, one of the most intriguing aspects of which is its undermining of certainty about origins. For, part of the unsettling effect of the performances is that while some of the figures Smith mimics are familiar to audiences (though, as I have said, usually only from their media representations), in many cases the spectator is acutely aware of watching imitations without knowing the originals. Giving priority, as it were, to the copy over the original, Smith radically and viscerally contests ideals of authenticity, in effect "deterritorializing" her characters and getting them to act on new common ground—the stage.

I want to conclude by reflecting on the various ways mimetic rivalry came into play around the production and reception of Smith's performances themselves. When it was announced that Smith would be coming to Los Angeles to do a show on the LA uprising, modeled after the work she did on Crown Heights, some local artists wrote a letter of protest to the Mark Taper Forum which was headlined in the local media. The artists complained that the Taper, which commissioned the piece, never features LA artists on the main stage, unless those artists have first gained celebrity in the New York theater world. As people of color living in Los Angeles, these artists argued, they were in a unique position to create art about the violence that had occurred in their own community.

It is interesting to note how these protests mimicked on the artistic plane the mimetic strife at the heart of Smith's performances. People from various ethnic and racial backgrounds ended up appearing to turn their anger on another person from a marginalized group who possessed an advantage they did not. Although most of those who protested were extremely careful to emphasize that the Taper was the target of their anger, not Smith herself, the press obviously relished the racial dimension of the controversy (it is hard to believe the press would have been as interested in a letter to the Taper protesting its marginalization of people of color if Smith hadn't been perceived as the target). Being judged as a kind of "outside agitator" in the theater world, Smith found herself in the midst of interracial and intraracial conflict, as artists of color from Los Angeles temporarily asserted their identity in terms of community as well as race—not unlike the blacks who lived in Crown Heights during the time in which Marshall's novel is set.

It was not only at the level of production that there arose a struggle over Smith's text akin to those her work represents, but also at the level of reception. Numerous postplay discussions, both those held at the Taper and those which took place more informally among theatergoers, revealed much resentment because Smith appeared to slight certain groups (e.g., non-Korean Asians) or to caricature a given group more than others. One person who was outraged over the way she was represented was Judith Tur, the only white woman in the Los Angeles version of *Twilight* and the character who expresses the most undisguised racist views in the play: "Let them go out and work for a living./ I'm sick of it./ We've all had a rough time in our life./ I've had a major rough time" (97). Such sentiments are of course the very stuff of mimetic rivalry—the perception that one's own oppression ("rough time") is equal to or greater than that of the other.

I must confess that I myself was disturbed by Smith's choice of a woman to be *the* voice of racism—after all, we live in a white patriarchy, not a matriarchy. I felt that Smith was not willing to consider how, like Jews, women as women have a history of oppression. Nor did she appear to recognize the fact that, like Jews and blacks, white women and black women have sometimes been partners and sometimes rivals in the struggle against oppression. An acknowledgment of the historic tensions between these groups would, I thought, have been more in keeping with Smith's overall project. On the contrary, however, it seemed to me that in its treatment of white women, Smith's text did not so much analyze the dynamics of scapegoating as enact it: while the white men interviewed for *Twilight* exhibit an entire range of human responses to the beating of Rodney King and its aftermath *except* the most virulent form of racism that, for example, led one of the policemen who beat Rodney King to joke about "gorillas in the mist," white women remain unrehabilitated.[8] This is especially evident in the Broadway version, which contains the portraits of two additional rather ghastly white women. Here I have to admit to my own implication in the rivalry inspired *by* Smith's work in *Twilight*: after seeing the way white women were portrayed in this version my first reaction was one of anger. I did not initially consider my privileged relation to women of color, but rather thought primarily about my own oppression. I even briefly considered not publishing this chapter: if Smith was not prepared to acknowledge my oppression as a woman, I felt, I would not recognize hers as an African American.

121

Both of the white female characters who have been added to the text are upper-middle-class women (class is a category which complicates the binaries of racial difference but is not brought to bear sufficiently in Smith's choice of interviewees). One of these is a Brentwood mother who worries about the way the threat of gang violence interferes with her child's prom night—and lest we miss the message that this woman is a tad out of touch with the real victims of police brutality and gang violence, a video image of a gated community is projected behind Smith when she mimes this character.[9] The other woman added to the latest version of *Twilight* is a real estate agent, portrayed in an extremely caricatured way, who laments the closing of the Polo Lounge at the Beverly Hills Hotel where during the "riots" she and her friends would "huddle together" until two or three in the morning (153). This woman, whose name is Elaine Young, seems to be a figure of ridicule partly because of the plastic surgery problems she has had: silicone implanted in her cheeks exploded, causing her to have thirty-six operations to restore her face. As a result, she has become an activist in the war against silicone implants.[10]

While Young's plight as Smith performs it is played largely for comic effect (thus inviting us to see the woman's problems as the grotesque consequence of vanity and privilege), one can detect faintly in the text a thread with which one could construct a more feminist analysis. The thread would link the aging white woman, Elaine Young, to the baby girl of Elvira Evers, a Panamanian woman from Compton who was shot during the uprising and whose baby while still in the womb received the bullet in her elbow. Shortly after the child was born, her mother subjected her to another kind of body piercing: "We don't like to keep the girls without earrings. We like the little/ girls/ to look like girls from little" (i.e., from a very early age); "she was seven days,/ and I/ pierced her ears" (122). There is a hint here and in Elaine Young's story of a violence different from the choke-holds, baton blows, and drive-by shootings that preoccupy the media in times of racial strife, a violence inflicted by patriarchy—even when enacted by women— on the female body to brand it with the mark of gender. Such violence, often more sanctioned than the violence done to Rodney King or Gavin Cato or Yankel Rosenbaum, is less likely to be perceived as the stuff of drama, especially by male theater reviewers and male-dominated award committees.

As a consequence of Smith's privileging of racial hierarchy over gender hierarchy, issues of gender return to haunt the text with the specter of mimetic rivalry. But if the work does not extricate itself from the dynamics it illustrates, it does point the way out. In particular, it suggests the necessity for us, on the one hand, to remain judicious in our assessments of blame for our various oppressions and, on the other hand, to recognize not just the wrongs that are done to us but the privileges which make our lives so enviable to those without our advantages.

In focusing so much on individual responses to Smith's work, we must not overlook the *institutional* forms of mimeticism at play around Smith's performances—evidenced, for example, in the Mark Taper Forum's unabashed desire to follow the New York theater scene, rather than attempt to foster artists a little closer to home. What complicated the rather straightforward workings of mimetic desire in this case, however, was the fact that *Fires in the Mirror* had had such an impact in New York partly because it opened around the same time that the uprising in LA occurred—a fact which reviewers seldom failed to notice. In one sense, then, *Twilight*, commissioned with the idea that Smith would do LA's very "own" riot, was a copy of a work that already seemed to mirror that riot. Yet when *Twilight* was nominated for a Tony Award, the director of the Taper, Gordon Davidson, crowed: "We're the most active and productive theater in the area of new and challenging work in the United States. Somebody else can add 'the world.'" In a gesture of artistic imperialism that is strikingly ironic in light of Smith's project, the white producer implicitly denies all debts, blithely treading on the sensitivities of the people of color who felt overlooked by his choice in the first place, and explicitly puts himself solidly at the point of origin.

The feeling of ownership that many of us who live in Los Angeles experienced after the uprising (a friend told me she never felt that Los Angeles was really "her" city until those explosive days in April 1992) had positive aspects to it insofar as it gave rise to a sense of responsibility at the local level on the part of people who had previously lacked commitment to the city. However, such commitment needs to be accompanied by an awareness not only of the differences between any two places in the way racism is experienced—say, between Crown Heights, Brooklyn, and Los Angeles, California (e.g., in Crown Heights two groups appeared to be locked in an agonistic struggle with one another; in Los Angeles, as *Twilight* brings out, many more ethnic groups were involved in events that seemed far less centered than those which had occurred in Crown Heights)—but also of the similarities. After all, racism in this country is a transcommunal phenomenon—as the numerous "copycat riots" following in the wake of the LA uprising attest.

The phrase "copycat riot" is obviously a dismissive one, particularly as it is taken up in journalistic practice; it implies that such uprisings are "mere copies," without their "own" rationale and specificity—a view that never of course stands up under rigorous analysis. To repeat: repetition is always repetition-with-a-difference and, as we have seen throughout, it is necessary to adopt a double vision, seeing the sameness *and* the uniqueness in various experiences of oppression and of protests against oppression. Each of the two models I began by outlining—the humanist, which stresses identity, and the posthumanist, which stresses difference—is thus inadequate for theorizing this approach.

Speaking of Plato's banishment of the artist from the republic, Christopher Prendergast writes that the mimetic artist through "his doublings and multiplications . . . introduces 'improprieties' (a 'poison') into a social system ordered according to the rule that everything and everyone should be in its/his/her 'proper' place. He disturbs *both* the law of identity *and* the law of differentiation," and in short is "excommunicated not because [his work] is a threat to truth, but because it is a threat to order" (10, emphasis added). At the start of this chapter I suggested that Smith's performances were comforting to some precisely because she seemed to stay in her "'proper place,'" the space of the maternal. Indeed, at this point I think it is necessary to add one more variable to the Boyarins' formula and say that race, space, and *gender* make for a "deadly discourse": for an example we could cite the black nationalist Leonard Jeffries, who in *Fires in the Mirror* laments the censoring of the term "Mother Africa" from the television version of *Roots*. The nationalist fantasy is often a gendered fantasy, and women must resist not only staying in place, but allowing themselves to be represented *as* space.

Yet the view of Smith as "container" of the multitudes is, as I suggested earlier, in part belied by the nature of the project itself which involves her in a constant traversal of borders. One might in this light see Smith's continual deflection of the question so frequently posed to her by journalists, "Where are *you* in this piece?" not as a refusal to take a political position but a refusal to be pinned down: if, as I would argue, the black woman has traditionally occupied the most fixed place in this country's representational practices, her departure from that role constitutes perhaps the most threatening sign of disorder, more threatening certainly than the work of the implicitly white male artist evoked by Plato and Prendergast. In this regard, we might look at a revealing moment in the Los Angeles version of *Twilight*, when Stanley Sheinbaum tells of driving on the freeway the night of the riots and receiving his first clue that something was wrong when he saw a black woman in a Mercedes carrying a hammer.[11] This account invariably provoked a response of hilarity in audiences (and indeed was mentioned again by Sheinbaum in the *Los Angeles Times* in a letter attempting to defend Smith's use of humor in *Twilight*). The laughter was undoubtedly a response to what seems a carnivalesque crossing of borders involving unexpected intersections of class, gender, and race (presumably the sight of black men driving expensive cars and bearing submachine guns would be less apt to signal something oddly out of place). I think we can take this image of the woman on the freeway as emblematic of Smith's artistry, which also involves such carnivalesque crossings. And in response to the journalists' recurrent question, "where are *you* in all this?" we might recall the title of Smith's series and say that she is "on the road," in a kind of permanent exile, hammering out justice.

125

7

DO WE GET TO LOSE THIS TIME?

Revising the Vietnam War Film

❏

If there ever was a purely masculine genre, it is surely the war film. That women in the genre represent a threat to the male warrior is revealed in a time-worn convention: whenever a soldier displays a photograph of his girlfriend, wife, or family, he is doomed to die by the end of the film. The convention is so well known that it is parodied in *Hot Shots,* a spoof of the very popular film *Top Gun.* Playing off the nicknaming of fighter pilots, one of the early scenes in *Hot Shots* shows the hero's side-kick slamming a locker door on which is taped a family photo. He then introduces himself to the hero as "Dead Meat."

Feminist critics of the war film, most notably Susan Jeffords, have convincingly argued that the genre is not only *for* men but plays a crucial role in the masculinizing process so necessary to the creation of warriors. Through spectacle (bombs bursting in air) and sound (usually heavy rock music), pro-war fantasies like *Top Gun* mobilize the kind of aggression essential to the functioning of men as killing machines. So too, problematically enough, do many anti-war films. Indeed, it is frequently noted that films like *Platoon* not only do not effectively protest the war but actually participate in and, in a way, extend it, to the point where the spectator him- or herself becomes the target of the warrior-filmmaker's assault. As Gilbert Adair, in a thoughtful critique of *Platoon*, puts it:

> It is surely time that film-makers learned that the meticulously de-   127
> tailed aping of an atrocity *is* an atrocity; that the hyper-realistic de-
> piction of an obscenity cannot avoid being contaminated with that
> obscenity; and that the unmediated representation of violence con-
> stitutes in itself an act of violence against the spectator. (159)

Moreover, just as it is the goal of war to crush opposing viewpoints and vi- olently secure the opposing side's assent to the conqueror's truth, films like *Platoon* "bully" us into "craven submission," as Adair puts it, by pointing "an accusatory finger" and asking, "'How do you know what it was like un- less you've been there?'" (169). Such questions are often literally addressed to women in the Vietnam films: "Who the hell are you to judge him?" the uncle, a vet (Bruce Willis), rebukes his niece (Emily Lloyd) in Norman Jew- ison's *In Country* when she expresses dismay at the racist remarks she finds in the diary her father kept before being killed in the war. Thus, since "being there" has so far been out of the question for women, who are pro- hibited from combat, their authority on any issue related to war is discred- ited from the outset and insofar as they may be inclined to question or op- pose war (except in and on the terms granted them by men), they find themselves consigned to the ranks of the always-already defeated.[1]

Given the extent to which war has been an exclusive masculine preserve it is not surprising to find the critics themselves desiring generic purity, ex- pressing discomfort when bits of "feminine discourse," for example, ele- ments of melodrama or the love story, invade and "contaminate" the war film. One of the earliest films about the Vietnam War, *Coming Home,* which David James criticizes because it "rewrite[s] the invasion of Vietnam as erotic melodrama," is a case in point ("Rock and Roll," 91). While com- mentators like John Hellman have found much to praise in films that rewrite the invasion in terms of *male* genres—the Western (*The Deerhunter*) and the detective genre (*Apocalypse Now*)—*Coming Home*'s incorporation of female genres has often provoked derision. Of course, *Coming Home* is not really about the war, but about its aftermath, and thus it is situated in a tradition of films about veterans' adjustment to civilian life. Nevertheless critics have faulted it for focusing less on the problems of returning veterans than on the clichéd love story.

Coming Home is about a disabled veteran, Luke (Jon Voight), returning to civilian life and meeting Sally (Jane Fonda) who is married to a Marine serving in Vietnam and whose consciousness about the war is raised when she serves as a volunteer in a VA hospital. This consciousness receives a gigantic boost when Sally makes love with Luke, who brings her to climax orally, giving her her first orgasm. Critics have struggled to understand this scene in symbolic terms. Jason Katzman writes, "[*Coming Home*] uses the love story as a metaphor for the impotence of an entire country in understanding Vietnam. . . . Sally's ability to reach an orgasm with Luke where she could never before with her husband Bob (Bruce Dern), is one of the more widely discussed symbols" (12).

It is not clear to me what exactly the woman's orgasm is a symbol *of*; but it is clear that the event was less satisfying to some male critics than it was to *her*. Albert Auster and Leonard Quart, for example, express uneasiness about this plot element although they do not really specify the source of their discomfort: "Unfortunately," they write, "Sally's transformation seems unconvincing and mechanical, especially in the emphasis it places on her achieving orgasm . . . while making love to Luke" (50).

Suppose, however, we take the orgasm to be an end in itself, rather than a symbol or a metaphor for something else. Suppose, in fact, that one of the problems with Vietnam war films in particular is their relentless exploitation of experiences and events for the significance they have solely to the soldiers who fought in the war rather than to the men's loved ones, allies, or enemies. I suspect that the critics' discomfort stems from the vividness with which the film demonstrates the point that men's losses may be a gain for women. Kaja Silverman has identified a similar theme in *The Best Years of Our Lives,* William Wyler's 1946 film about men returning from World

War II and attempting to adjust to civilian life. Silverman heralds the film as a kind of feminist milestone in the history of what she calls "libidinal politics," since at this moment of "historical trauma" in which men came back from war mutilated both psychically and physically, nonphallic forms of male sexuality emerged (52–121).

One might argue that from the point of view of women on the homefront, *Coming Home* is even more important in this regard: unlike *The Best Years of Our Lives,* in which the women must find satisfaction in an eroticized maternal relation to their men, *Coming Home,* based on a story written by a woman, was made at a time when feminists were vociferously proclaiming the myth of the vaginal orgasm and agitating for the requisite attention to be paid to the clitoris. Women were hardly passive beneficiaries of the historical vicissitudes of male sexuality (and male warmongering) but were actively demanding and sometimes winning their sexual rights. However attenuated the film's politics are in other respects,[2] it is important not to overlook the film's significant place in the ongoing struggles over sexual politics.

To see how far women have been forced to retreat from this position of sexual advantage, we need only briefly compare *Coming Home* to a film on the same subject made a dozen years later. In Oliver Stone's *Born on the Fourth of July,* a fictionalized version of the story of Ron Kovic—a war hero obsessed about his dysfunctional penis—the protagonist (Tom Cruise) reaches a low point when he goes down to Mexico and spends days and nights whoring, gambling, and boozing it up with other disabled vets. In one scene Ron appears to bring a whore to climax through manual stimulation; but in contrast to *Coming Home* which focuses on the woman's tears of joy and passion, in this film we see *the man* crying out of self-pity for his lost potency. (In *In Country* there is also a scene in which a vet is impotent with the young heroine, who is kind and understanding. Nowhere is there a hint that his hard-on might not be the *sine qua non* of *her* sexual pleasure, for the question of her sexual pleasure is not even on the horizon.) In a brief subsequent scene, the camera assumes the hero's point of view as he wheels himself around a whorehouse in which various Mexican women beckon him with lewd remarks. Racism and misogyny combine in a scene meant to demonstrate the depths of degradation to which the hero has sunk. This scene constitutes a typical example of the commonplace phenomenon in Vietnam films in which exploited people (in this instance, the Mexican prostitutes) are further exploited by the films themselves for the symbolic value they hold for the hero. Thus do the films perpetuate the social and cultural insensitivity that led to America's involvement in the war and the atrocities committed there.

The film *Casualties of War* presents another example of this phenomenon. In this film, as Pat Aufderheide argues, the rape and murder of a Vietnamese peasant girl by American soldiers signify "the collapse of a moral framework for the men who killed her. The spectacular agony of her death is intended to stir not the audience's righteous anger at the grunts . . . but empathy for the ordinary fighting men who have been turned into beasts by their tour of duty" (88). Equally extreme and still more bizarre is a scene in *Born on the Fourth of July* in which Kovic and another vet quarrel over which of them has killed more babies. The implication is that the superior person is the one who has killed the most babies since he has to carry a greater burden of guilt![3]

It is eminently clear from *Born on the Fourth of July* that historical trauma does not necessarily result in a progressive politics—libidinal or otherwise. Nor is the phallus necessarily relinquished by men who have suffered from such trauma. As Tony Williams has shrewdly observed in his discussion of the film, the trip to Mexico allows Ron to "confront his dark side . . . , confess his sins to the family of the man he shot, and gain the phallus (if not the penis) by speaking at the 1984 Democratic convention before an audience mainly composed of silent . . . and admiring, autograph seeking women" (129). Previously in the film, when Ron is released from the hospital he goes to see his girlfriend from high school. She, however, is so caught up in anti-war activities, that she is unable to connect with him. As Ron wheels through her college campus, he declares his love for her, and the camera focuses on her walking beside him but looking in the direction of a group of activists about to hold a meeting. The proper role for a woman, the film makes clear, is that of silent supporter of male protestors, not independent actor, in the anti-war movement. The feminism which grew up partly in response to this attitude is, needless to say, nowhere evident in the film.

In addition to *Coming Home,* one other film is noteworthy not only for its incorporation of a love story, but most importantly, for the emphasis it places on the effects of the war and the war's aftermath on women.[4] In the film *Jacknife* Ed Harris plays Dave, a pent-up, alcoholic vet whose anti-social attitudes and behavior are ruining the life of his schoolteacher sister (Kathy Baker) with whom he resides. A friend called Megs, played by Robert DeNiro, comes to visit Dave and attempts to break him out of his shell; in the process Megs falls in love with Dave's sister. Dave violently opposes the relationship and works to sabotage it, although not entirely aware of what he is doing. One night when his sister and Megs are at the prom (she chaperones, but clearly they are both attempting to capture something lost in their youth), Dave comes to the high school, sees old trophies and an old picture of himself, and smashes the glass cases. After he runs off, his sister attempts to go on with the evening as if nothing had happened, while Megs is understandably distracted and distraught. Astonishingly, the film does not demonize the woman for resenting the way her brother's trauma has circumscribed her life. Indeed, it shows that the brother needs to accept a certain amount of responsibility for casting a pall on her existence. At the end we see him in group therapy coming to terms with the fact that he betrayed Megs one time in battle and coming to terms as well with what he sees as his own cowardice.

Rick Berg, a combat veteran, has written in an influential essay, "Losing Vietnam," that "the vet can begin to overcome his alienation" only when he recognizes that Vietnam's "consequences range throughout a community" (65). While for the most part Berg's concern is with issues of class, *Jacknife* has the merit of focusing on the vet's recognition of the way the war affects the relations between the sexes. The film is certainly not without many of the problems characteristic of films about post-Vietnam life. For instance it never, of course, even alludes to the feminism that arose from anti-war activity; on the contrary, the sister is cast in stereotypically spin-sterish terms ("I know what I am," she says, not, however, voicing the dreaded term), and to her the goal of a life of her own is having a husband and family. The ending of the film is especially problematic in simplisti-cally suggesting that somehow the union of Megs and Dave's sister will allow the couple to capture the lost innocence of their high school days. Nevertheless, if the film accomplished nothing more than granting Baker the line, "Don't you want a point of view?" when her brother says he won't take her, a woman, fishing with his friend, it would have done more than almost any other Vietnam film in granting woman an independent subjec-tivity and hinting at the possibility that she can be the maker and not just the bearer of meaning.[5]

The ending of *Jacknife*, with its nostalgic promise of a return to inno-cence, is characteristic of the genre. "Return" is a constant motif in Viet-nam films, as many critics have noted. In the Rambo-type films, there is one heroic man's return to Vietnam so he can "win the war this time." For all its apparent liberalism, the same concern is detectable in *Born on the Fourth of July*. Ron's activism at the end of the film is *explicitly* associated with warfare: turned out of the Republican convention the veterans have stormed, Ron uses militarist language in instructing his men to return and "take the hall." Not only is Kovic thus positioned as a victorious warrior, a man who wins the war against the war, but in taking the hall he reverses another ignominious defeat, a wrestling match he lost in high school, to the tremendous disappointment of his mother and girlfriend sitting in the bleachers.

The notion of return is also present in the constant process of "metaphorization" that occurs in these films, which as we have seen make everything and everyone (raped women, murdered babies, etc.) refer back to and stand in for the American soldier (or veteran) and his plight. Differ-ence and otherness are recognized only to the extent that they are seen to signify something about the American male. Some feminists have identi-fied metaphor, which reduces differences to versions of sameness, as basic to Western "phallocentric" thought; in making this point they draw on the paradigmatic Freudian scenario whereby the male reads the female body in terms of his own standard—the penis, which the female body is judged to be lacking.[6] Now, given the crisis in America's "phallic" authority that opened up with the loss of the war and given the occasionally literal severing of the penis from the phallus which symbolizes it, it is not surprising to see metaphorical operations such as those I have described move into high gear in representations of Vietnam. Thinking again of the coming in *Coming Home,* we can see why a feminist would appreciate the sex scene in that film, might prize its brief acknowledgment of feminine difference, and want to insist that sometimes a clitoris is just a clitoris, and a woman's orgasm simply that.

133

This rather lengthy preamble is designed to put in relief the achievement of Nancy Savoca's understated little film *Dogfight,* since it is easily lost in the midst of the loud, frantic, spectacular representations with which we have been bombarded by so many male directors of Vietnam films. *Dogfight* is a film about a group of Marines about to be shipped overseas (they don't know it but they are destined for Vietnam). The group of men set up a "dogfight," which turns out to be a dance, to which each of the Marines is supposed to bring an ugly date. The man who finds the ugliest woman will be the winner and receive a cash prize. One of the four men, Eddie (River Phoenix), is unsuccessful at convincing the women he encounters to go out with him; more or less giving up on the attempt he goes into a diner and meets Rose (Lili Taylor, padded up a bit for the role), a waitress whose mother owns the diner and who, when he first sees her, is picking out a folk tune on her guitar. He invites her to the dance, and after some hesitation she accepts. One of the interesting aspects of the way the film sets up the initial sequence is that the spectator is not sure whether or not Eddie really considers Rose to be "dogfight" material, a question that the film in fact never clears up.

At the end of the evening Rose discovers the purpose of the dogfight, slugs Eddie, and leaves in a rage. Remorseful, Eddie goes to the apartment over the diner where Rose lives and gets Rose to agree to go out with him for the night. Scenes of their evening out, which is sweetly romantic despite periodic arguments (Rose is a budding peacenik), are intercut with scenes of Eddie's three friends, who spend their last night in the States brawling with sailors and watching pornography in a theater as a prostitute fellates them, chewing gum in between bouts. At the end of the evening they go to a tattoo parlor and get tattoos of bees on their arms (each has a last name beginning with "B") to mark their loyalty to one another. Eddie and Rose sleep together and in the morning he goes off to meet his bus. After a very brief battle scene set in Vietnam, Eddie returns, wounded, to San Francisco, and the film very movingly presents us with the point of view of a man who sees an entirely different world from the one he left (figure 7.1). Flower children fill the street: one of them walks past Eddie and softly asks, "Hey, man, did you kill any babies over there?" For all the preoccupation of films like *Born on the Fourth of July* with the soldier's readjustment to civilian life, in my view no other movie captures as vividly as this scene the estrangement and confusion of the returning vet. Eddie goes into the diner which Rose now runs and encounters a more mature woman; as they look at each other, they are at a loss for words, and in a mournful ending the two embrace.

I want to argue against the grain of the voluminous criticism written about Vietnam war movies and to propose that precisely *because Dogfight* is a love story and gives us a woman's perspective on war and the warrior mentality, it is less compromising in its opposition to war than any other film in that most paradoxical of genres, the anti-war war movie. The anti-war sentiment is not only present in *Dogfight*'s narrative but is conveyed at the level of style: much of the film's subversiveness lies in the peacefulness and restraint of its pacing, rhythms, and soundtrack. There is a sweetness in the encounter between boy and girl that is genuinely moving. At the same time it must be said that this film is less sentimental than most Vietnam films, which Andrew Martin has convincingly shown to be for the most

Figure 7.1. River Phoenix as Eddie coming home in *Dogfight*. © 1991 Warner Bros. Inc.

part male melodrama. To measure the gap between the sentimentality of some of these films and *Dogfight*'s uncompromising view of the cruelties of which people are capable and which, after all, have some bearing on our desire or at least our willingness to make war, we need only compare one event, the prom that is featured prominently in Vietnam films, with a very different one in Savoca's film—the dogfight. The latter is, to say the least, an event for which it is difficult to muster up the same sort of nostalgia inspired by the former.

The eponymous event of the dogfight may be seen as the antithesis of the prom scenes in *Jacknife* and *Born on the Fourth of July,* both of which nourish us in the dangerous illusion of a pre-war era of lost innocence and unimpaired relations between the sexes. In *Born on the Fourth of July* Ron Kovic, on the eve of his departure for military service, runs through a storm in his old clothes and arrives soaked at the prom to dance with his starry-eyed girlfriend. In *Dogfight*, of course, the "dance" is the cruel event of the dogfight itself (staged, like the prom in *Born on the Fourth of July,* on the eve of the men's departure for Vietnam). Rose finds out about the point of the dance, the dogfight, in a scene that takes place in the ladies room. One of the girls, Marcy, who has gone toothless to the affair and earned the prize for the man who brought her, stands in front of the bathroom mirror putting her teeth back in and tells Rose about the rules of the contest. "The thing that gets me," Marcy concludes, "is how great they think they are. Did you ever see such a pack of pukes in your life?" Rose is, naturally, appalled and marches out to Eddie and punches him, confronting him directly with his cruelty and lack of feelings for others. The script, written by ex-Marine Bob Comfort, has the infinite merit of focusing here on the anger and humiliation of the object, rather than the sad plight of the subject, of the cruelty.

Yet in creating Rose, who in the original script was supposed to be excessively overweight, Comfort intended to make the woman serve as a "metaphor" for the Marine, her unacceptable looks symbolizing his "outsider status." Comfort has publicly expressed his unhappiness with Savoca's changes in his script, and one can only speculate that his feeling of dispossession, his sense of dis-Comfort, as it were, stemmed from director Savoca's resistance to turning the heroine into a metaphor, a reflection of the hero. According to Savoca, in the original script Rose "was more of a catalyst for change," and, she says, "this bored me and Lili to tears." They resolved to make the character someone in her own right. Importantly, however, the transformation in the female character does not occur at the *expense* of the male character (almost a primal fear of men when women make art); on the contrary, Savoca maintains, "as her IQ comes up, so does his. Because rather than reacting to a thing, he's reacting to a complicated person. Something happens between two people and not just between this guy and his revelation." Savoca continues:

> We decided that the first thing to do was give her a passion—so that regardless of what she looks like there's something going on within herself. And that something is music. . . . He becomes attracted to

her because she has a love in her that goes beyond their small world and the rigid narrow existence he's used to living — and not because one day she takes out the ribbon in her hair and, oh my god, she's stunning.[7]

In view of the narcissistic self-referentiality of many male-directed Vietnam films, which repeatedly and utterly disqualify women as authorities in matters of war and peace (we recall Ron Kovic's girlfriend being judged harshly by the film *Born on the Fourth of July* for turning away from Kovic and toward the anti-war demonstrators), we can perhaps appreciate Savoca's audacity in having her heroine's aspirations and values point a way out of the trap in which the soldier finds himself. Indeed, we might say that, by extension, just as Eddie is required to treat Rose as a person with an independent subjectivity who has the potential for giving him a glimpse of more expansive horizons, so too does Savoca's encounter with Comfort's text strengthen it while respecting and underscoring its powerful indictment of a society which devours young working-class men and spits them out.

Rose is a young girl who dreams of changing the world, of possibly joining the civil rights movement in the South or engaging in some other form of social activism; she also aspires to be a folk singer and during their date she argues with Eddie throughout the evening about the most effective means of changing the world: he, of course, has opted for guns; she for guitars. That the aspirations and values of the heroine are expressed in her love of folk music is particularly appropriate. Vietnam was, as more than one critic has noted, America's rock-and-roll war, and many of the films about the war are edited to supercharged rhythms of the Rolling Stones and similar groups. Even if the lyrics of many of these songs are intended to make an ironic or critical comment on the war, the music itself often serves to pump up the testosterone level, working viscerally against the anti-war sentiments supposedly being promoted.[8] Such music, as David James has argued, is always at least ambivalent ("Rock and Roll"). In this regard, then, we might compare the nihilistic song by the Stones, "Paint It Black," that ends Stanley Kubrick's anti-war, anti-military film *Full Metal Jacket* with the Malvina Reynolds song that Rose haltingly sings sitting at a piano in a nearly deserted café as Eddie looks on: "The grass is gone/ the boy disappears/ and rain keeps falling like helpless tears."

138   Eddie and his friends do disappear, and only Eddie returns. When he comes back to San Francisco, the world has changed drastically, and he is viewed with disdain and suspicion by the flower children milling around in the street. Eddie limps into a bar across the street from Rose's café wearing his uniform. When the bartender sees Eddie's tattoo he shows him his: a girl who jiggles and performs a "belly dance" on his protruding gut. Eddie asks about Rose, describing her to the bartender as kind of chubby; the bartender responds, "She ain't no prize," and one of the men chimes in, "Yeah, like you're really something, eh Carl?" At one point the bartender asks Eddie if he served in Vietnam. When Eddie responds in the affirmative, the bartender, at a loss for words, says, "Yeah, bummer," and walks away. "No charge on that," says the owner of the bar when Eddie gets a second drink. "Thank you," Eddie replies. "Thank *you*," says the man quietly, but he can't look Eddie in the eye.

Such moments convey the pathos and isolation of the returning veteran more eloquently than a thousand bombastic moments in an Oliver Stone movie. They strike a note of pure loss, prolonged through the final shots when Eddie goes across the street to see Rose and she too seems not to know what to say or do. They embrace, though this is clearly not the embrace of two people destined to live happily ever after; it is an act of mutual consolation over all the sorrow and loss that has occurred in the intervening years, including the severing of their slender connection, which of course cannot ever be reforged. Warner Brothers Studio, encouraged by a preview audience's positive response to the first part of the movie (some of the crowd found the dogfight idea hilarious), exerted intense pressure on Savoca to change the ending to make it more upbeat. Finally, an exasperated Savoca asked sardonically, "Do you want us to change the ending so we win the war?"—apparently not realizing that that was *exactly* what

Hollywood wanted and what movie directors for the last decade or so have been all too happy to provide.

Dogfight, in a certain sense, may be seen as the second in a two-part series Savoca filmed on relations between the sexes. Her brilliant film debut was a movie, *True Love* (1989), that gained a certain cult following among women. Drawing on some techniques of documentary, *True Love* is a dystopian "wedding comedy" which focuses on the rituals leading up to the big day. Donna (Annabella Sciorra) and Mikey (Ron Eldard), the engaged couple, battle over whether or not Donna will get to go out with Mikey after his bachelor party. Throughout the film, Savoca cuts between the group of guys (Mikey and his friends) and the group of girls (Donna and hers), showing us two worlds that are so separate, their inhabitants might as well live on separate planets. "Sometimes she says things to me and I don't understand what the fuck she's talkin' about," says Mikey at one point. As the boys party on throughout the night, getting drunker and drunker (while the camera angles and positions get wilder and wilder), the girls just hang out waiting, talking of marriage, home decorating, and the like. At one point they go to watch a male stripper, but it is clear they do so defiantly, in order to prove their ability to have the same kind of fun as the boys—thereby, of course, proving the opposite. The climax of the movie occurs during the wedding itself when Mikey proposes to his friends that they go out for a while on the wedding night. He begs Donna to let him go just for an hour or two with the boys, and she runs crying into the ladies room, where she is followed first by her friends and then by Mikey. The film ends inconclusively, although one senses the two will go on with married life, living it as happily or rather as unhappily as most.

True Love documents better than almost any film I have ever seen the asymmetries of life as it is generally lived by the two sexes in modern America. It submits to a trenchant analysis the relations between men that are glorified and idealized by the overwhelming majority of Hollywood films. *Dogfight* continues in this vein, alternating scenes of the developing relation between Eddie and Rose with scenes of Eddie's friends out on the town boozing and whoring. From wedding to war and home again, Savoca's first two films, taken together, cover the same territory as Michael Cimino's lengthy and controversial Vietnam film *The Deer Hunter* and may be read as a rewriting of that film in feminist terms.

Roughly the first third of *The Deer Hunter* depicts a wedding that takes place in a highly sex-segregated working-class community of Russian Americans, just as *True Love* is situated in a working-class Italian American section of the Bronx. In an excellent analysis of *The Deer Hunter*, Susan Jeffords argues that the wedding sets up the basic conflict of the film, which is most clearly played out in relation to the character of Nicky (Christopher Walken) who is killed off by the film, precisely because his loyalties are divided between the world associated with women (sex, marriage, domesticity) and his affiliation with men—specifically Michael, played by Robert DeNiro. Jeffords writes, "One must either live all of the points of the code ('discipline, endurance, purity') or not attempt it at all; . . . one must fulfill either the masculine or the feminine, but not both" (95). Of course, these two options are not equally valued by the film, for the character who chooses the feminine comes home a paraplegic; rather, its primary emotional investment is in the relations between men, in particular, between Nick and Michael, whose friendship is highly idealized by Cimino. Jeffords goes so far as to claim that "Vietnam is . . . not the subject of *The Deer Hunter* but merely the occasion for announcing the primacy of the bonds between men" (99).

While many Vietnam films, most notably perhaps *Full Metal Jacket,* have exposed the misogynistic aspects of military life, none of them focuses as unwaveringly as *Dogfight* on the more unappealing aspects of the male bonding which is part and parcel of the misogyny—the dirty jokes, the lies about sexual prowess, the animal behavior and brawling, the humiliation of those farther down the pecking order and so on. Soldiers who fought in Vietnam were, after all, just boys out of high school (a fact we're inclined to forget when a thirty-something Robert DeNiro is the star). *Dogfight* goes

Figure 7.2. The four B's in *Dogfight*. © The Academy of Motion Picture Arts and Sciences.

very far indeed in contravening one of the most basic assumptions of Hollywood war films in regard to women and male bonding, suggesting *not* that men must give up ties to women and families in order to survive, but that the unthinking loyalty to the all-male group, an ideal promoted by military life and by much of our civilian culture as well, is what threatens their survival. The point may seem obvious, but it is never made in Hollywood films.

To emphasize the irrationality of these bonds the film includes a discussion at the dogfight in which the boys explain to the girls how it is their surnames all begin with the same initial. One of the four explains that they had to line up by alphabetical order when they were in infantry training. Rose conversationally concludes, "So you got to be friends by standing in line?" There is an awkward pause, and then Marcy, the toothless girl, guffaws loudly. The guys call themselves the four B's, and the film makes much of the ritual in which they get themselves tattooed with bees on their arms—all except Eddie who is with Rose. When Eddie rejoins the group the morning after sleeping with Rose, he tells one of his friends, Berzin (Richard Panebianco), that he has learned from Rose that Berzin had fixed the dogfight. Berzin in turn tells Eddie that when he was getting his tattoo he saw him with Rose—not with the gorgeous officer's wife Eddie has lied about having spent his last night with. In a rare moment of honesty between men Eddie asks his friend Berzin, "How'd we get to be so full of shit like this . . . such idiots?" All these lies are "bullshit," Eddie says. Berzin replies:

> Let me tell you something about bullshit. It's everywhere. You hit me with a little, and I buy it. I hit you with a little, you buy it. That doesn't make us idiots. It's what makes us buddies. We buy what the Corps hands out, and that's what makes us Marines. And the Corps's buying all the bullshit from President Kennedy and President Kennedy's buying all the bullshit from everybody in the U.S. of Fuckin' A and that's what makes us Americans.

It's still bullshit," Eddie insists. "Right, and we're in it up to our goddam lips, Buddy. . . . I don't know if I'm making sense, but [here he rolls up his sleeve to show the bee tattoos], this makes a hell of a lot of sense to me. There's no bullshit in this." At this point, one of the four "bees" farts loudly; the guys all start laughing and joking again about the officer's wife. In a chilling gesture Eddie tears up the address Rose has given him and throws the pieces out the window of the bus, where they are scattered to the wind. The act of renouncing association with women would in the logic of most war films help to secure the man's safety, which as I noted at the outset, is endangered whenever men keep mementos of their attachments at home.

In *Dogfight* the outcome is very different. The film devotes about one minute of screen time to depicting the men in combat (thereby avoiding the contradictions involved when films rely on combat sequences for their anti-war message). In this brief scene we see the four young men sitting around playing cards, and one of them brings up a joke: "What did the ghost say to the bee? 'Boo, bee.'" As two of the four "bees" laugh at a dumb pun which condenses various themes of the film—male bonding (the four bees), the degradation of women (the crude reference to a part of female anatomy), and death (the ghost), mortar falls into their midst and apparently kills Eddie's friends. It might be said that, at the fantasmatic level, Eddie is allowed to survive *because* his loyalties were at least temporarily divided between the male group and a woman—the very reason, in Jeffords's argument, that Nick in *The Deer Hunter* must be killed off.

In Savoca's previous film, *True Love,* the heroine Donna resents the all-male group but recognizes its primacy. The night before the wedding Donna takes Mikey aside and cuts both their hands to intermingle their blood, like "blood brothers," she explains. The acknowledgement of the primacy of male bonds, along with the yearning to become a member of the privileged male group, is something that is also expressed in representations of Vietnam created by women. In her discussion of Bobbie Ann Mason's *In Country,* for instance, Jeffords shows how the heroine longs to have the same kind of understanding of war that men have and how finally the novel confirms "collectivity as a function of the masculine bond" (62). When Sam/Samantha, who is named after her father, goes to the Vietnam War Memorial, she is able to touch her own name and symbolically become part of the collectivity from which she has felt excluded. In *Dogfight,* however, the woman stands for a higher form of collectivity than the military group exemplified by the four bees—and her vision of a better world achievable through artistic endeavor and political activism (*not* through any essentialized categories such as feminine nurturance) is presented by the film as admirable, if vague and a bit naively idealistic.

On the film's horizon is a faint glimpse, barely discernible, of another kind of collectivity. Taking place on the eve of a feminist revolt which would gain momentum in the seventies, *Dogfight* reminds us, most particularly in the casting of folksinger Holly Near as the mother of a heroine who believes in the power of music to change the world, of a time when *women* would bond together in lesbian separatist spaces, pre-eminent of which was the woman's music festival. Additionally, in locating Rose and her mother in a place called "Rose's Coffee Shop," which is handed down from mother to daughter, beginning with Rose's grandmother, the film privileges matrilineality and presages the alternative economies which feminists would be attempting to devise.

The fullness of that story, though, is left to another time, another film. For Savoca and her husband, screenwriter Richard Guay with whom she works closely, the principal concern is the relation, or more accurately nonrelation, between the sexes. One finds a fairly persistent pessimism in Savoca's work about the possibilities for meaningful union between male and female. But the connection between Rose and Eddie when it does occur is luminescent. The physical part of the relationship begins after Rose has sung for Eddie in the café. He takes her to a musical arcade where they put money in all the machines and dance to a cacophony of music box tunes. Then as the music winds down, it is as if the raucous soundtrack of every Vietnam film ever made were being stilled, the rhythm cranked down and a temporary truce called in the hostilities between men and women. The noisy soundtrack is replaced by the sound of two people awkwardly embracing, fumbling to get their arms right, breathing unevenly in excitement and surprise at the intense pleasures of newly awakening sexuality.

When Eddie goes to Rose's bedroom, they begin kissing to the tune of a Malvina Reynolds song playing on Rose's phonograph machine; then Rose goes into her closet "to change." Eddie whisks out of his clothes and stops when he remembers to go through his wallet to find a condom. He slips it under the bib of a teddy bear on Rose's bed and quickly gets into the bed. Rose comes out wearing a long flannel nightgown, and Eddie is dazzled: "You look good, you look real good." The process in which Rose goes from being perceived as possible dogfight material to being looked upon as a vision of loveliness is complete and entirely believable, without the film's ever stopping to make a point of it (figure 7.3). As if responding to the commentators who have criticized Vietnam representations for seldom acknowledging that warriors are just boys, the film in this scene touchingly evokes precisely the liminal space between childhood and

Figure 7.3. River Phoenix (Eddie) and Lili Taylor (Rose) in *Dogfight*. © 1991 Warner Bros. Inc.

adulthood so crucial to the future of humanity (its end—in war; its beginning—in sex).

Because the movie is about teenagers, Warner Brothers thought it should be marketed as a teen comedy—the ghetto to which so many women directors are relegated in Hollywood. Such a confusion might seem laughable on the face of it, but the fact that the movie is as much about a teenage *girl* as it is about boys makes it especially vulnerable to being judged trivial. Nor is *Dogfight* alone in being patronized because of its protagonist. In an article entitled "Men, Women and Vietnam," Milton J. Bates writes of Bobbie Ann Mason's novel *In Country*: "Mason, having elected to tell her story from a teenage girl's point of view, cannot realistically venture a more mature critique of the War or sexual roles. Why inflict such a handicap on one's narrative?" (29). One might as well say that *Huckleberry Finn* is handicapped by having a young boy as its protagonist and that consequently Mark Twain cannot venture a mature critique of American society or slavery! I am arguing, however, that having a teenage girl as (co)protagonist provides Savoca with a unique vantage point from which to advance an important critique of the war mentality and especially of war narratives—a critique, in part, of their exclusive emphasis *on the white male soldier's point of view*.

146

Discussing the sex scene in class, one of my students remarked that this was the first time in the movies she had seen a man ask a woman if it was okay to proceed in his sexual "advances." It is in such small details that the subversive nature of women's popular cinema often lies. This detail might be dismissed as another instance in which "the invasion is rewritten as erotic melodrama." But I would counter that in being anti-invasion on a very minute scale, the film points to the existence of other subjectivities and other desires besides those of the white male hero. In so saying, I do not, I hope, commit the same error I lamented in mainstream representations of Vietnam and implicitly offer Rose as a metaphor for Asia. I do, however, mean to suggest that in the film one man is shown to take a crucial *step* toward recognizing otherness in the variety of forms it takes; the movie thus prepares the ground for the emergence of an anti-war sensibility, even though it doesn't go the entire distance.

The film itself respects the integrity and independence of its viewers as well and never bludgeons them with the moral. Rather than beginning by condemning the men for their barbarous treatment of women, for example, the film depicts the staging of the dogfight in such a way that the point of the men's search for ugly women, which may initially strike us as somewhat amusing, only gradually becomes clear. We tend to identify with Eddie until Rose learns about the dogfight, and then we find ourselves implicated in his lack of sensitivity and his propensity for cruelty. This development, along with the film's somber finale, angered preview audiences who wanted the comfort of a happy and predictable ending: boy loses war but at least wins girl (the boo-bee prize).

The anger is certainly understandable. The war itself seemed to many Americans to have had the wrong ending, and rather than mourning its loss, they have fallen victim to a widespread melancholia, in which they cling to the lost object rather than letting it go.[9] According to Sigmund Freud, when people are unable to mourn a loss and put it behind them, they internalize it, preserving it within themselves, and become inconsolable. Turning inward, they appear narcissistic. This malady is what Freud calls "melancholia" ("Mourning and Melancholia"). Having denied loss, denied the fact of having lost the war, America internalized the war and cannot seem to move beyond the question of what this loss has meant to itself, rather than to others who were also affected by it. *Dogfight* points to the necessity of moving beyond narcissism and coming to terms with the losses we incurred in being vanquished—the necessity, then, of mourning.

147

And in mourning who better than women to lead the way? In her important study, *The Gendering of Melancholia,* Juliana Schiesari, following and reassessing Freud, discusses mourning as a social ritual that has generally been performed by women. Melancholia, in contrast to mourning, is a category by which a solitary male elevates and glorifies his losses (a comrade; a lover; a war) into "signifiers of cultural superiority" (62). A literary critic, Schiesari is speaking primarily of poets and other creative writers who through masterful elegiac displays put their own exquisite sensibilities forward for us to admire, offering themselves as objects to be pitied for the losses they have sustained, and—in some cases—hoping to acquire immortality, paradoxically, through creating for posterity a work which supposedly acknowledges death. For our purposes, Oliver Stone, who cannot seem to stop making movies about Vietnam, might be seen as an example of the inconsolable melancholic. A quintessentially melancholic scene would be the one in *Born on the Fourth of July* in which we're asked to focus on *Kovic's* pain and guilt when he has to talk to the parents of a dead buddy. Schiesari concludes that mourning is a social ritual which "accommodates the imagination to reality" while melancholia accommodates reality to the imagination. In her capacity as mourner, too, then, woman stands for the collectivity over male individualism.

Doing the work of mourning, accommodating the imagination to reality, the film confronts us both with the reality of our losses and, concomitantly, with the real—as opposed to figural—status of woman. The struggle to establish this reality by asserting a female vision and female authority was waged at several levels of the text's production and reception. First, in order to make the female character of equal importance to the male, Savoca had to take on scriptwriter Comfort, who was displeased at some of her revisions. Second, many of the changes were decided on during the filming and were worked out collectively between cast and crew, most particularly between Savoca and Taylor. Finally, after preview audiences responded unfavorably to the film's ending, Savoca refused to comply with Warner Brothers' attempts to get her to change the ending. She conceded that Warner Brothers had the authority to do what they liked with the film, but she demanded that her name be taken off the project if the ending was reshot. Warner Brothers executives called River Phoenix and Lili Taylor, but both refused to reshoot the ending without Savoca. Savoca believes that neither she nor Taylor counted for much with the studio but thinks that Phoenix's refusal to reshoot forced Warner Brothers' decision to stop pursuing the issue (whereupon, according to Savoca, the project was dumped "into the toilet"). I like to think that Phoenix's role taught him something about resisting the orders of a male power structure and the desirability of sometimes deferring to the vision of a woman—in this case, Nancy Savoca, who elicited from him one of the finest performances of his tragically short life. Fittingly, Phoenix ended up being eloquently memorialized in a work that asserts the legitimacy of female authority.

8

A WOMAN'S GOTTA DO . . . WHAT A MAN'S GOTTA DO?

Cross-Dressing in the Western

❏

A male reviewer wrote of The Ballad of Little Jo, *"The film made me want to go home and watch* Bonanza.*" And I thought: You want to go back to the Western where there's no woman around telling these three guys that they're not okay and where the Chinese man in the kitchen has no dick? That's where you want to go back to?*

Well, you can't. It's over.

—Maggie Greenwald, director of The Ballad of Little Jo

In the encyclopedic volume *The BFI Companion to the Western,* Edward Buscombe writes in his lengthy and highly informative introduction, "It seemed as though at the very moment of [the Western's] creation the West was suffused with a rosy tinge of nostalgia" (52). In view of the resistance on the part of some white male critics to new developments in the genre, perhaps it could be said that male viewers who want to go back to the always-already nostalgic cowboy stories of old are imbued not with what Mary Ann Doane, in speaking of the female viewer, has called the "desire to desire" but with the nostalgia for nostalgia. Indeed, Buscombe himself seems to fall victim to this malady when he laments the directions taken by the genre in the sixties and seventies: "The withering away of the traditional audience for the Western had led by the 1970s to a free-for-all, where in order to find a market everything was tried at least once. There were Westerns for children, for blacks and hippies, for liberals and conservatives." The list continues for a paragraph, and the next paragraph begins, "There were good Westerns, too"(!)(51)—all of which, it turns out, have white men as protagonists.

In the nineties some white male critics seem again to sense that something is "withering away" and to feel renewed solidarity with the more traditional heroes who are presumably being crowded out of their terrain.[1] Yet I would argue that while these critics identify with the cowboys they consider to be a vanishing breed, in reality they more closely resemble the railroad speculators seeking to gobble up all the land and to deprive anyone else of the territory they might legitimately claim for themselves. Thus, whether intentionally or not, they will often ensnare works such as Mario Van Peebles's *Posse* (1993) or Maggie Greenwald's *The Ballad of Little Jo* (1993) in a Catch-22 logic: on the one hand, a film like *Posse* is liable to be dismissed as conventional—therefore derivative. Part of the problem of its being derivative, it is implied, is that it is false to the specificity of African American existence (thus do ostensibly liberal white critics appear to speak on behalf of African Americans in the very process of eliminating them as competitors in the arena of popular culture).[2] On the other hand, *Posse* is liable to be seen as a product of the marketplace's cynical strategy of trying everything at least once, as Buscombe puts it. The film may have a novel theme or unconventional characters, but these are regarded as mere gimmicks. Whereas films like *Posse* and *The Ballad of Little Jo* are doubly disqualified in these ways, a film like *Unforgiven* (1992) gets the benefit of the doubt in both directions. It is proclaimed truly revisionary—simultaneously a real Western and a work of art.

Certainly few reviewers in the mainstream American press have any stake in considering why marginalized groups would want not to discard but to rework stories that have, after all, shaped the fantasies of most people in this culture. Still less do reviewers want to consider what happens to the genre when, say, the shoot-out pits black cowboys against the Ku Klux Klan, or when the railroad companies deprive black people of living in the townships they have formed—as in fact happened after the Civil War. Are such plots not radically revisionary and recognizably Western? Are they not true to an ever-growing awareness of the American West as containing diverse realities that suggest the comparative poverty of some of the older myths? For if, as Richard Slotkin has observed, the Western is caught up in a "dilemma of authenticity"—cultural tradition's tendency to define "the west as both an actual place with a real history and as a mythic space populated by projective fantasies"—then the plots of the new Westerns might, as in the example here, be expected to refigure the relationship of historical reality to myth in ways that merit close mapping (234).[3]

151

There are many compelling reasons to undertake such a mapping of *The Ballad of Little Jo,* not the least of which is that it does indeed reflect the new directions being taken in histories of the Old West which have increasingly focused on gender and on the ethnic and racial diversity of nineteenth-century frontier society. Further, as an imaginative work of popular art, the film provides an occasion to examine the history of male and female "projective fantasies" of the Old West and the Western landscape from the pioneer days to the present and to see how the very border between male and female worlds of popular culture shifts when a woman is working on what has hitherto been exclusively masculine territory. Whereas an earlier generation of feminist culture critics posited a strict binary opposition between men's fantasies and women's fantasies of the West and the Western landscape, and often actually reinforced the segregation of men and women in the popular culture sphere—either by bemoaning the "transvestism" forced on the female reader/spectator of Westerns or by asserting the superiority of female fantasies (of home and garden) to men's fantasies (of the desert and the range)—a film like *Ballad* forcefully challenges this binary system, stirring up the kind of "gender trouble" celebrated by theorists such as Judith Butler. In this regard, the film furnishes an opportunity to chart the distance feminist cultural criticism and theory have traveled in the past two decades.

Looking at *The Ballad of Little Jo* in a historical context, moreover, might help shed light on the current fascination with cross-dressing not only in feminist theory but, equally important, in popular culture and high culture (I am thinking not only of films such as *To Wong Foo, Thanks for Everything! Julie Newmar* [1995] but of such films as *Orlando* [1993] and *The Crying Game* [1992]). In a fascinating article titled "Balladry's Female Warriors: Women, Warfare and Disguise in the Eighteenth Century," Dianne Dugaw discusses the popularity of the cross-dressed female warrior in Anglo-American balladry, an art form that flourished from the mid-eighteenth to the mid-nineteenth centuries among the working class. Dugaw notes that ballads drew on the experience of many women in the working classes, who, for a variety of social and economic reasons, sometimes disguised themselves as men, often to join the military. In this regard it might be argued that the nineteenth-century dime novels, which I discuss below, inherited and prolonged the life of the character of the female cross-dresser so popular in the Anglo-American ballads. It is likely as well that both of these genres spoke to the actual experience of westering American women whose rugged lives necessitated their violation of feminine norms.

Given this history, it is highly interesting that Greenwald, without conscious knowledge of the ballad tradition, chose the ballad form (episodic verses, accompanied by ballad music) to contribute to the resurgence of interest in cross-dressing at the present time. Dugaw contends that the eighteenth century was "obsessed at all levels with disguise and cross-dressing" (15). Referring to popular theories of carnival as a space in which hierarchies of class and gender were temporarily upset, she writes:

> For people in the eighteenth century, masquerade served not simply
> as a means of reversing roles or suspending authority for a day, *but
> rather as an end in itself, as an experiment with identity.* Ballads about
> women pretending to be men became best sellers, and people of all
> classes regularly feigned being who they were not on virtually any

day of the week. In the eighteenth century disguise became a social fad, a literary trope, and a settled and ongoing way of conceptualizing behavior. (15, emphasis added)

So, too, the current craze for cross-dressing in film and popular culture may also reveal a desire to put identity into question, a desire that may not be limited to a small coterie of feminist and queer theorists in the academy.

153

Finally, I want to look at *The Ballad of Little Jo* to consider how it deals with ethnic and racial diversity, for I believe it provides a way to see—and to see beyond—the unconscious racial dimensions of certain white female fantasies of the American West (both past and present) as well as of the theories of these fantasies in feminist scholarship. Here I do not wish simply to gesture toward a need for greater inclusivity in white feminist literary and film criticism, but to show precisely how the binary thinking of some feminist culture critics who have focused primarily on sexual difference has sometimes rested on untheorized assumptions about race. This is not, however, to deny the force of gender binarisms even on nonwhite American culture and criticism. To take an example that is especially pertinent to the present discussion—in that the protagonist of *Ballad* becomes romantically involved with a feminized Chinese man (figure 8.1)—King-Kok Cheung has shown how some Chinese men have responded to Chinese women writers' alleged emasculation of Chinese men by stressing a warrior tradition and asserting the value of "fighting" over "feeling." In this respect, Chinese American letters are waging even today a conflict similar to the one that Jane Tompkins claims is at the heart of a "literary gender war" historically played out between the dueling genres of male Western narratives and female domestic, or sentimental, fiction.

I want to begin by measuring the distance traveled by *The Ballad of Little Jo* from the classical Western, choosing as my example of the latter one of the films singled out for special praise by Buscombe and almost every other fan of the Western: Sam Peckinpah's *Ride the High Country* (1962).

Figure 8.1. Suzy Amis (Jo) and David Chung (Tinman) in *The Ballad of Little Jo.* © 1993 Fine Line Features. Photo by Bill Foley.

The film is set on the eve of the Western's decline and thus powerfully evokes that sense of nostalgia so pervasive in the genre. In the film, two aging cowboys, played by Randolph Scott and Joel McCrea, team up to deliver gold from a mining camp to the bank in the nearest town. At the beginning of the film, the two men, formerly partners, accidentally meet at a Wild West Show, in which one of them has been acting the part of Buffalo Bill. After deciding to take this final job, the men hire a younger man to accompany them, and on the way they encounter Elsa Knudsen (Mariette Hartley), a young woman living alone with her fanatical father, who, it is hinted, has been incestuous with his daughter. To get away from her father, Elsa invites herself along on the journey to the mining camp, where her fiancé resides with his all-male "white trash" family, who assault the girl on their wedding night. Describing the initial scene in which Elsa appears, Jim Kitses writes, "The enemy of feeling and instinct, the Knudsen household is deeply repressive, the girl Elsa stunted and hiding herself in ill-fitting men's clothes, growth and self-knowledge finally impossible here" (156). At the end of the film, when all the conflicts have been resolved, "Elsa's growth," Kitses writes, is signified by the girl's "finally accepting a suitable costume" (158). As this description suggests, the film's narrative reveals with exceptional clarity how anxiety about the decline of male potency (and the threat of male sexual perversion) is linked to the fear that the Western is nothing but a show, nothing but theater, and that in such a world women may easily move out of their appointed place, and chaos will reign.

That a costume can be fraught with the kind of meaning and moral significance Kitses assigns to it suggests how even today a Western heroine like Little Jo who achieves "growth and self-knowledge" precisely through dressing as a man may represent a threat to male moviegoers. I would suggest that some of the hostile reaction of male critics to Greenwald's film stems from the fear that the phallus may in fact not be in its usual place: hence the sense of lack or "incompleteness" experienced by some of the male reviewers, the feeling that Little Jo's actions and choices need to be explained in more detail—the costume seen through and the "real" woman revealed.[4] Of course, such a demand is seldom made of male heroes, whose legendary status (one thinks of Shane, for example) is maintained through secrecy regarding their feelings, motives, and origins. Western heroes are supposed to be enigmatic: "Who *was* that masked man?" Indeed, to supply a hero with motives that lie outside him would diminish his phallic self-sufficiency, which is revealed in his typically tautological appeal to a gendered identity whenever he is asked to give a reason for his actions: "A man's gotta do what a man's gotta do." By contrast, the woman must be psychologized and understood, for she represents an intolerable double enigma: the enigma of the Westerner superimposed, as it were, on the enigma of woman.

Not that what is known about the "real" Jo Monaghan, on whom the character is based, clears up the mystery surrounding the woman. All that is known of her is that she was an Eastern society girl who had a child out of wedlock and was disowned by her family. Josephine Monaghan gave the child to her sister to care for and came out West, taking on the identity of a man sometime during her journey. "Her existence," says Greenwald, "was pretty meager and lonely," although she apparently was able throughout her life to send money to the sister for the care of the child.

Greenwald fleshes out this bare-bones plot by having her heroine, played by Suzy Amis, assume the identity of a man after she narrowly escapes being raped by two Union soldiers (Jo buys men's clothes, cuts her hair, and scars her face by cutting it with a razor); she enters the mining camp of Ruby city and boards with a man named Percy (played by Ian McKellen), until one night Percy gets drunk and cuts up a prostitute. At this point, Jo takes on a job as a sheepherder working for a man named Frank Badger (Bo Hopkins, figure 8.2), who is destined to become her life-long friend. Jo lives out in the wilderness with no company for months on end, teaching herself to tend the animals, learning to shoot the wolves that prey on the flock, and finding a degree of fulfillment in the solitary life. Eventually she buys her own flock and a homestead near Frank's.

One day in town Jo encounters Frank Badger and a group of men "having a little fun" by taunting a Chinese man, "Tinman" (David Chung), whose neck they have placed in a noose.[5] Jo forces them to cut the man loose and in return agrees to take him on as a house boy. The two eventually end up as lovers, although their relationship reaches a crisis point when Jo, tempted to return home to her son, almost sells her ranch to the Western Cattle Company, which has been tyrannizing homesteaders who refuse to sell their land. When she decides to stay, she and Frank are forced into a shoot-out against the company's hired thugs.

Figure 8.2. Bo Hopkins (Frank Badger) punches Suzy Amis (Jo) in *The Ballad of Little Jo*. © 1993 Fine Line Features. Photo by Bill Foley.

The film skips over many years, as a title informs the viewer, and fades into a long shot of Jo laboriously carrying water from the well and collapsing before she can get it to the house. By the time Frank gets her into town she is dead. As the undertaker prepares the body, the townspeople gather in the saloon to toast their friend, Little Jo Monaghan. Just as they are raising their glasses, the undertaker rushes into the saloon to tell them the secret of Jo's identity, and in a comical scene they all rush to look at the body. As they stand gazing down at it, the one woman in the group begins to laugh. In a darkly humorous penultimate scene, the townspeople put the corpse of Little Jo on her horse and tie her to the saddle so that a photograph may be taken of her. At the end, Frank enters Jo's cabin in a rage at the hoax perpetrated on him and begins to tear the place apart; in the process he comes across an old photograph of Jo (taken by the man whose child she bore), which gives him pause, and in the final image of the film, the viewer sees this photograph juxtaposed with the one in the newspaper of the cross-dressed female corpse seated on a horse.

Figure 8.3. Suzy Amis (Jo) and Sam Robards (Jasper Hill) in *The Ballad of Little Jo*. © 1993 Fine Line Features. Photo by Bill Foley.

By making Jo's first lover be the photographer who takes both the Monaghan family photograph and the individual photograph of Jo herself, Greenwald calls attention to woman's status in classic narrative as object of the gaze. Becoming in effect a victim of her biological femininity after she is seduced by the photographer, Jo is forced to become a man to avoid sexual victimization (figure 8.3) after she is cast out for bearing a child. At the end, when her sexual identity has been discovered, it is a female photographer who takes the picture—the woman behind the camera (a double, perhaps, of the director) serving to provide visual verification of the heroine's successful male masquerade.

Greenwald's idea for the scene in which the corpse is placed on the horse came from looking at books of Western photography, which she notes are filled with photographs of dead people. In fact, when she first saw the photograph of the real Jo in the newspaper clipping she thought it was a death photo. Greenwald says that photography books were her primary research tool and that she wrote the screenplay surrounded by these books. For Greenwald,

> Anything that was real was far more fascinating than anything you could make up. For instance, looking at the photographs it occurred to me to ask: what happens when you suddenly decide to build a town in the middle of a forest? You end up with tree stumps in the middle of the road and mud all over the place. Where do you get materials to build? The buildings are shelters in these photographs—well, what are they made of? And you suddenly notice that something's got a piece of paisley and that part of a roof or a window may be someone's scarf. It was a matter of using anything that was available to work with. I felt it was important to give the film that kind of texture. (Modleski "Interview with Maggie Greenwald" 8)[6]

159

Contributing to the rich texture is the film's interest in the details of work performed in the Old West—the laborious tasks involved in gold mining, for example. Although the details of women's work are depicted, such as the tending of the sick in the scene in which Frank Badger's wife, Ruth (Carrie Snodgress), doctors the ailing Tinman, spoon-feeding him kerosene, cutting up onions and taping them to the bottoms of his feet, and so forth, most of the work that is shown is work that was usually done by men. It is interesting that a woman director conveys the details of this work and of the material reality of the West more lovingly than have most male directors working in this action-oriented genre. In lingering over such details, the camera shows a fascination with things in themselves, with processes rather than goals; indeed, it might be said (were not such observations so discredited these days) that in this respect the film takes a traditionally feminine approach to the depiction of traditionally masculine activities.

One episode in *Ballad* shows the heroine learning how to tend sheep and to survive on her own in the wilderness. The first time a coyote preys upon her flock, Jo cowers in her covered wagon, terrified by the bleating of the sheep, the snarling of the coyote, the frantic barking of her dog. She determines to learn how to shoot, and scenes of target practice are intercut with amusing scenes in which Jo attempts to disentangle ungainly sheep from the brambles and then tries to get them to move as they continue to lie there. Such scenes, pleasurable in themselves, may be compared with the brief early scenes in *Unforgiven* in which Will Munny (Clint Eastwood) slides around with his pigs in the muck. These scenes establish the initial degradation of the hero, whom one character describes as a "broken-down pig farmer," and seem to be included solely to make the eventual resuscitation of Munny's gunslinger persona that much more spectacular. The pigs, in themselves, are of no interest.

In *West of Everything*, Jane Tompkins argues that animals in the Western, for all their ubiquity, are invisible. Speaking of cattle, she writes, "Lending their energy and life to the moving picture, epitomizing its goal, yet hardly ever recognized for what they are—sentient beings like ourselves, capable of pleasure and pain—cattle are an enabling condition of Western narratives. They *cannot* be seen for themselves." She argues that if they were to be truly seen, the Western would be rendered impossible, because the "relation humans have" to animals "is the same one they have to their own bodies and emotions" (118–19). The denial of the body is the fundamental truth of the male Western hero, Tompkins asserts. In *Ballad*, however, the sheep are at least in part seen for themselves; moreover, there is a recognition of a similarity between humans and animals—in this case between Jo and the sheep. The feminizing of sheep and the activity of sheepherding in the Old West is not new: for example, in *The Ballad of Josie* (1967), a comic Doris Day movie with a title uncannily similar to Greenwald's, the heroine sets up a "sheep farm in what has traditionally been cattle country, provoking a range war."[7] (In fact, historically sheep were despised because of their association with "inferior peoples": "the dislike of sheep . . . carried class and racist overtones" because sheepherding was "traditionally an occupation of Spanish-speaking natives of the Southwest or of Indian peoples such as the Navaho" [Buscombe 218]).

Greenwald revives and tacitly politicizes the rather clichéd association between women and sheep: just as Jo learns to protect the sheep from predators, so is she herself, in the course of the film, transformed from sexual prey to a woman who is in control of her life. The day after the coyote attacks the sheep, Jo comes down from her wagon and is confronted with the sickening sight of a sheep's bloody carcass. Later, when she shoots a coyote that is attacking the sheep, the camera cuts to a shot of Jo sewing and then cuts again to a low-angle shot of Jo on her horse, silhouetted against the Western landscape, wearing a huge coat made of the dead animal's fur. Rather than signify a transcendence of the animal body, the sequence and its final image suggest an apt metaphor for the female cross-dresser in the West—a sheep dressed in wolf's clothing.

Crossed-dressed heroines are not without precedent in the West or the Western genre. There was a significant subgenre of nineteenth-century dime-store Westerns featuring women dressed as men. These women did not appear on the scene all at once, however, but were part of a more gradual transformation of the Western heroine from, in Henry Nash Smith's words, "the merely passive sexual object she had tended to be in the Leatherstocking tales" to a more active protagonist. One early plot device, notes Smith in *Virgin Land*, involved a form of cross-racial masquerade: the heroine was sometimes an "Indian girl able to ride and shoot who later proves to be an upper-class white girl captured long ago by the Indians." He goes on to write, "A much more promising means of effecting a real development in the [white] heroine was the ancient device of introducing a woman disguised as a man or wearing male attire" (112). Calamity Jane of the Deadwood Dick series by Edward L. Wheeler is the most famous female cross-dresser in the Western and was, of course, a figure who survived well into the twentieth century. In Wheeler's series, Jane, not unlike Jo, has a genteel background but has been transformed into a "ruthless Amazon" by a "great wrong," her lover's desertion of her. Jane's marital prospects have suffered as a result of her having "grown reckless in act and rough in language," and the reader is informed that she will probably never marry (H. Smith 118). By contrast, in the 1953 musical comedy *Calamity Jane*, starring Doris Day, Calamity does marry, thus returning to proper femininity, but only after a great deal of "gender trouble" has occurred (including a scene in which Wild Bill Hickok, having lost a bet, attends a musical performance—of a female singer who is not who she claims to be—dressed up as an Indian squaw with a papoose; like the earliest heroines cited by Smith, his masquerade also has a cross-racial dimension).

The proliferation of masquerades, all seeming to originate from Calamity's transgression of gender norms, verges on exposing the Western as primarily about costume, poses, and theater.[8] But, of course, various forms of travesty, especially gender impersonations, have always been the stuff of comedy; laughter is precisely what keeps audiences from seriously examining the rules and hierarchies they delight in seeing temporarily subverted. It is perhaps the desire for the reassurances provided by comic laughter and the comic ending that led some of *Ballad*'s detractors to complain about the film's humorlessness. Critics like the one who faulted Greenwald for failing to exploit the "humor and suspense *inherent* in the story" (emphasis added) apparently want a Western version of *Victor/Victoria* (1982) (Levy 68). In fact there is much humor in the film; however, as the woman's laugh at the end of the film suggests, the joke is on someone else for a change—not on the transvestite but on the people who were so easily fooled by the impersonation, the very people, paradoxically, who care the most about maintaining distinctions between the sexes (hence the early scene in *Ballad* in which Frank Badger and some other men force Jo at gun point to remove her shoes to show that her socks are not patterned in yellow and black stripes like those of a "dude" whom they had recently encountered).

The disappointment in not being presented with a cowgirl version of *Victor/Victoria* is no doubt what led some critics to deplore the film's lack of "psycho-sexual cross-currents"; no doubt they had expected the kind of (invariably comic) plot in which the transvestite finds herself desired by a member of her own sex (Rainer). There does in fact remain in the film a small bit from a larger sequence, later dropped, in which a young girl named Mary falls for Jo. Thus, the suggestion of an attraction between

162

women is at least registered in *Ballad*, although to be sure the film's psychosexual energies lie elsewhere—in, precisely, a questioning of the Western *male's* sexuality.

Much of this questioning of male sexuality goes on around the figure of Percy, the misogynist who "had a wife," but who found wives to be too much trouble (as he informs Jo while competently skinning and cutting up a rabbit for stew); now, he says, he visits the girls in their tents every once in a while. He is curious about Jo, seems attracted to "him," and initiates "him" into manhood, teaching "him" how to smoke, for example. But one night a drunken Percy slashes up a prostitute because, as he explains to Jo, she would not "put it in her mouth." Greenwald was very conscious of creating in Percy a character to embody a question seldom asked in the Western genre and then only disingenuously: "Who are those men? Conventional Westerns are full of these marginalized men who are alone . . . and you don't know who they are and they never really connect, and they are someone's side-kick, or they're someone who is scary and bad and does one good deed. The Western is full of them. Who are they? And it's not just Westerns, but stories about seamen or pirates, anybody who has run away" (Modleski "Our Heroes," 10). Usually, such questions, when they are asked at all in the Western (as in the lyrics of the song in John Ford's *The Searchers* [1956]—"What makes a man to wander, to turn his back on home?") must remain rhetorical. But while most Westerns unselfconsciously play out homoerotic relations between men, like Doc Holliday and Wyatt Earp, Greenwald pauses to register the men's sexual ambiguity. The casting of McKellen was particularly inspired since, as an openly gay actor who is clear about and confident in his sexuality, he throws into relief the problems of the sexually confused but straight-identified character.

After Jo has spent some months in the line camp, she returns to Ruby City and is confronted by Percy, who has read a letter sent to Jo by her sister and has consequently discovered her true identity. Percy attempts to rape Jo, feeling betrayed just as Frank Badger ultimately feels betrayed by the revelation that Jo is a woman, but she draws a gun on him, saying, "I'll never forget the look on that woman's face as long as I live." This recogni-

163

tion of a common bond between Jo and the prostitute is an important aspect of the film's "projective fantasy." Given the historical division between "respectable" women and prostitutes in the West, and given the emphasis on this division by films such as the classic John Ford Western, *Stagecoach* (1939) (although to be sure, Ford reverses the usual values), such solidarity is to a certain extent utopian rather than indicative of actual class relations between women in the West. But it is more than that. The early sections of the film provide a feminist analysis of the grounds for such solidarity when it shows how Jo's sexual fall and subsequent banishment from her high-society family would have led her straight into prostitution had she not struck on the idea of disguising herself as a man (indeed, unbeknownst to her, she is in fact sold to the Union soldiers by the tinker who pretends to befriend her at the beginning of the movie). The job of "reuniting women" who, in the words of Western historian Patricia Limerick, "would have refused to occupy the same room" is the job not only of the historian but of the artist as well (52).[9]

Limerick and other revisionary historians of the American West stress the diversity of the West and the Western experience in relation not only to gender but also to race and ethnicity. To give a portrait of such diversity is also Greenwald's aim—achieved most notably in the depiction of the Chinese man who becomes Jo's lover and thereby sets the "psycho-sexual cross-currents" raging. Of all the ethnic and racial types of men peopling the landscape of the Western genre, the Chinese man has been the most invisible.[10] This invisibility is ironic considering the centrality of Asia and the Asian man to the construction of the great white myths of the West. Not only was Asia Christopher Columbus's intended destiny, but it also figured largely in the thinking of the advocates of manifest destiny in the early years of the nation. Henry Nash Smith has shown how in the history of American thought the intense desire for intercontinental link was gradually displaced by a preoccupation with internal borders, marked and remarked by the westward-moving frontier. This internal movement, of course, was made possible by the construction of the railroad, much of which was built through exploiting the labor of Chinese immigrants. In having Jo and Tinman become sexually involved, the film forges a connection to Asia undreamed of by proponents of manifest destiny (except perhaps in their worst nightmares); at the same time, by stressing the toll his labor has taken on Tinman, the film provides a new, but certainly authentic, take on the Western convention of the evil railroad. A similar reworking of generic convention occurs in the scene in which the white men threaten to lynch Tinman. While the lynch mob is a familiar sight in Western movies, it is certainly never acknowledged that the lynching of Chinese men in the West was part of a pattern of violence periodically visited on them by white men. Yet one male historian who reviewed *Ballad* ignored the fact that the film brings to light a mostly unacknowledged historical reality—the massacring of Chinese men by white men (Chen 46–47, 137, 139)—and complained instead about the "savage" depiction of white men in the movie (White "Little Jo," 63). That this historian has earned his reputation by calling into question the ethnocentrism of Western myths is sobering testimony to the defensiveness white men continue to display when in rare instances they find themselves sidelined (see White "Race Relations").

In the nineteenth century the white establishment had a stake in not recognizing Asians as distinct from other nonwhite groups in America. Limerick discusses the dilemmas of racist legal thinkers and Americans in general who in the nineteenth century were "wrestling with the questions raised by Western diversity" and attempting to maintain a fiction of a "bipolar West composed of 'whites' and 'Indians'" (261). If, as Marjorie Garber has argued, the transvestite represents a "category crisis" with respect to gender (16–17), it might be said that the Asian represented a category crisis with respect to nineteenth-century theories of race. In 1854, Limerick notes, Chief Justice J. Murray wrote an opinion designed to include Chinese people in a "unified racist theory" so that discriminatory legislation could be made to apply to all nonwhite peoples: "'Ethnology,'" he wrote, "having reached a 'high point of perfection,' disclosed a hidden truth in Columbus's error. It now seemed likely that 'this country was first peopled by Asiatics.'" Therefore, Murray ruled, any statute discriminating against "Indians" applied to Asians as well (Limerick 261). Thus it may be seen that the tendency of the Western genre to jumble up all racial groups into an undifferentiated mass has a long and ignoble history. In this light, Greenwald's decision to give a central role to the nearly invisible Chinese man and to give him as well a specific history of oppression (which he recounts to Jo in bed by telling her where he got the various scars on his body) may be said to strike a blow against the bipolar racial thinking so characteristic of American thought and myth. And, as seen in Greenwald's treatment of women from different backgrounds, part of the projective fantasy is to suggest a link between oppressed people, in this case between the white woman and the Asian man.

In making the connection Greenwald draws on a complex history of relations between white women and Chinese men. In the late nineteenth century, Chinese men were often seen as competitors with white women for jobs, since Chinese men not employed by the railroad were limited to "service-sector" jobs typically held by women (hence, when the Western does afford a rare glimpse of a Chinese man, it is in the feminized role of houseboy—Hop Sing on the television show *Bonanza* being perhaps the most egregious example). Sarah Deutsch points out that in the last part of the century antagonism on the part of labor unions toward Chinese men was fomented around the issue of women's sexuality: the unions claimed that "white women were drifting into prostitution because Chinese competition undermined their wages"; the unions thus called for boycotting employers of Chinese immigrants. "Yet white women were not party to the movement, and the boycott forced out of business several white female lodging house keepers who employed Chinese male servants. When these women asked the police for the much-vaunted 'protection,' the police refused" (116).[11]

"The Western is haunted by the fear of miscegenation," writes Pam Cook (242), while Slotkin points out that the stake of much Western fiction and film is "the defense of Western civilization (represented especially by the women and children of the White race) against savagery (represented by non-White natives and European tyrants)" (265). Given this stake and given the specific psychosexual and psychosocial dynamics governing historical relations between white women and Chinese men (in which white women's sexuality was at issue, even though the "emasculated" Chinese man was at times viewed as a competitor *with* rather than *for* the white woman), it was a risky decision on Greenwald's part to pose questions of sexuality and gender around the relationship of a white cross-dressing woman and a Chinese "houseboy" who has been physically debilitated by his years of working on the railroad. Considering how high the stakes are, it is particularly noteworthy that the characters are complex and the relationship lacking in sentimentality. One line in the film especially seems to prepare the viewer for a sentimentalized portrait of the love between Jo and Tinman, only to subvert it in a thoroughly humorous way; the line speaks volumes about the taboos the characters have violated and the utterly circumstantial nature of events that have resulted in this violation. When Jo and Tinman lie in bed after first making love (where he also teaches her to smoke opium), she shows him the old picture of herself and he says, "I like you better as you are." Jo smiles and readies herself for the compliment she expects when she asks, "Why?" and Tinman replies, "Because that white girl would never have done this with me." Jo and Tinman are both also capable of a certain amount of cruelty toward one another and in their anger even taunt one another with the other's gender deficiencies: Jo at one point calls Tinman "an ailing Chinaman"; on his part, when she briefly entertains going away and being a woman again, putting on a dress and smiling coyly at Tinman, he flies into a rage: "What kind of girl could you be somewhere else? What man would want you? You have no hair. Half your face is destroyed with that ugly scar. You can't even make a pie," and he plunges his hand into the mess of a pie she has concocted. Their roles (her masculine one, his feminized one) having been forced on them as a result of the gendered nature of their oppression (her sexual victimization,

167

the exploitation of his labor on the railroad), each nevertheless comes to find some pleasure and an abiding satisfaction in the other and in the work each does.

At points in the film Greenwald is unable to avoid simply reversing the roles in depicting the relationship between Jo and Tinman. For instance, Jo first experiences desire for Tinman when she rides by him on a horse as he bathes in a stream (figure 8.4). The shot is taken from Jo's point of view, and while he looks exceedingly virile, the gaze nonetheless fetishizes the image. At other times the film conveys a kind of fluidity in the sexuality that prevents it from settling into stereotype. One time when Jo and Tinman are in bed together, the camera begins with an extreme close-up of Tinman's long, dark hair, slowing panning upward; the shot is briefly disorienting until the viewer sorts out the fact that the hair belongs to the man and not the woman. The kinds of dissonances celebrated by lesbian postmodern feminists such as Butler, in which sex, gender, and "performance" (to say nothing of race and class) are at odds with one another, are at play throughout much of Tinman's portrayal (137).

It is not surprising that a couple of critics were uncomfortable with the portrayal of Tinman, charging Greenwald with, as Ruby Rich put it, being unconscious of the stereotype she was invoking—by which I assume she means the stereotype of the feminized Asian man (although Rich also finds much of the play with gender roles in this relationship "subversive").[12] Now, as I have shown, Chinese men in America were often made to perform work traditionally relegated to women and were prevented from doing the kind of work a man's supposedly "gotta do" to be a man. Rather than ignore the historical reality, *Ballad* reveals the performative aspects of the racial stereotype, just as it shows gender to possess a performative dimension. For example, Tinman puts on an exaggerated display of servility whenever Frank Badger comes around, so the viewer sees that the Hop Sing manner is an act. When Tinman is sick, Frank commiserates with Jo because he knows the two have a close relationship; he reassures her by saying that if Tinman dies, he will get Jo another Chinaman. Jo gives him a withering look, to which Frank, as ever,

Figure 8.4. Suzy Amis (Jo) and David Chung (Tinman) in *The Ballad of Little Jo*. © 1993 Fine Line Features. Photo by Bill Foley.

is oblivious. "By God," he observes, "they make damn fine cooks and housekeepers, don't they?"

Toward the end of the film Jo must make the kind of decision that most Western heroes face: whether to embrace the way of life associated with the East, with domesticity and civilization, or to remain apart from the forces encroaching on the wilderness and to live out her life as a rugged individualist. Of course, for the male Westerner, domesticity and civilization are very often represented by a woman from the East.[13] In Jo, the conflict is necessarily played out as an internal one. The threat to the wilderness way of life in *Ballad* is represented by the cattle companies that are buying up all the land and intimidating and slaughtering those who refuse to sell, like the Russian family Jo befriends. After witnessing the murder of the Russian woman, Jo is heartsick and feels torn between the desire to go back to her son, who has recently been told his mother is dead, and the desire to stay with Tinman, participate in elections ("You are a free white man," says Tinman, "and someday soon you will vote"), and fight the cattle company. In this weak moment she agrees to sell. But as Tinman lies sick in bed, possibly dying, Jo stands near the Eastern man from the cattle company who is signing the deed of transfer and looks out the window at his wife in the carriage scolding her son for running around and getting dirty. Then Tinman, a man from a different East, appears in the doorway and Jo smiles. She tells the director of the cattle company she has changed her mind. This scene is crucial not only because it satisfies generic requirements but because it suggests the extent to which Jo has grown to love her way of life and actually chooses it. Just as Suzy Amis's performance seems more and more natural as the movie progresses, so too does Jo seem to grow into a life she would never have chosen at the beginning.

That a heroine retains the viewer's sympathy and in a sense relinquishes her child not primarily for his own good, but because in fact she has found a way of life she loves and does not want to give up, is subversive in the extreme, given the tendency of popular narrative to demonize mothers who do not act out of pure self-sacrifice. The significance of Jo's decision to remain a "man" and not go back to her son and assume her "proper" role in the domestic sphere can be most fully appreciated by situating the film in a historical tradition of women's fantasies and of the feminist scholarship that has explored these fantasies. In her study of the Western genre Tompkins, who herself has affirmed the "sentimental power" of women's domestic fiction of the nineteenth century, argues in *West of Everything* that Western myths developed as a response to the female domestic novel in which women asserted the superiority of their sphere over the male public sphere. Tompkins's view is that male genres like the Western and female genres like domestic fiction actually waged something like a literary gender war, with the Westerner rejecting all that the domestic heroine represents—values associated with the home and the private realm of emotions and interpersonal relationships. Tompkins and other feminist scholars have responded to the Western's denigration of femininity by affirming the moral and political values of women's sentimental fiction, despite the constraints it places on heroine and readers alike.

Thus, while Tompkins herself speaks of an ambivalence toward the Western hero and at times expresses regret that male and female fantasies became so polarized, she nevertheless seems to privilege the sentimental fiction written by women and seems as well to support its views against the values of Western fiction and film. Indeed, Tompkins's own approach to the topic is sentimental, as when she avers that she cried upon realizing she had excluded Indians from her book. This substitution of "female" emotion (crying) for "male" action (rewriting) testifies to the glaring need to find a way to bring "male" and "female" worlds into closer proximity (10).

At one point Tompkins invokes Annette Kolodny's book *The Land before Her* to argue that "when women wrote about the West, the stories they told did not look anything like what we know as the Western. Their experience as well as their dreams had another shape entirely" (Tompkins *West of Everything*, 42). Because Kolodny's text has led scholars to such conclusions, it is worth taking a look at it, even though it covers the period before the settling of the Far West. Kolodny is one of the few literary critics who have examined women's writings in order to understand women's fantasies—in this case of the Western landscape; her project is thus consonant with my own. Kolodny's thesis is that westering women viewed the wilderness in a way wholly different from the men, who saw the land as virgin territory to be conquered and subdued. Over and over again, Kolodny reads the writing of these women as projecting onto the frightening landscape "a garden's narrow space," in which women were engaged in "innocent . . . amusement"; thus women were able to avoid "male anguish at lost Edens and male guilt in the face of the raping of the continent" (7). Further, while men were invested in "the fantasy of the solitary, Indian-like hunter of the deep woods" and "sought sexual and filial gratifications from the land, . . . women sought there the gratifications of home and family relations" (12). Indeed, metaphors of intimacy, she notes, pervade women's writings (8).

For any modern-day reader who might be disappointed with aspirations that by today's standards seem "tame," "paltry," and "constricted," Kolodny cautions against judging the women who wrote about the West according to "the ideological predispositions of late twentieth-century feminism" (xiii). One might appreciate the historian's tact while at the same time pointing out the impossibility of entirely preventing oneself from imposing "projective fantasies" onto the texts of one's pioneering forebears. Kolodny herself, for example, seems to indulge her own such fantasy when she speculates that the popularity among female readers of the captivity narratives written by women taken prisoner by Indians may be attributed to a displaced resentment toward their husbands, who without consulting them brought them into the wilderness. "The anger such women felt (but dared not express) toward the husband who had staked the family's future on the availability of rich lands on the frontier might thus, through the captivity narrative, vicariously be displaced onto the dark and dusky figure of the Indian, a projection of the husband's darker side" (33).

Note the racism of the psychodynamics outlined by Kolodny, in which the Indians who were themselves victims of white male colonialism serve as scapegoats for women's hostility toward their husbands. If white women's dependence on white men actually served to exacerbate racism (and Kolodny's analysis is persuasive on this point, although she herself does not arrive at precisely this conclusion), such fantasies obviously cannot be represented as wholly positive alternatives to male fantasies. Insofar as *Ballad* suggests the desirability of striving for female self-sufficiency, it points the way out of a system in which the oppressed turn their resentment onto one another rather than onto those in power.

Looking at the fantasies discussed by Kolodny, a viewer of *Ballad* can see what was lacking in these early fantasies or what was perhaps buried deep within them. From the perspective of a twentieth-century spectator identifying with Little Jo, I would project two hypotheses back onto the texts of frontier women. I would speculate first that the captivity narratives were not devoid of psychosexual interest for their women readers. Kolodny's insistent yoking of eroticism with male aggression in effect denies the possibility of female sexuality altogether and thus reinforces the sexual repressiveness of domestic fantasies, the repressiveness that led to Josephine Monaghan's banishment from her family. Second, I would speculate that the very terror of the wilderness expressed by women in captivity narratives and other writings may have been a source of pleasure, if not to the writers, then to their readers. Kolodny's desire to posit a counterfantasy—of the garden, settlement, family—to male fantasies of conquest in the wilderness leads her to downplay the possibility of women's attraction to the sublime in nature, that is, to what in nature is wild and dangerous (and, hence, often associated with the masculine).[14] Yet it is precisely a relation to the sublime in nature that *Ballad* offers viewers, inviting them to contemplate the magnificent vistas through which the heroine roams.

It is significant, however, that the film's beautiful landscapes do not simply reproduce a clichéd "masculine" view of the West. Asked why she chose not to shoot in Cinemascope, given her interest in conveying the vastness and majesty of the landscape, Greenwald responded that had she done so, the images would have been "out of proportion with the story. It would destroy the intimacy." Recalling Kolodny's observation that "metaphors of intimacy" abound in women's fantasies, it could be said that Greenwald is not countering one, male, perspective with another, female, one, but is combining them to produce a text that pushes beyond differently gendered views, inspiring in the spectator both awe at the grandeur of the landscape and a sense of the intimate pleasures of interacting with the land and its diverse inhabitants.

174

Like Kolodny, Tompkins, and other feminist literary critics from their generation who contributed to, as well as analyzed and critiqued, the polarization of male and female fantasies and male and female genres, feminist film theorists in the 1980s and early 1990s also tended to reject male genres and rehabilitate female genres, in particular the melodramas known as "women's films" which were often based on novels written by women and which were in a direct line of descent from the sentimental and domestic fiction privileged by many feminist literary critics. Indeed, women who watched and enjoyed male genres such as the Western were said to suffer a kind of psychic transvestism, a condition that was largely deplored. Given the centrality of the figure of the female transvestite in feminist film theory, *The Ballad of Little Jo* presents itself as the perfect text from which to survey the history of the metaphor in feminist film theory.

While film critic Mary Ann Doane was far more critical than her literary counterparts of popular texts made by and/or for women, and saw them as reinforcing conservative notions of woman's place, even she attempted to recuperate "female texts" by developing a theory according to which the female spectator could accomplish a resisting reading of these texts through performing a kind of feminine masquerade. Drawing on the work of psychoanalysts such as Joan Riviere and Luce Irigaray, proponents of the theory of feminine mimesis, Doane suggested (in "Film and the Masquerade") that the female spectator can adopt an ironic distance from femininity by exaggerating (miming) its traits and hence exposing its artifice. The performance of such a masquerade was a way for the female spectator to evade psychic transvestism, to refuse the alien, masculine identity forced onto women by male-oriented Hollywood genres.

Other feminist critics such as Laura Mulvey (in "Afterthoughts") also saw transvestism in a negative light but argued that the female spectator never wholly gave herself up to it. Rather—and on this point many film theorists agreed (Rodowick; de Lauretis *Alice Doesn't*)—the woman viewer was said to experience at best an "oscillation" between male and female roles that is uncomfortable, difficult, and even tragic. As Mulvey wrote, the heroine's "oscillation, her *inability* to achieve stable sexual identity, is echoed by the woman spectator's masculine point of view" ("Afterthoughts," 70; emphasis added).[15] And again, "For women (from childhood onwards) trans-sex identification is a *habit* that very easily becomes *second Nature*. However, this Nature does not sit easily and shifts restlessly in its borrowed transvestite clothes" ("Afterthoughts," 72; emphasis in original).

It is interesting that Mulvey theorizes her concept of the female spectator's transvestism by analyzing the 1946 Western *Duel in the Sun,* a film that relies on the very dynamic Henry Nash Smith detected in the early dime novels in which the heroine's unfeminine behavior was explained by her being an Indian (who later proves really to be white). In this film the heroine, Pearl Chavez (Jennifer Jones), is the half-breed daughter of an Indian mother and an English father. (The father, played by Herbert Marshall, has a rather extraordinary last name for one of his nationality; yet the point of making him British and hence really Anglo seems to be to support the legitimacy of Pearl's *first* name.) Like the heroines of the stories cited by Smith, Pearl's active, "masculine" pursuits—riding and shooting—are clearly associated with the Indian part of her identity. But unlike the fiction referred to by Smith, *Duel in the Sun* does not happily resolve the heroine's two identities by making one of them disappear; rather, being a melodrama, it plays them out as a tragic conflict that ultimately destroys the heroine.

Mulvey suggests that in *Duel in the Sun* the brothers to whom Pearl is attracted—the good, progressive man of the law (Joseph Cotten) and the sexually dangerous outlaw (Gregory Peck)—represent, respectively, the feminine (passive) and masculine (active, phallic, sexual) sides of Pearl. She goes on to speculate that, like Pearl, the female spectator is torn between masculine and feminine identifications and is involved in a kind of perpetual oscillation between these two poles. What Mulvey did not note was the extent to which the transvestism (the woman's masculine identification) was made as visible as it was because it was projected onto an other, to whom the norms of femininity never fully applied in the first place. (It scarcely seems accidental that Lillian Gish plays the mother of the two men and is the model toward which Pearl futilely aspires, given Gish's role in *Birth of a Nation* as the archetypal pure white woman whose sexuality the Ku Klux Klan defends against the threat of rape by black men.) Just as in the fantasies analyzed by Kolodny, then, the female spectators in Mulvey's analysis (and to the extent that race was unremarked as a factor in her theory, Mulvey herself) were able to displace unacceptable feelings and desires onto the "dark and dusky" other.

Some years after Mulvey wrote about *Duel in the Sun,* Sue-Ellen Case wrote an article in which she criticized many white feminist film theorists, not for racism but for heterosexism. Case criticized these theorists for not acknowledging that concepts like masquerade and transvestism are traceable to the butch/femme role-playing common in some lesbian cultures. Although this was not her primary intention, in bringing the "butch" into the conversation Case was affirming a figure who had been erased or implicitly condemned in much feminist film theory. By focusing on the lesbian, Case's polemic sheds light on a key reason for the various displacements at work in the fantasies and theories of female fantasy I have been discussing: underneath the transvestite's garments frequently lurks . . . a dyke. Surely the bogey of the lesbian (especially the mannish lesbian) accounts for some of the tenacity with which feminists have held to the theory of the masquerade, for it allows woman to be ultrafeminine (in a male-directed sense) and resistant at the same time.

The positive valuation Case places on the role of the "butch" coincides in the era of queer theory with a widespread reassessment of transvestism in cultural studies, most notably elaborated in Marjorie Garber's voluminous *Vested Interests*.[16] While much of this work has in my view tended to overemphasize the parodic aspect of butch/femme role-playing and transvestism (thus perhaps unwittingly supporting those who, like the male critic of *Ballad*, believed humor to be inherent in cross-dressing), some feminists have begun to go beyond a notion of parody in accounting for the effects and affects of cross-gender behavior. Arguing in a vein similar to Judith Butler, Teresa de Lauretis notes in *The Practice of Love* that in lesbian butch/femme role-playing, one experiences "the uncanny distance, like an effect of ghosting, between desire . . . and the representation, because the representation doesn't fit the actors who perform it" (109–10). But whereas Butler and others have focused on the parodic aspects of drag, de Lauretis suggests that butch/femme role-playing may be the source of erotic attraction as well as of humor. Indeed, de Lauretis sees the parodic element of cross-dressing and cross-gender imitation as much more characteristic of a *male* homosexual aesthetic than a female one (105n.). (At the same time that I raise these issues in the context of a discussion of *The Ballad of Little Jo,* I am uneasy about once again eliding lesbian difference; the lack of homoeroticism in the film disappointed some critics, notwithstanding the evidence of heterosexual activity in the "real" Jo Monaghan's life.)[17]

The character of Little Jo thus appears at an opportune moment in women's cultural history to embody a condition—the transvestism of the male-identified woman—that in film theory has hitherto functioned primarily as a metaphor. In making a serious, that is, nonparodic, Western about cross-dressing, Greenwald both conveys the pleasures of transsex identification and suggests that what feminists have said of the masquerading woman is also true of the transvestite: she is not (to use Irigaray's words in *Speculum*) "wholly absorbed" in and by the role. Thus, on the one hand, the film depicts a woman who acquires many admirable traits in becoming a man and even proves herself to be in some respects more manly than the men (but then as Eve Kosofsky Sedgwick has observed, "Some-

177

times masculinity has nothing to do with . . . men" [12]). For example, whereas Jo feels deeply the solace of open spaces and comes to love the long solitary winters in the line camp, the men who take on the job go crazy without any company (and here we might recall that even the Lone Ranger was never *really* alone). On the other hand, Jo's presence as a woman in the midst of men serves to throw into relief some of the more questionable aspects of masculinity—the aggression, the misogyny, and so forth. In addition, the film foregrounds the fact that masculinity is crucially inflected by race, and in doing so it helps to deconstruct the entire category.

Through the character of Little Jo, a figure at once male and not male, *Ballad* suggests that being assigned to only one of two gendered alternatives may be the true source of peoples' "restlessness," to recall Mulvey's word. Rather than simply being forced to assume an alien identity and take up "the masculine point of view," the woman transforms the Western itself when she enters its landscape wearing the clothes that allow her to range freely across it. Doomed neither to comic laughter nor to tragic failure, the heroic figure in *The Ballad of Little Jo* represents one intriguing answer to the question asked so often by feminist critics about the female personae in and at the films of yesteryear: Who *was* that cross-dressed woman?

9

SOMETHING ELSE BESIDES A MOTHER

Reflections of a Feminist
on the Death of Her Mother

❏

I take my title from the melodramatic film *Stella Dallas* which occasioned a debate about the feminist potential of a film that seems to glorify female self-sacrifice.

I had thought to call this chapter "My Mother's Vagina." This would be a reference to Nancy Miller's rather notorious autobiographical snippet entitled "My Father's Penis," published in her book *Getting Personal*. "My Father's Penis" deliberately breached the decorum so characteristic of Miller's feminist critical and theoretical writing, but I hate to think Miller might feel responsible for initiating a vulgar game of one-upmanship in the "getting personal" department. Can there be a doubt, though, as to who would win such a game? Is not the exposure of the mother's vagina (the vagina of the dying mother, no less) the ultimate act of autobiographical disclosure? Is it not even more intimate, shocking, and unassimilable than exposing one's own sexual organs?

My impulse to play "you-show-me-your-father's-sex-organ-and-I'll-show-you-my-mother's" comes from a very deep place in my psyche where there lies a granite determination to deny primacy to the father and elevate the mother in his place. Yet in order to explain I need to begin by talking about my father.

I have already mentioned that my father was older than my mother by seventeen years, and he terrified her and my brother and me with his anger and his moods. It was not that my father was a physically violent man, although there was violence in the family background. His brother Tony had been a policeman in New York City who one day shot his wife and children and then killed himself. My parents naturally did not like to discuss this incident, but once I asked my mother what made my uncle commit this atrocity. She answered, "I don't know, but they do say his mother-in-law was a terrible woman."

Like so many feminist daughters from Mary Wollstonecraft to Dorothy Allison, I considered it my duty to protect my mother from my father's anger, although it will come as a surprise to nobody familiar with dysfunctional families (thus perhaps to nobody at all) that she did not particularly want to be saved. My desire to rescue women who were treated unjustly was enacted time and again in my youth and adolescence and often ended in my being rejected by everyone. Once when some girls were ganging up on my friend Eileen in the eighth grade, I rushed to her defense and was berated for not minding my own business. The next day when I sat down at the lunch table, all the girls, including Eileen herself, got up and sat at another table.

Simplistic as it sounds, I consider my career to have been an extension of the impulse to save the mother—hence the subject of my book *Feminism without Women,* which was an attempt to defend the very category of "woman" against those theorists who wanted to abolish it and against those men who were seeking to occupy center stage within feminism itself. A lot of the objects of my rescue missions have been about as grateful for my interference as my mother was. Sometimes feminist conferences have reminded me more than a little bit of my high school days. When games of inclusion and exclusion are being played, for example, around issues of political or theoretical correctness, I feel like I'm being dragged back to moments that are almost primal in their psychic intensity. I find myself in the presence of the same old desires, the same rejections, the same feelings of betrayal—in the presence, in other words, of the uncanny. The force of the uncanny is such that no matter how far or freely we seem to travel we find ourselves intermittently coming to a place we thought to have left behind.

Growing up, I would not only argue with my father when he was being mean to my mother (whereupon I would be reprimanded by my mother), but I took it upon myself to articulate desires that I knew she possessed but did not dare express to my father. Certain extreme instances stand out in my mind, like the Good Friday she said to my brother and me, "I wonder if your father will want to go to Confession tonight. I hope so." "Why don't you ask him?" my brother and I said for the millionth time. "It's up to your father," she replied as always. At dinner I said, "Dad, Mom wants to go to confession tonight." She glared at me and shushed me, claiming she had said no such thing. But my father just said, "If you want to go, why don't you say so?" I recalled this moment many years later when my mother told me about a woman in our family, a full-time housewife, who would spend all week looking forward to leaving her children home with her husband so that she could get out on Friday nights to shop for groceries. My mother said that every once in a while B. would come home on a Friday and say magnanimously, "Oh, why don't you stay home and I'll do the grocery shopping for you tonight?" Clamping down on my irritation I asked my mother tightly why this woman didn't just say she wanted to do the shopping herself. And my mother replied, "There's many a one that *would* say that, these days. That's why they're all getting divorced."

Not for the first time I reflected on the ludicrous gap between us feminist thinkers who speak about women's "desire" in very grandiose terms, envisioning realms of endless *jouissance*, and women in the "real world" who are afraid their husbands will divorce them if they express a desire to shop for the family groceries.

As for my own desire, it seems as though I always had separatist tendencies. I longed to have my mother to myself. She was so relaxed when we were alone together, and so tense around my father. She was more like one of us than a parent. That even my father saw her that way was bizarrely confirmed a couple of years before he died. I was home on a visit, and we were sitting around the table laughing and joking; my father, whose mind was rather nimble for an 85-year-old but who nevertheless had his lapses, waved derisively at something my mother said and turned to me to say, "She was always stubborn, just like *all* my children." My father realized immediately what he had said, and he and I stared at each other in shock. My mother, who was hard of hearing, kept asking, "What did he say? What did he say?" And my father whispered, "Don't tell her."

I never until this moment reflected on the irony of my father's actual statement, which pronounced my mother, who never asked anything of my father, much less insisted on it, to be "stubborn."

For a few blissful years starting when I was about ten years old, my father got a job which required him to live away from home during the week, so we saw him only on the weekends. Then we had great times. When my father was home, he would often curtly order us to turn off the TV so he could go to bed early or listen to a game on the radio. But on nights he was gone we would get into our nightgowns and pajamas early and stay up late watching *Maverick* or *The Fugitive.* We would make buttered popcorn or fudge which consisted solely of butter, sugar, and chocolate, gorging ourselves and glorying in the fact that no one was around to make fun of us for getting fat. On Friday nights, if my father said he was going to be late returning home, we flouted both him and the spirit of our religion in general, refusing to eat the smelly frozen fish which was the only kind of seafood available to us at that time and eating instead an entire meal of strawberry shortcakes, made with wild strawberries I would pick.

But when my father didn't come home by the time he was expected, I would have hysterical fits, crying uncontrollably and getting sick to my stomach and vomiting. I was in a panic because I was sure that he had died (the fact that he was, in my eyes, so old made it seem to me likely that this could occur at any time). I didn't have to read much Freud before I understood that I was experiencing unconscious guilt because I actually wished him dead. I did need to read and think a lot more, though, before I understood that he had become for me the "bad object" theorized in Kleinian psychoanalytic thought. I know now that I must have been more angry at my mother than I have ever been able to admit; every weekend, after all, she would abandon me all over again to side with my father when he ridiculed or demeaned me. But all I really perceived was the injustice and cruelty of his behavior.

I don't think it invalidates my feminism that men have come to occupy a place in my psyche as bad object. On the contrary, given existing power relations, they are in some ways made for the rap. Yet insofar as anger at the father is derivative of a deeper anger at the mother, it will be easier to forgive him and nearly impossible to achieve psychic reconciliation with her.

In the end I did kill my father. And I did it precisely by doing something special for my self-abnegating mother. Determined to give her the recognition she would never claim for herself, I threw a big surprise party for her seventieth birthday. At this event, my 86-year-old father, who was frail and on a strict diet, partied so hard and danced so much that the next day he took to his bed and never got up again. He was taken to the hospital a few weeks later where he died. Yet even as I killed him, my father, as fathers have a way of doing, snatched victory from the jaws of defeat. I had in fact inadvertently helped him to die the way he had wanted to die. Some years previously my father had begun writing me letters in which he, a simple carpenter who came from peasant stock, struggled to come to terms with death and to articulate his spiritual beliefs. In one of these letters he expressed a desire to die on the dance floor, since dancing had been his great passion in life. He wrote:

> The God that suited me best is a female called Mother Nature. I
> lived mostly by her dictates and I think of going out of existence on

this earth by her. She has not helped me as yet in my lift off to space, so maybe she is strictly an earthly God. I hope she doesn't numb me with her needle (a stroke). I would rather she have my dancing friends pick me up off the dance hall floor after a bit of exertion, either on a sentimental waltz or a lively polka.

My father hadn't *only* been a tyrant. In fact he had a playful side that I had always admired but had great difficulty connecting up to emotionally. Whereas many of my friends worked hard in life to measure up to their parents' expectations, my father would always ask at the end of phone conversations in which I told him of my career successes, "But are you having *fun?*"

The son of Polish immigrants who grew up in Brooklyn and then moved with his parents to a little farm in the country, my father was a carpenter who specialized in restoring old houses. He loved his work and did it intuitively, sensing the original architecture of the buildings rather than consulting books about country homes. Being poor, he purchased an old gas station and built a house out if it for us, and we lived in it while he slowly fixed it up over the years. Our house was full of clever, fairy tale touches, like the small dead tree my father uprooted, preserved, and put in our hall as a coat rack (my father the ogre and the friendly woodcutter by turns). He also played the fiddle by ear and painted, and he was always taking up new interests like art history or astronomy. Although he had only completed eighth grade, he read all my high school textbooks and many of my college ones. But his greatest passion in life was dancing. He met both his wives (the first who was seventeen years older than he, the second, seventeen years younger, both pregnant before the wedding) at dances.

When I was young my parents went out dancing all the time. In his seventies he resumed dancing, taking my mother out on Saturday night, following a country and western band they particularly liked all around the county. I once went with them when I was home on a visit. My father, as I had witnessed so often in my youth, danced with a deceptively understated grace and elegance, and never showed off. The night I accompanied them to the bar I watched as one young woman after another came over and asked my silver-haired father to dance. It was not primarily that they wanted to flatter a cute little old man, although he *was* flattered, but that their own boyfriends or husbands—slouching at the bar in jeans and T-shirts, drinking beer and scratching themselves ("bums," my father might have called them)—couldn't or wouldn't do anything so compromising to their masculinity as dance a waltz or a foxtrot.

To this day I do not dance. "Let me lead," my father would snap when as a young girl there was no way for me to get out of trying it one more time. Or he would lean into my ear and command, "RELAX," and I would stiffen and trip over his foot. So it was that fun itself became fraught between my father and me.

One day a few years before he died a letter from him arrived in my mail—the first I had ever received from him. It was, as he called it, "a letter of appeal" to me, the educated daughter, to help him organize his memories and to assist him in sorting through his beliefs, especially about spiritual matters. He felt alone in his struggle to come to terms with dying. "Ma has her novels," he wrote, as if *she* were the one responsible for shutting *him* out, and he didn't want to disturb her beliefs about the Catholic religion. He was very happy and excited—almost like a little boy—when I agreed to help him write a memoir and a collection of his thoughts about spiritual matters. He was concerned about how I would address these letters so that no one else would read them. He sneaked behind my mother's back to phone me, anxious to work out our private system of communication, worried that his "descendants" would disapprove of the heretical turn of his thoughts.

It was ironic in view of his role within our family that in his letters this son of Polish immigrants who was so proud of his eighth-grade education in a parochial school (in the last years my father would practice diagramming sentences the way he remembered the monks taught him and send them to me to correct) began to question the patriarchal religion he had been taught, and tried to formulate one based on a matriarchal principle. This was partly owing to the fact that he was thinking a lot about his mother. He revealed in the correspondence that he identified with her as a member of a class inferior to that of her husband: "I adopted a simple philosophy by my mother's teaching rather than by my father, who seemed to be one step higher than the peasant class because he was a *brabia*—the son of a farm owner." His mother, the peasant, was always "a bit resentful" of her husband who was educated enough to read.

In searching for a matriarchal principle, my father was struggling to accept the fact of mortality and repudiate the idea of a hereafter. He criticized the Catholic church for instructing "man to adore God instead of teaching him to live a useful life and to help those around him": "What need is there for me to adore the All Powerful? . . . With Mother Nature's gift of instinct, plus my mother's peasant philosophy of hard work, along with a bit of music for pleasure, I lived a useful life."

In my father's new religion, I was designated the "death goddess," like the Valkyrie in German mythology.

> While I think of my Mom on one end of the spectrum and you on the other, I felt induced to communicate with you, by making a bit of a scientific connection. The whole idea is based on the matter of atoms and genes. We are all one when it comes to explaining the soul in universal life. It makes me feel that "Mom" started me off right and perhaps you can send me off the same way, so we are all one in that light.

I forgave my father a great deal in these last years. I was so deeply moved that he had chosen to treat death as his last great experience, that he went so lucidly through the process of dying, and I was deeply honored that he had elected me as his usher. Of course, little did he suspect when he appointed me how literally I would play the role of what Freud, in an analysis of the daughter's role in *King Lear*, calls "the destroyer." According to

Freud in his essay "The Theme of the Three Caskets," the psychic "truth" of the play's final scene can be arrived at by reversing the situation in which Lear carries the dead Cordelia. Freud writes:

> One might say that the three inevitable relations man has with woman are . . . that with the mother who bears him, with the companion of his bed and board, and with the destroyer. Or it is the three forms taken on by the figure of the mother as life proceeds: the mother herself, the beloved who is chosen after her pattern, and finally the Mother Earth who receives him again. But it is in vain that the old man yearns after the love of woman as once he had it from his mother; the third of the Fates alone, the silent goddess of Death, will take him into her arms. (75)

And so in a sense I ended up being mother to my own father and came to occupy the site of the uncanny ("she who has stepped into the place of the Death-goddess, has kept certain characteristics that border on the uncanny," Freud notes [73]). And yet, Freud is surely right: despite my feeling greatly reconciled with my father in his late years, he will never have gained from me the unconditional love that his mother bestowed on him and that seemed to sap all the energy from my mother as she gave and gave and gave, ruthlessly suppressing the "stubborn" stirrings of will and desire.

After I had escorted him down to the underworld, my father, like an Alfred Hitchcock character, seemed to communicate with me from beyond the grave. Six weeks after his death my mother discovered some notes my father had written to me shortly before he died but never sent. They arrived in my mail unannounced one day. They read:

> February 15, 1990: I was happy to participate in Clare's birthday party to end what I called my active life. I am not strong enough to do exercise of any sort and feel that it will continue that way. Each time I come to these spasms I become more helpless to help myself and makes more work for Ma.

Mother Nature does not guarantee me anything. No matter how I conduct myself, she makes me a freer man. How would I know what's in store. I would say everyone else is in the same boat, up till this time. Excuse if I repeat, I'm just consoling a frail creature.

February 16: We're absorbed by birds, it's all we got to mix with living things since I can't swing into society. Most people who feed birds do not favor starlings because they are a scavenging lot. We enjoy watching them pounce on left over chicken, in a flock, getting rid of garbage.

First of all, my soul is part of the universe not merely of the body.

I'll have to get a new pair of glasses when I go back into the atmosphere. There just won't be any connection of my body and soul. Excuse me for writing these notes spasmodically.

February 17: I'm just trying to stumble on a few reasons for all this wonder, and it helps me, Tania, you are a great help to me to have you listen to me talk.

I was transmitted into this earth through the atmosphere, so I assume my spirit was responsible for the creation of my body through contact with the earth—by a chemical marriage.

And then a doodle, with the ink literally trailing off at the end:

A bug has a feeler and I have a brain
I love to prattle while singing in the rain.

What strikes me every time I read these (to me almost unbearably) poignant notes is how my father actually experienced death as a shedding of the mortal coil. He liked to read my old college textbooks which I had left behind, and perhaps he had read some of the American transcendalists. Regardless of where he acquired his terms and ideas, the point is that they gave him a way to experience his death as a process of disembodiment and dissolution, as a soaring of the spirit beyond its earth-bound limitations: the last waltz and then the "lift off."

My father actually wrote one more letter after the notes I quoted above, though I received it before them. The letter was more formal than anything else he had written to me:

March 8, 1990:
Dear Tania:
Ma has been urging me along to receive communion. So I decided to leave this world as I came in and was brought up. Rather than to adopt any other theory, I drop my stubbornness against miracles and leave this earth peacefully.

Father Sinisky and I came to a good understanding, and so I came to this conclusion, to give up the struggle with my feeble mind.

Ma is greatly pleased and so am I. I am sure you will be pleased to see me get back to earthly things for my remaining days.

Pop

In the end my father was the "stubborn" one who was required to give way, and my mother's will, strong in its unquestioning fidelity to the highest male authority, prevailed. To me it is the ultimate irony that after years of deferring unquestioningly to my father she asserted herself in the final moments of his life in order to reconcile him to patriarchal religion and God the Father: She connived with the priest on a plan for him to "drop by" and persuade my father to receive the last rites.

At last my mother and I had become the Oedipal rivals psychoanalysis tells us we were destined to be—rivals in the matter of my father's death and in the disposition of his afterlife. She wanted him for patriarchy and I for (the idea of) matriarchy. Whereas I had been grateful to discover, however belatedly, a gap between my father and the Father, my mother did her best to suture it back up.

Always possessed of a sense of the high significance of his life, my father exited appropriately: he died on Good Friday, April 13, 1990.

As I think over my father's dying and the way I have written about it, I am forcefully struck with the number and the weightiness of the narratives that are culturally in place to shape his experience and his and my understanding of it. Norse mythology and Shakespearean tragedy lend depth and tragic resonance to a perfectly ordinary event: the death of an 86-year-old son of Polish immigrants—a carpenter who lived in a home he converted from a gas station, who enjoyed doing puzzles in the morning newspaper and who loved nothing more than dancing. Outstripping Freud, however, my father went ahead and once he was "reconverted," slotted himself into the Greatest Story Ever Told, mapping his death onto that of Jesus Christ himself. I recall coming in on the plane from California the day after his death, and as we descended I was crying and staring at the brilliant globe of the setting sun, which, exactly at the moment the plane touched ground, disappeared below the horizon. Hackneyed or grandiose, the stories and symbols seemed to furnish themselves abundantly to confirm the monumental nature of the occasion.

The second thing that strikes me, indeed stuns me, about the way my father understood and wrote about his death is how thoroughly it conforms to feminist theories of narrative. In *Alice Doesn't* Teresa de Lauretis writes of the way woman in male narratives represents space—most particularly the womb or tomb. Yet I doubt that many women have been called upon so explicitly to function as a kind of death receptacle and thus to occupy the site of the uncanny, as I was when my father placed me on the other end of the "spectrum" from the mother who brought him forth. There can scarcely be many sensations more uncanny than experiencing oneself *as* the uncanny in someone else's story, perhaps above all in one's father's story.

But given the relative paucity of symbols and narratives with which to make sense of it, how does a daughter tell the story of her mother's death? The difficulty here is compounded by the fact that in their respective deaths my father and mother seemed to me to confirm Simone de Beauvoir's observation that in patriarchal society man equals transcendence, woman immanence. While my father withered away until he became just a little stick and, even as he experienced bodily suffering, imaginatively projected himself into space, becoming more and more preoccupied with metaphors of flight and dissolution, my mother at the age of 72 was stricken with a muscle disease—polymyositis—that as it progressed made it more and more difficult for her to move at all and then when she took massive doses of steroids to stave off what she always called "The Disease" she swelled to grotesque proportions. Hard of hearing for many years, she rapidly developed the most extreme form of macular degeneration, and so was to all intents and purposes blind. While my father's needs and whims were minutely catered to by my mother as he lay dying fully and properly, rounding out his life and getting it all into perspective, my mother was left to cope with much more on her own, although she was aided by relatives and, later, before she went into a nursing home, by a part-time home-care helper.

The doctor warned us at the outset that this would be one of the worst deaths, worse than cancer, he said. And indeed my mother's suffering was extreme, both from the disease and such side effects of the medication as broken bones in her back (steroids thin the bones), diabetes, bladder problems that required her to wear a catheter permanently, and so forth. She seemed to be trapped in a body which had all but shut down, and the doctor was constantly counseling her to go into a nursing home, but she managed to stay out longer than anyone believed to be possible. Moving into a one-room apartment, she barely got around with a walker. Her lungs were weakened by a lifetime of heavy cigarette smoking, and just getting off the toilet or pulling herself out of a chair made her wheeze and gasp for breath alarmingly. She would lean on the walker for a while until the breathlessness subsided a bit and then haul herself across the room she couldn't really see, wheezing and gasping after each step. When I visited her, my mother gave the home care assistant time off because I was there to help out. I wish I could say that I lovingly tended to my mother's bodily needs, but the fact was that the intimacy somewhat repelled me, and I tried to mentally detach myself from the tasks of putting on a bra over her blobby, sagging skin, rubbing lotion onto her scaly legs, clipping chunks of massive in-

191

grown toenails (these tasks were, however, nothing compared to the kinds of things my sister-in-law, who lived nearby, sometimes had to do, like wiping her up after an accidental bowel movement).

One night when I was at her place, the catheter became unhooked, and we had to call the visiting nurse, Kitty, who checked on my mother every few days. My mother, to whom this had happened before, briefly mentioned how terribly embarrassing it was to undergo the procedure of reinsertion, but then characteristically pulling herself together, said briskly and sensibly, "But, what are you going to do? It can't be helped." When Kitty arrived, she put my mother on the bed, raised her legs as if she were a baby being diapered, and asked me to hold the flashlight so she could see clearly to insert the catheter tube. I trained the beam on my mother's vagina and forced myself to look straight at the hole trying to assume a clinical detachment, so that I was seeing it without really seeing it (the Freudian concept of disavowal all too clear to me now). There I was, staring down into the place where I emerged and *my* story began.

"No body existed less for me; none existed more," says Simone de Beauvoir of the naked body of her dying mother, in words that evoke Freud's notion of the uncanny, which he described as a sensation one has when one encounters something that seems both strange and familiar (19). For Freud the mother's womb is the site par excellence of the uncanny. Freud, however, did not spend much time thinking about the impact the sight of the mother's naked body has on the female subject. He did of course notoriously theorize that the male subject comes to understand sexual difference and difference itself by reading it off the body of the mother (reading her as lacking because of the absence of a penis), thereby putting woman into the role of bearer rather than maker of meaning, as Laura Mulvey memorably put it.

Yet I must face the fact that to a certain extent I, too, like the most patriarchal subject, put my mother into this role and relegated her to the status of a nonsubject, this undemanding woman who wholeheartedly accepted her servitude and who spent her life cooking and cleaning for her family and for others (cleaning motel rooms, preparing and serving school

SOMETHING ELSE BESIDES A MOTHER

lunches). To me she was someone who had no story of her own. Of course, my reasons for maintaining this view of her were partly "feminist." In my view her independent will and desire, like that of so many women, had been sucked out of her by her parents and then by her husband and her children. One strong image of her that the last years of her life impressed upon my psyche was that of a dumb suffering animal, helpless and uncomprehending. When she died I sometimes had dreams like the one in which a little dog had died, and I sobbed and sobbed uncontrollably, and even in the dream I knew I was displacing my grief from my mother to the little dog.

And yet it was striking how much went against this view, and how much, in the final analysis, I needed to see in my mother an independent subjectivity at work.

The night the catheter came undone my mother had warned me that the nurse would probably ask me to hold the flashlight (and I was thinking, no, God, please, no, not the flashlight), and it was characteristic of her to prepare me. Her concern for us in the midst of her own adversity was astounding. From time to time my mother would call me and call my brother to tell us about particularly frank conversations she had with the doctor in which he would strongly suggest that her days were numbered. My mother went out of her way to solicit such information and heroically faced death so that she could prepare my brother and me and diminish as much as possible our shock and pain when she died.

After one horrible confrontation with some of my relatives who said that everyone in the family considered me a bad daughter because I didn't come back to live with my mother in the summers, I was so devastated that I went crying to my Mom, who certainly ought to have been spared. I stayed up half the hot summer night drinking beer, while she smoked cigarettes and assured me that she felt nothing but pride in me and was more than satisfied with the number and length of my visits. I would say, "You know, I have my work." And she would say, "Of course you have your work." And then as we talked on into the night she said, "And it's not just your work; you have your *life*." And I thought, surprised, "Yes, I have my life." So there was my mother who had given me life, giving me *my* life. (I can't express how grateful I feel about the fact that over the years she never so much as hinted that she wished I had married, borne children, reproduced her life.) And suddenly now that I was the chief beneficiary of her sacrifices, I saw them in a whole new light—as gifts, willingly bestowed, rather than obligations exacted from a martyred housewife.

Trouble had been simmering for some time between me and other family members. They took it for granted that the unmarried daughter, even if she did live and work three thousand miles away, should be her mother's chief caretaker, and before the incident in which they confronted me, they dedicated themselves to emphasizing constantly the pain and suffering my mother was undergoing. For example, they would tell me on the phone how depressed my mother was, and I would say, alarmed, "She is?" and they would say, "Well, of course she is," and then say over and over, "Put yourself in her place, Tania" (as if a daughter could help putting herself in her mother's place, as if part of her struggle is not to get out of that place). Apparently they thought that I did not sufficiently appreciate the gravity of my mother's condition, and if I could just be made to see how dire it was, I would cave in. As a result I was continually feeling desperate about my mother and was of course wracked by guilt.

Sometimes they made me think she was dying, and in a panic I would begin readying myself to fly back on an emergency basis, but my mother would put a stop to the plans, emphatically stating that she was not that bad and she did not want me to come home. When I would tell this to the others, they would say, "You know she'll never tell you how bad she really feels." And I did know that, for wasn't her refusal to speak up for herself the source of my deepest complaint about her? My mother was, in fact, furious whenever she discovered we had been talking amongst ourselves in order to get or give information that we felt she was withholding. She felt infantilized, and she continually sought to make us promise that we would not talk about her behind her back. I was of course only too happy to oblige her and support these somewhat paradoxical assertions of her right to be her usual selfless self.

The expectation of family members that as the daughter without family of her own I should give up my life to tend to my Mom made me feel as if nothing I could do would be perceived as generous: sacrificing my entire life would have been merely performing my duty, and anything less was reviled because it *was* less. To what extent, though, had I, in seeing my mother as blindly adhering all her life to her "duty" as wife and mother, put her in a similar no-win situation—one in which she merited no gratitude on my part because she did nothing freely? My freedom, I now see (conveniently, I admit), depends on my acknowledging hers, circumscribed though it was. If she gave me *my* life, I could only accept it by giving her hers: that is, by granting her a life in which she had some choice and thus the power *to* give.

My mother even gave me a dispensation for my future life. One day she said to me, "When I die I want you to be happy." Stunned that even my self-abnegating mother would go that far, I said, "Well . . . can't I feel just a little sad?" She laughed and said, "No, that's not what I mean; I mean I don't want you to have any regrets whatsoever."

I once related this conversation to a friend, a feminist who idealizes the moment of lesbian feminism when many women were able to achieve a sense of solidarity by invoking flattering generalizations about women. I said that whereas my father had been thinking of death in very private and personal terms, my mother was thinking about how her death would affect *us*. My friend chalked up this difference to the differences between the sexes, and though I no doubt elicited, intended to elicit, this conclusion, I was nettled when she proffered it. I felt that the extraordinary generosity manifested by my mother in such extreme circumstances was not receiving its due; such generosity could not be fully explained by appealing to some deterministic view of motherhood (be it biological or cultural, anti-feminist or feminist), for it was also an individual act of sublime courage and love achieved in a struggle against overwhelming fear and pain and sorrow.

195

It is to me exceedingly ironic that my mother, with her clear and unwavering ideas about what is expected of a woman, lived up (and died up) to these ideas in such a way as to make me see more clearly than I ever had the limitations of essentialist thinking.

I mentioned my mother's remark at the funeral service when the priest, who was new and young, asked us if we had anything we would like to say about Mom (a question which struck most people dumb since the practice of speaking directly to parishioners like this was a new one in that church). He recognized the magnanimity of it, and spent a bit of time elaborating on it. He recalled the times he had visited my mother, and he spoke to my mother's close friend, my sister-in-law's mother, of their friendship, mentioning how often he had seen them sitting together on the porch of my Mom's apartment in the middle of town on summer afternoons.

I was amazed at how consoling this service was to me. I remembered how bitter I felt at my father's funeral when the old alcoholic priest, after winning my father's soul, said a generic Mass and even forgot to tell the organist to show up. At my mother's Mass, my nephew, who had been asked to select a text from the Bible, read a passage about Christ's death and resurrection. I had asked him to read a passage from Job, of course, but my nephew talked me out of it, feeling that his choice was more in tune with my Mom's views and desires, and he was right. I was still insisting on *my* stories about my mother, trying to make one last-ditch complaint on behalf of this long suffering woman who, to my mind at the time, should have cursed God before she died.

When my nephew read the passage, I winced at the pronouns, reminded again of how women always have to fit themselves into men's stories, which, like the story of Christ, are supposed to comprehend them. It is notoriously difficult to find tragedies that deal with the subject of an aging, ailing, or dying woman. But if the subject has not leant itself to high drama it is the very stuff of the "debased" form of tragedy, melodrama. And, indeed, I believe my mother's funeral was a comfort to me for the very reasons that melodrama appeals to many women. All the melodramatic elements were present that day in abundance: the tears, the stirring music which the priest, who had been an opera singer, sang at various points in the mass, the scene in which the astonishing virtue of the self-sacrificing heroine is, at last, publicly recognized and acclaimed, a scene in which elemental and therefore undeniable relationships are asserted with primal force: "She was my Mama," cries Annie's daughter Sarah Jane in *Imitation of Life* when she returns just in time for the funeral after having denied her black mother and tried to pass as white. Hollywood history is full of films about wives and mothers who sacrifice themselves, and often their very lives, for husbands and/or children. The plot is typically about a woman who passes up a chance to have her own story, so that those she loves may have theirs, but part of my point has been that this *is* a story. It is not, however, even in my mother's case, the whole story.

When my father died, my mother, who had spent years taking care of this increasingly demanding man, determined to take advantage of her remaining time; she planned outings with senior citizens, took her first plane trip to see me in California, and looked forward to going to Ireland with her (comparatively) well-traveled sister. We were tremendously excited to think of her making these journeys, and all of us were in shock when she deteriorated so rapidly. Nothing makes me angrier than when people, clearly holding some romantic belief about old folks pining away when their beloved partners die, nod sagely upon hearing that she went downhill soon after my father died. MY MOTHER WANTED TO LIVE.

If there was any doubt about this it was cleared up the time when, having become so ill, she was knocked out by the sheer exhaustion of performing some simple task like pulling herself out of a chair or finding something on the table. She cried hard for about thirty seconds (my Mom who never cried), and said, "Your Aunt Bobbie is always criticizing Helen [a neighbor] for constantly being on the run. She says 'Helen's always running—running here, running there. She never stops running.'" Then my mother abruptly pointed at me and hollered so loud I jumped, "RUN. While you can."

Indeed, till the very end my mother took advantage of each moment despite the pain and difficulty the least exertion caused her. If people said they were going to visit her and were vague about when they should be expected or were late in arriving, and if in the meantime my brother came and asked her out for lunch, she would go. "I don't wait for anybody anymore," she announced.

There wasn't much she could do, but she could eat, albeit with considerably diminished appetite, and she liked to go to restaurants. My brother and sister-in-law thus made a point of taking her out often, and sometimes she would be taken by her sisters and her brother. It was a tremendous ordeal for her to get dressed, get the little catheter strapped to her leg, struggle down the icy sidewalk, position herself to be stashed in and then extracted from the car, and then try to find her way into the restaurant with the walker when she couldn't really see where she was going, and when the doctor said that a fall could kill her. She was very aware of the fact that people were staring, and teenagers giggling, at the sight of the heavy, balding, swollen old lady who was laboriously making her way across the room. When she got settled and received her food we would cut it up for her, and then she would eat. First she would look down at her plate, her eyes shifting in that strange manner of people who suffer from macular degeneration when they try to fix their peripheral vision on an object. She would stab at the plate with the fork, most of the time not knowing what she was picking up (every bite's a surprise, she once said), and then, her muscles being weak, she would prop her elbow on the table and her forearm would shake so much it was lucky if there was any food left on the fork when it got to her mouth. Of course much of it spilled on her, and my poor fastidious mother was a mess even with a napkin tucked into her blouse.

She was capable of finding humor in her situation. She laughed about the time when she was having more than the usual difficulty picking up her food, and finally her brother leaned over and said softly, "Clare, turn the spoon around." Nevertheless, she also felt deeply humiliated at such times, which only made her efforts to get all she could out of her remaining days the more heroic. My brother is certain that she kept herself out of a nursing home one final time because she was so determined to get to the annual pancake breakfast at the local Firehouse. This was toward the end, after she had been sent to the hospital with pains, never diagnosed (and always recurring), that came in waves and wracked her body so much that she grabbed the rails of the hospital bed and went into paroxysms. Although at these times she prayed to die, the lure of the pancake breakfast won out on this occasion, and she was released from the hospital. When she came back to the hospital again, though, she was sent from there to the nursing home, and since by this time she couldn't even prop herself up when she slumped to one side or another, she knew there was no alternative.

In her book about her mother's death Simone de Beauvoir writes:

> My mother encouraged one to be optimistic when, crippled with arthritis and dying, she asserted the infinite value of each instant but her vain tenaciousness also ripped and tore the reassuring curtain of everyday triviality. There is no such thing as a natural death: nothing that happens to a man is ever natural, since his presence calls the world into question. (106)

It is striking that it was her conventional mother who taught the life-long companion of Jean-Paul Sartre one of the greatest existential lessons. In Beauvoir's account, the mother in the very act of dying affirms life, offers hope, demonstrates transcendence and thus gives the lie to the notion of woman's immanence (i.e., her identity with "the natural"). The mother of this feminist daughter conveys a very different message from the one little Sigmund Freud learned when his mother rubbed her hands together to show him epidermal "dust" as a sample of the dust to which we are all destined to return. Like Beauvoir's mother, my mother too revealed not only the inevitability of death but the "infinite value" of life.

Today feminists seek images and representations and stories that enable a rethinking of the relation between body and spirit (or desire, or imagination, or whatever one chooses to call "spirit") and thus surmount the ages-old dualism in which the feminine stands for the former and the masculine for the latter. In her book *The Female Grotesque,* Mary Russo argues the need not only to affirm the female body in its grotesque manifestations—the grotesque and the feminine being so often linked—but also to search for female figures who at the same time embody possibility, error, and risk and hence open up spaces of freedom for women (spaces in which untold stories may emerge). She finds two such figures in the female acrobat and the aviatrix, who according to Russo demonstrate that the female body is "process and semiosis—a grotesque that moves." But I want to propose a humbler figure as emblematic of female striving and female journeying—of woman moving *through* space, rather than representing it. I offer not the somewhat grandiose figure of the aviatrix proposed by Russo or of the nomadic subject proposed by Rosi Braidotti or of the woman-in-exile I myself invoked early in this book. Rather, I offer the image of my mother with her walker, dragging her grotesque body blindly across the cavernous hall in the Firehouse at the pancake breakfast, and a second image that comments on the first: my mother pointing at me and exhorting me, in anguish and in anger, "RUN. While you can."

200

NOTES

NOTES TO THE INTRODUCTION

1. Because consciousness-raising was the way women's stories were told at the dawn of the latest wave of feminism and because my book is about storytelling—about "real" women telling "true" stories, as well as about fictional stories created by women, it seems important to insist on the accomplishments of consciousness-raising in the face of those who focus on its supposed failures.

I would strongly disagree with claims that consciousness-raising didn't subversively "rearticulate gender norms" (Kaplan 160). Interestingly, most people seem to have forgotten or never known that one of the successes of early feminism was to get the term "woman" put into general use—as opposed to the then far more common terms "lady" and "girl." That gain alone caused a seismic shift in gender norms. But that is only one among myriad triumphs of consciousness-raising. Whenever a woman believes that her body is her own and chooses abortion (or indeed *chooses* to have the baby); whenever rape gets taken seriously as a crime against women; whenever a battered woman finds shelter and ceases thinking of herself as one who deserves abuse; whenever a woman feels entitled to forms of fulfillment other than child rearing; whenever a woman successfully prosecutes a man who has sexually harassed her rather than accepting it as part of her job—whenever these things occur, some credit is owing to the women who engaged in consciousness-raising, naming and identifying practices not heretofore recognized as part of women's reality. I think consciousness-raising had a profound impact on the material lives of women of all classes and races, and is something its practitioners can be proud of.

NOTES TO CHAPTER ONE

1. Wendy Brown 73. Brown rebukes "North Atlantic feminists" who naively "seek to preserve some variant of consciousness raising as a mode of discerning and delivering the 'truth' about women." Yet how can a feminist deny the positive consciousness-raising effects of Hill's testimony about her experience of

sexual harassment? Brown is, of course, drawing on Michel Foucault's *The History of Sexuality: An Introduction*.

2. The phrase "legitimation crisis" is a key phrase in discussions about postmodernity: the decline of the "public sphere" is said to result in crises of authority and language— crises that Jurgen Habermas deplores and that, to a certain extent, Jean-François Lyotard celebrates. Nancy Fraser, who has written extensively on these debates, has published an article on the Thomas/Hill hearings, "Sex, Lies, and the Public Sphere: Some Reflections on the Confirmation of Clarence Thomas." The idea that the body of the raped woman signifies the deconstructive ideal has actually been seriously entertained by at least one critic. See Warner's discussion of the novel *Clarissa*. And see Castle's response.

3. I was recently reminded of the importance of storytelling and credibility in a case I've become acquainted with concerning the sexual harassment of a student. When the male supervisor to whom a complaint was issued heard the accusation, he continually reiterated that he believed the accused. Interestingly, however, the accused had not been confronted with the complaint and so had *not yet denied* it. That patriarchy survives in part through men's transforming into law and truth each other's stories, which at a certain point don't even need to be told since they assume the status of the "already told," seems to me a point that cannot be stressed enough; as Judith Resnick and Carolyn Heilbrun write: "Women lawyers know the risks of repeating stories already told, of law not as a vehicle for changing but for reaffirming the arrangements of the status quo." For Resnick and Heilbrun, "The feminist interruption of 'law and literature' occurs at the juncture between the texts of the powerful and the readers of the powerful" (1940–41). Out of the struggle that takes place at the level of interpretation—in lower courts, law classes, and other arenas—comes the possibility of generating feminist counterstories that legislate other truths, beyond the "already read"—truths that will not be dismissed as the delusional ravings of hysterics.

4. See Josef Breuer and Sigmund Freud, especially the case study of Fraulein Elisabeth von R. (135–81).

5. Indeed, Cornell's refusal to adopt "the masculine" at any point is striking for a writer who insists on the need to go beyond binary logic. "Since we are in this bipolar world of gender identity, we can *only* proceed to what is Other through *mimesis*. The *other choice* is to repudiate the feminine, as MacKinnon does, and by so doing to reduce our desire to the fantasy of symmetry" (156; emphasis added). But why the binary thinking? Given Cornell's reliance on Irigaray, who

declares woman "the sex which is not one," it seems curious that for the purposes of her polemic against MacKinnon she accepts the either/or terms offered to gendered subjects in patriarchy. See Patricia Williams's discussion of the importance of the notion of "rights" in the history of civil rights activism for an eloquent argument about the necessity of retaining certain terms that have figured importantly in (white, male) law (145–65).

6. Patricia Williams 11. For a summary of the debates within the theory of feminist jurisprudence over the application of studies like Gilligan's *In a Different Voice,* see Whitman.

7. Quoted in Bray 95.

NOTES TO CHAPTER TWO

1. Those who work with battered women tell us that men often get ideas from pornographic or violent stories in the media and moreover use these stories to threaten their wives. A feminist ethnographic study of the effect of representations of violence on battered women which had not already prejudged the issues would, I believe, be most illuminating.

2. See the review by Georgia Brown, "Sympathy for the Devil." Amy Holden Jones, the film's screenwriter, responded to a negative review in the *Los Angeles Times* by referring to reviews like Brown's and claiming that her film is a "woman's film."

3. A sampling of the literature includes not only *Loving with a Vengeance,* but Snitow, Radway, and Crane.

4. In referring at times to extra-textual information, particularly biographical information, I realize I am taking a risk, since critics have long seen women's texts as narcissistic. I want to make clear first, that I am trying to show how these biographical bits connect up to larger psycho-social issues, but second, that such information, while it can lead us in a direction we might not otherwise have thought to follow, must yield an interpretation that can be supported by the text itself.

5. I am thus taking strong issue with Clover's criticism of the film's "ecstatic investment in powerlessness and victimization." Clover writes, "It would be one thing if *The Piano* had something bright to say about that investment but I don't see that it does. . . . To the extent that it comments on its own dynamic, it does so by an accumulation of winks and nods. . . . But the accumulation is just that, and it goes nowhere in particular" (22). To sustain this judgment, Clover, like

virtually all of the other commentators on the film, virtually ignores the role of the daughter.

6. I must confess to having been one of those who probably over-romanticized the girl's pre-Oedipal relation with the mother.

7. See Clover's excellent discussion of the resemblance of the story to that of the Christian martyr (21–22).

8. This symbolic reenactment of the mother's disappearance and return recalls, of course, Freud's discussion in *Beyond the Pleasure Principle* of the *fort/da* game (8–11).

NOTES TO CHAPTER THREE

1. See in particular, de Lauretis's response in *The Practice of Love* to a host of critics who, drawing on an important article by Jean Laplanche and Jean-Bertrand Pontalis, have argued that the reader of a book or the spectator of a movie takes up a variety of fantasy positions in relation to the text. Among these critics are Penley, Cowie, and Cora Kaplan. Kaplan's reading of *The Thorn Birds* makes a similar argument and takes issue with my point that in Harlequins the reader identifies almost exclusively with the heroine. I disagree with Kaplan as regards the older Harlequins, but, as I will be discussing, changes in the formula of romances do now facilitate more mobility on the part of the female romance reader. For an intelligent, if "postfeminist," discussion of shifting point of view in romances, see Kinsale.

2. See Greer's chapter on "Romance," 167–85.

3. Amy Garawitz brought this wonderful line to my attention.

4. See Adorno, and Gendron's comments on Adorno's essay.

5. On her web page Snoe acknowledges choosing the pseudonym to suggest the universal appeal of romance.

6. This comment was made during my phone interview with Beverly Jenkins.

NOTES TO CHAPTER FIVE

1. If one accepts the view that the blues was an authentic expression of black female sexuality, uncontaminated by white culture, then West's appropriation becomes one of simple theft. However, Ann duCille argues that the blues emerges out of a tradition of white minstrel shows and blackface vaudeville acts.

"A number of blues stars," she notes, "including Ma Rainey and Bessie Smith, began their careers touring in minstrel shows and tent performances that followed black migrant workers from harvest to harvest." That borders are crossed from both sides of the black white divide (although not with equal freedom or with equivalent gains in a racist society) is, I think, part of the point of the film. See duCille 164 n. 10.

2. I use the name Sandra to designate the film's persona.

3. Rather than simply dismissing Bernhard because she effects a substitution of race for gender (as if these two categories did not significantly overlap), white feminists would do well to use the film as an occasion to reflect on white feminism's own relation to blackface. I can only briefly suggest how such a reflection might proceed. White feminism as it evolved in the seventies and eighties was often accused of formulating a political theory and practice around white middle-class women's issues and then to have invited black women to join the ranks. Sometimes this theory sought to derive racism—and, it follows, its effects on identity formation—from sexism (Sandra influences Diana, not the other way around). "Racism is sexism extended," Shulamith Firestone wrote, or, in other words, "Without *me*" your experience of oppression would be nonexistent—or at least inexplicable (122). Most frequently, claims to commonality with blacks on the part of white feminist theorists of the last couple of decades were couched in the form of analogies. An impressive essay by Lisa Hogeland entitled "*Invisible Man* and Invisible Women: The Sex/Race Analogy of the 1970s" looks at the centrality of Ellison's metaphor of invisibility for racial oppression and suggests how protean cross-racial analogizing could be. In this case, white feminists' insistence that women in patriarchy shared a plight in common with African Americans shifted the terms of cross-racial masquerade from "black like me" to "invisible like me." Finally, some of the most subtle kinds of blackface adopted by white feminists can be found in certain anthropological writings of white feminists in the seventies. To take a single example (a highly interesting one in the context because it involves a woman who forcefully articulated the need for a shift in the alliance this book investigates [see Rubin "Thinking Sex"]): Gayle Rubin's powerful, influential, and by now classic, essay "The Traffic in Women," looks to various tribal cultures that have figured largely in anthropological studies in order to understand the laws that enforce the oppression of *all* women: Without the *Trobriand Islanders* we're nothing. A full analysis of the sex-race analogies that pervaded the writings of feminists (and not *only* white feminists) may be found in Hogeland's striking and finely nuanced essay referred to above.

4. For another analysis of the film that draws on the work of Rogin but reaches somewhat different conclusions, see Pellegrini (49–64).

5. Bernhard seems to have anticipated Philip Roth's discussion of Irving Berlin in *Operation Shylock*:

> I heard myself next praising the greatest Diasporist of all, the father of the new Diasporist movement, Irving Berlin. "People ask where I got the idea. Well, I got it listening to the radio. The radio was playing 'Easter Parade' and I thought, But this is Jewish genius on a par with the Ten Commandments. God gave Moses the Ten Commandments and then He gave to Irving Berlin 'Easter Parade' and 'White Christmas.' The two holidays that celebrate the divinity of Christ—the divinity that's the very heart of the Jewish rejection of Christianity—and what does Irving Berlin brilliantly do? He de-Christs them both! Easter he turns into a fashion show and Christmas into a holiday about snow. Gone is the gore and the murder of Christ—down with the crucifix and up with the bonnet! *He turns their religion into schlock.* But nicely! . . . If schlockified Christianity is Christianity cleansed of Jew hatred, then three cheers for schlock. If supplanting Jesus Christ with snow can enable my people to cozy up to Christmas, then let it snow, let it snow, let it snow! Do you see my point?" I took more pride, I told them, in "Easter Parade" than in the victory of the Six Day War, found more security in "White Christmas" than in the Israeli nuclear reactor. (157–58)

I am indebted to Maeera Shreiber for referring me to this wonderful passage.

6. In an extremely interesting article on interracial male relationships, Susan Fraiman discusses the way women operate as a kind of "switch point" in relations between men of different races. Here we see the black woman as a kind of switch point between two women, one a Jew, the other virtually an archetype of desirable white Christian femininity.

7. In a brilliant discussion of how race figures in white lesbian theory of the "queer" variety, Biddy Martin discusses how the woman of color functions as a sign of difference and suggests that this enables the white woman "to avoid any hint of identification, too much femininity, or perhaps too much lesbian feminism" (86).

8. Probyn draws on Valerie Smith's work, quoted here, to make the opposite point from the one I am making; she argues that Bernhard exemplifies Smith's point about black woman as signifying "material concerns" (156–57).

9. Of course, Madonna is another pop cultural figure who has aligned herself

politically with gay men—with black gay men, in particular, in her voguing phase.

NOTES TO CHAPTER SIX

1. See Sandra Richards for an illuminating discussion of Smith's early work.

2. Craig Owens provides the most cogent description of postmodern art that I've read. See especially "The Allegorical Impulse: Toward a Theory of Postmodern Art," Parts 1 and 2, 52–87.

3. For a discussion of the Ancient Greeks' view of woman as "the mimetic creature *par excellence*," see Zeitlin 79.

4. For an excellent application of Irigaray's reading of Plato to the issue of women and theatre, see Diamond.

5. It is extraordinary that in Felman's book, which explores the "crisis of witnessing" opened up by the Holocaust, Felman does not seem to consider the obscenity of our eagerness to consume Holocaust stories and images as part of this crisis.

6. See Mercer "Black Hair," for a discussion of how even before the Afro, black hair style, which appeared to imitate white styles, was actually more independent of these styles than later generations of African Americans tended to believe.

7. Unfortunately, Smith's decision to emphasize only the divisions between blacks and Jews around the Crown Heights incidents meant passing up an opportunity to reveal aspects of solidarity that actually existed at the time of the Crown Heights riots. Cornell West in a discussion of black-Jewish relations castigates the media for perpetuating the belief of most Americans "that the black community has been silent in the face of Yankel Rosenbaum's murder." The media "seem to have little interest in making known to the public the moral condemnations" emanating from black ministers in particular. West concludes, "Black anti-Semitism is not caused by media hype—yet it does sell more newspapers and turn out attention away from those black prophetic energies that give us some hope" (78–79).

8. Yet Smith could have chosen to include an interview with the female California Highway Patrol officer who broke the code of silence during the second, federal, trial of the police officers and cried on the witness stand over what she witnessed of the King beating—thus providing key testimony that resulted in the guilty verdict against Sergeant Koon and some of his men.

9. This character does not appear in the book *Twilight: Los Angeles, 1992*

which was apparently rushed into print before the Broadway version was completed. The book thus includes, in Smith's words, "some of the material . . . performed both in the play's Los Angeles version for the Taper and in the version presented at the New York Shakespeare Festival. It includes additional interviews that were not included in the stage versions" (xvii).

10. The Broadway version has Young speak at two different times, but only one part of the interview is included in the book. Young's tale of the horrors of plastic surgery does not appear in the printed text of *Twilight*.

11. This does not appear in the printed version.

NOTES TO CHAPTER SEVEN

1. See the chapter, "A Father Is Being Beaten" in my *Feminism without Women*.

2. As David James reminds us, though, *Coming Home*'s "unequivocal assertion that the invasion is *wrong* distinguishes it from all other films made in Hollywood" (James "Rock and Roll," 90).

3. One might be tempted to read the scene as satiric; yet the entire film presents its hero and its subject with such hysterical immediacy and apparent overidentification that it lacks the distance necessary for a satiric commentary.

4. This film too has been criticized for involving a "love story" which, writes Katzman, "digressed from the film's more interesting element, which was Dave's healing process" (21).

5. These are Laura Mulvey's terms in "Visual Pleasure and Narrative Cinema."

6. See Mulvey's "Visual Pleasure."

7. All quotations are from an interview I conducted with Nancy Savoca on November 30, 1994.

8. In addition to James "Rock and Roll," see Reitinger.

9. J. Hoberman speaks of the war's "bummer of a finale that's left us with a compulsion to remake, if not history, then at least the movie" (41).

NOTES TO CHAPTER EIGHT

1. That masculinity itself is at stake in defenses of the Western can be seen in the language of male hysteria used by some commentators on the genre. Thus, Tag Gallagher ends a spirited critique of his fellow critics with the observation that "genre criticism tends to delete the sensuous from the dialectic between sen-

suousness and logic that creates art; in doing so such criticism emasculates cinema of its aesthetic dimension and transforms it into an effete conceptual vehicle. Art becomes an academic exercise, pornography or propaganda, raped of its capability, its *aesthetic* capability, to give us knowledge of ourselves and our world" (214).

2. The highly dismissive blurb on *Posse* in Leonard Maltin's *Movie and Video Guide 1997* calls the film "conventional" and "politically correct" (meaning, I suppose, that it is not about white guys).

3. In her book on spectatorship, Judith Mayne draws on the work of feminist historian Linda Gordon in order to account for various positions that female spectators can take up in relation to the cinema. Mayne's discussion allows us to see why the Western, as described by Slotkin, is a perfect genre with which to consider the relation between women's history and mythmaking: "Gordon notes that contemporary women's history has moved in two different directions: the one, empirical in scope, seeking to uncover the truth of women's lives that have been obscured by the falsehoods of previous generations of historians; the other 'rejecting the possibility of objectivity,' defining history as myth-making and storytelling" (Gordon 22; Mayne 75).

4. "Many scenes seem incomplete or uncommented on" (Kronke 14).

5. The name is their Anglicized version of the man's Chinese name.

6. All quotations from Greenwald are taken from my interview of her which was published in *Film Quarterly* ("Our Heroes"). If no page number appears in the text, the reference is to a remark that was edited from the printed version.

7. This is the summary of the film given in Buscombe (24). Cook's lengthy entry on women in Buscombe's *BFI Companion to the Western,* some of which addresses the issue of cross-dressing, is by far the most interesting and complex discussion of women in the Western that I have read. It is, as well, one of the most astute discussions of the genre.

8. See also the 1935 film *Annie Oakley* directed by George Stevens and featuring Barbara Stanwyck in the title role. Henry Nash Smith sees in early Westerns a pronounced manifestation of "the nineteenth-century fondness for disguises on the stage and in fiction, a taste which encouraged actors to exploit mimicry and make-up as a form of sensationalism" (92).

9. Despite this statement, Limerick's sole intent in the eight scant pages she devotes to women in the West is to disabuse "anyone inclined to project a sentimentalized hope for women's essential solidarity in the past" (50).

10. Since I have been discussing both prostitutes and Asians, I should not

neglect to point out the especially oppressed status of the Chinese women who often served as prostitutes in the American West and were "controlled as virtual slaves" (Limerick 268). For a discussion of Chinese prostitutes and their relation to anti-Chinese sentiment and anti-Chinese labor agitation, see Cheng and Bonacich. For a lovely film about a Chinese woman who is sold into slavery in the Old West, see Nancy Kelly's *Thousand Pieces of Gold* (1990), which is based on a fictionalized biography written by Ruthanne Lum McCunn.

11. But there were also occasions on which white women acted out of a threat to their self-interest. As Julie Roy Jeffrey writes, "Chinese laundries . . . threatened women who made money by washing clothes. In Helena, Montana, the operation of Chinese laundries constituted such a serious threat that the town's laundresses warned the Chinese in a newspaper article to leave town or suffer the consequences" (123).

12. Richard Fung, however, seems to regard the film as something of a landmark in its treatment of Chinese men: "It is only recently that Chinese men have begun to function as regular sexual beings on the screen, mostly in films by white directors, like *The Lover, Dragon*, and *The Ballad of Little Jo*" (296). Is it significant that of these one, *The Lover*, was based on a novel by a woman (Duras) and another, *Ballad*, was written and directed by one?

13. It is true, however, that as John Cawelti points out, the hero also experiences an internal conflict, "a divided commitment" (53).

14. Thus, when Kolodny encounters a passage that speaks about the sublime in a novel about a woman who makes her home with the Shawnee, she labels as "atypical" a female character who says, "For the first time in my life I felt the force of liberty and the wild, sublime pleasures of an unshackled spirit. Every new thought which awoke in my heart in that deep wilderness was full of sublimity and wild poetic strength." Kolodny calls this character "an unwonted and morally ambiguous Eve at home in a wilderness usually reserved for the isolate American Adam" (202). For a different view from Kolodny's (or rather from the inferences Tompkins draws from Kolodny's text), one more consonant with my own, see Myres.

15. The instability of mechanisms of identification with respect to gender, sexuality, and race is being affirmed by scholars such as Diana Fuss. Well before Fuss, some feminist critics used psychoanalysis to stress the importance for feminism of the failures of identification. The point was to show how the construction of "woman" is fraught with perils that are in the interest of feminism to exacerbate in order to subvert the oppressive aspects of the construction. See, for example, Rose.

16. But see also Epstein and Straub. Numerous collections of essays that follow up on the insights of queer critics like Garber and Butler include Burroughs and Ehrenreich; and Senelick (the latter specifically deals with the performing arts).

17. Most of these critics, as Greenwald and I discussed in the interview, were, however, straight white men.

WORKS CITED

Abatemarco, Tony. "When Will the Taper's Power Brokers Wake Up?" *Los Angeles Times* 17 August 1992: F3.

Adair, Gilbert. *Hollywood's Vietnam: From "The Green Berets" to "Full Metal Jacket."* London: Heinemann, 1989.

Adorno, Theodor (with the assistance of George Simpson). "On Popular Music." *Studies in Philosophy and Social Science* 9.1 (1941): 17–48.

Allen, Richard. "The Transitional Object, Fetishism, and *The Piano.*" *Issues in Psychoanalytic Psychology* 17.2 (1995): 185–201.

Althofer, Beth. "*The Piano,* Or *Wuthering Heights* Revisited, Or Separation and Civilization through the Eyes of the (Girl) Child." *Psychoanalytic Review* 81.2 (Summer 1994): 339–42.

Apter, Emily. *Feminizing the Fetish: Psychoanalysis and Narrative Obsession in Turn-of-the-Century France.* Ithaca: Cornell UP, 1991.

Aufderheide, Pat. "Good Soldiers." *Seeing through the Movies.* Ed. Mark Crispin Miller. New York: Pantheon, 1990. 81–111.

Auster, Albert, and Leonard Quart. *How the War Was Remembered: Hollywood and Vietnam.* New York: Praeger, 1988.

Barr, Geraldine (with Ted Schwarz). *My Sister Roseanne: The True Story of Roseanne Barr Arnold.* New York: Birch Lane Press, 1994.

Barr, Roseanne. *Roseanne: My Life as a Woman.* New York: Harper and Row, 1989.

Bates, Milton J. "Men, Women and Vietnam." *America Rediscovered: Critical Essays on Literature and Film of the Vietnam War.* Ed. Owen W. Gilman, Jr., and Lorrie Smith. New York: Garland, 1990. 27–63.

Berg, Rick. "Losing Vietnam: Covering the War in an Age of Technology." *From Hanoi to Hollywood: The Vietnam War in American Film.* Ed. Linda Dittmar and Gene Michaud. New Brunswick: Rutgers UP, 1990. 41–68.

Berlant, Lauren, and Elizabeth Freeman. "Queer Nationality." *boundary 2* 19.1 (1992): 149–80.

Bhabha, Homi K. "Freedom's Basis in the Indeterminate." *October* 61 (Summer 1992): 46–57.

Bilbrough, Milo. Interview with Jane Campion. *Cinema Papers* (May 1993): 4–11.

Bourne, Jenny. "Homelands of the Mind: Jewish Feminism and Identity Politics." *Race and Class* 29 (1987): 1–24.

Boyarin, Daniel, and Jonathan Boyarin. "Diaspora: Generation and the Ground of Jewish Identity." *Critical Inquiry* 19.4 (Summer 1993): 693–725.

Braidotti, Rosi. *Nomadic Subjects: Embodiment and Sexual Difference in Contemporary Feminist Theory.* New York: Columbia UP, 1994.

Bray, Rosemary L. "Taking Sides against Ourselves." *New York Times Magazine* 17 November 1991: 56+.

Breuer, Josef, and Sigmund Freud. *Studies on Hysteria.* Trans. James Strachey. New York: Basic, 1957.

Brooks, Peter. *The Melodramatic Imagination: Balzac, Henry James, Melodrama and the Mode of Excess.* New Haven: Yale UP, 1976.

———. *Reading for the Plot: Design and Intention in Narrative.* New York: Random House-Vintage, 1984.

Brown, Georgia. "Say Anything." *Village Voice* 16 November 1993: 72.

———. "Sympathy for the Devil." *Village Voice* 13 April 1993: 49, 54.

Brown, Wendy. "Feminist Hesitations, Postmodern Exposures," *differences* 3.1 (1991): 63–84.

Brownmiller, Susan. *Against Our Will.* New York: Simon and Schuster, 1975.

Burroughs, Catherine B., and Jeffrey David Ehrenreich, eds. *Reading the Social Body.* Iowa City: U of Iowa P, 1993.

Buscombe, Edward. *The BFI Companion to the Western.* New York: Da Capo, 1988.

Butler, Judith. *Gender Trouble: Feminism and the Subversion of Identity.* New York: Routledge, 1989.

Campion, Jane. "Production Notes" for *The Piano.*

Carby, Hazel. "It Just Be's Dat Way Sometimes: The Sexual Politics of Women's Blues." *Radical America* 20 (1986): 6–13.

———. *Reconstructing Womanhood: The Emergence of the Afro-American Woman Novelist.* New York: Oxford UP, 1987.

Case, Sue-Ellen. "Toward a Butch-Femme Aesthetic." *Discourse* 11.1 (Fall-Winter 1988–89): 55–73.

Castle, Terry. *Clarissa's Ciphers: Meaning and Disruption of Richardson's Clarissa.* Ithaca: Cornell UP, 1982.

Cawelti, John. *The Six-Gun Mystique.* Bowling Green, Ohio: Bowling Green Popular Press, 1984.

Chen, Jack. *The Chinese of America*. San Francisco: Harper & Row, 1980.

Cheng, Lucie, and Edna Bonacich, eds. *Labor Immigration under Capitalism: Asian Workers in the United States before World War II*. Berkeley and Los Angeles: U of California P, 1984.

Cheung, King-Kok. "The Woman Warrior versus the Chinaman Pacific: Must a Chinese American Critic Choose between Feminism and Heroism?" *Conflicts in Feminism*. Ed. Marianne Hirsch and Evelyn Fox Keller. New York: Routledge, 1990. 234–51.

Chodorow, Nancy. *The Reproduction of Mothering: Psychoanalysis and the Sociology of Gender*. Berkeley and Los Angeles: U of California P, 1978.

Clark, Caitlin. *Baby It's You*. New York: Kensington-Precious Gem, 1997.

Clines, Francis X. "At Work with Anna Deavere Smith." *New York Times* 10 June 1992: C1+.

Clover, Carol. "Ecstatic Mutilation." *Threepenny Review* 15 (Spring 1994): 20–22.

———. *Men, Women, and Chainsaws: Gender and the Modern Horror Film*. Princeton: Princeton UP, 1992.

Cocks, Joan. "Augustine, Nietzsche, and Contemporary Body Politics." *differences* 3.1 (1991): 144–58.

Cook, Pam. "Women." In Buscombe 240–43.

Cornell, Drucilla. *Beyond Accommodation: Ethical Feminism, Deconstruction and the Law*. New York and London: Routledge, 1991.

Cowie, Elizabeth. "Fantasia." *mf* 9 (1984): 70–105.

Crane, Lynda L. "Romance Novel Readers: In Search of Feminist Change?" *Women's Studies* 23.3 (1994): 257–69.

Crenshaw, Kimberle. "Whose Story Is It, Anyway? Feminist and Anti-racist Appropriations of Anita Hill." *Race-ing Justice, En-gendering Power: Essays on Anita Hill, Clarence Thomas, and the Construction of Social Reality*. Ed. Toni Morrison. New York: Pantheon, 1992. 402–40.

de Beauvoir, Simone. *A Very Easy Death*. Trans. Patrick O'Brian. New York: Pantheon, 1965.

de Lauretis, Teresa. *Alice Doesn't: Feminism, Semiotics, Cinema*. Bloomington: Indiana UP, 1984.

———. *The Practice of Love: Lesbian Sexuality and Perverse Desire*. Bloomington: Indiana UP, 1994.

Deutsch, Sarah. "Landscape of Enclaves: Race Relations in the West, 1865–1990." *Under an Open Sky: Rethinking America's Western Past*. Ed. William Cronon, George Miles, and Jay Gitlin. New York: Norton, 1993. 110–31.

Diamond, Elin. "Mimesis, Mimicry, and the 'True-Real.'" *Acting Out*. Ann Arbor: Michigan UP, 1993. 363–82.

Doane Mary Ann. *The Desire to Desire: The Woman's Film of the 1940s*. Bloomington: Indiana UP.

————. "Film and the Masquerade: Theorising the Female Spectator." *Screen* 23.3–4 (September–October 1982): 74–87.

Douglas, Ann. "Soft-Porn Culture." *New Republic* 30 (August 1980): 25–29.

duCille, Ann. *The Coupling Convention: Sex, Text, and Tradition in Black Women's Fiction*. New York: Oxford UP, 1993.

Dugaw, Dianne. "Balladry's Female Warriors: Women, Warfare and Disguise in the Eighteenth Century." *Eighteenth-Century Life* 9.2 (January 1985): 1–20.

Duras, Marguerite. *The Lover*. London: Collins, 1985.

Eckman-Jadow, Judith. "*The Piano*, a Revisit to the 'Dark Continent': Response to Dr. Allen's Paper." *Issues in Psychoanalytic Psychology* 17.2 (1995): 202–16.

Epstein, Julia, and Kristina Straub, eds. *Body Guards: The Cultural Politics of Gender Ambiguity*. New York: Routledge, 1991.

Espen, Hal. "Kael Talks: Interview with Pauline Kael." *New Yorker* 21 March 1994: 134–42.

Fanon, Frantz. *Toward the African Revolution*. London: Writers and Readers, 1980.

Felman, Shoshana, and Dori Laub. *Testimony: Crises of Witnessing in Literature, Psychoanalysis, and History*. New York: Routledge, 1992.

Firestone, Shulamith. *The Dialectic of Sex*. New York: Morrow, 1970.

Foucault, Michel. *The History of Sexuality: An Introduction*. Vol. 1. Trans. Robert Hurley. New York: Pantheon, 1980.

Fraiman, Susan. "Geometries of Race and Gender: Eve Sedgwick, Spike Lee, and Charlayne Hunter-Gault." *Feminist Studies* 20.1 (Spring 1994): 67–84.

Fraser, Nancy. "Sex, Lies, and the Public Sphere: Some Reflections on the Confirmation of Clarence Thomas." *Critical Inquiry* 18.3 (1992): 595–612.

Freud, Sigmund. *Beyond the Pleasure Principle*. Trans. James Strachey. New York: Norton, 1961.

————. "Female Sexuality." Trans. Joan Riviere. *Sexuality and the Psychology of Love*. Ed. Philip Rieff. New York: Macmillan-Collier, 1963: 194–211.

————. "Mourning and Melancholia," *The Standard Edition of the Complete Psychological Works of Sigmund Freud*. Trans. James Strachey. Vol. 14. London: Hogarth Press, 1957. 243–58.

————. "The Relation of the Poet to Day-Dreaming." *On Creativity and the Unconscious: Papers on the Psychology of Art, Literature, Love, Religion*. Ed. Benjamin Nelson. New York: Harper & Row, 1958: 44–54.

—. "The Theme of the Three Caskets." *On Creativity and the Unconscious: Papers on the Psychology of Art, Literature, Love, Religion.* Ed. Benjamin Nelson. New York: Harper Torchbooks, 1958. 63–75.

—. "The Uncanny." *On Creativity and the Unconscious: Papers on the Psychology of Art, Literature, Love, Religion.* Ed. Benjamin Nelson. New York: Harper Torchbooks, 1958. 122–61.

Fung, Richard. "Burdens of Representation, Burdens of Responsibility." *Constructing Masculinities.* Ed. Maurice Berger, Brian Wallis, and Simon Watson. New York: Routledge, 1995. 291–98.

Fuss, Diana. *Identification Papers.* New York: Routledge, 1995.

Gallagher, Tag. "Shoot-Out at the Genre Corral: Problems in the 'Evolution' of the Western." *Film Genre Reader.* Ed. Barry Keith Grant. Austin: U of Texas P, 1986. 202–16.

Gallop, Jane. *The Daughter's Seduction: Feminism and Psychoanalysis.* Ithaca: Cornell UP, 1982.

Garber, Marjorie. *Vested Interests: Cross-Dressing and Cultural Anxiety.* New York: Routledge, 1992.

Gates, Henry Louis, Jr. *The Signifying Monkey: A Theory of Afro-American Literary Criticism.* New York: Oxford UP, 1988.

Gendron, Bernard. "Theodor Adorno Meets the Cadillacs." *Studies in Entertainment.* Ed. Tania Modleski. Bloomington: Indiana UP, 1984. 18–36.

Gilbert, Sandra M., and Susan Gubar. *The Madwoman in the Attic: The Woman Writer and the Nineteenth Century Literary Imagination.* New Haven: Yale UP, 1979.

Gilligan, Carol. *In a Different Voice.* Cambridge: Harvard UP, 1982.

Gordon, Linda. "What's New in Women's History?" *Feminist Studies/Critical Studies.* Ed. Teresa de Lauretis. Bloomington: Indiana UP, 1986. 20–30.

Goux, Jean-Joseph. *Symbolic Economies: After Marx and Freud.* Trans. Jennifer Curtiss Gage. Ithaca: Cornell UP, 1990.

Greer, Germaine. *The Female Eunuch.* New York: McGraw-Hill, 1970.

Habermas, Jurgen. *Knowledge and Human Interests.* Boston: Beacon, 1971.

Hellman, John. *American Myth and the Legacy of Vietnam.* New York: Columbia UP, 1986.

Hoberman, J. "America Dearest." *American Film* 13.7 (May 1988): 39–45.

Hogeland, Lisa. "*Invisible Man* and Invisible Women: The Sex/Race Analogy of the 1970s," forthcoming *Women's History Review.*

hooks, bell. *Black Looks: Race and Representation.* Boston: South End Press, 1992.

Howard, Linda. *Heart of Fire.* New York: Pocket Star Books, 1993.

217

Irigaray, Luce. *Speculum of the Other Woman*. Trans. Gillian C.Gill. Ithaca: Cornell UP, 1985.

————. *This Sex Which Is Not One*. Trans. Catherine Porter. Ithaca: Cornell UP, 1985.

Ivanov, Andrea. "Sexual Parody in American Comedic Film and Literature, 1925–1958." Ph.D. dissertation, U. of Southern California, 1994.

Jacobs, Harriet A. *Incidents in the Life of a Slave Girl*. Cambridge: Harvard UP, 1987.

Jacobus, Mary. Review of *The Madwoman in the Attic: The Woman Writer and the Nineteenth-Century Imagination*, by Sandra M. Gilbert and Susan Gubar. *Signs* 3.1 (Spring 1981): 517–22.

James, David. Rock and Roll in Representations of the Invasion of Vietnam." *Representations* 29 (Winter 1990): 78–98.

————. "The Vietnam War and American Music." *The Vietnam War and American Culture*. Ed. John Carlos Rowe and Rick Berg. New York: Columbia UP, 1991. 226–54.

Jeffords, Susan. *The Remasculinization of America: Gender and the Vietnam War*. Bloomington: Indiana UP, 1989.

Jeffrey, Julie Roy. *Frontier Women: The Trans-Mississippi West, 1840–1880*. New York: Hill & Wang, 1979.

Jenkins, Beverly. *Indigo*. New York: Avon, 1996.

————. Phone Interview. 15 September 1997.

Johnson, Barbara. "No Short Cuts to Democracy." *Fires in the Mirror: Essays and Teaching Strategies*. Ed. Pamela Benson. Boston: WGBH Educational Print and Outreach, 1993. 9–11.

Jones, Amy Holden. "A 'Proposal' Intended for People, Not for Critics."*Los Angeles Times* 19 April 1993: F3.

Joyce, Brenda. *Violet Fire*. New York: Avon, 1989.

Kamuf, Peggy. "Replacing Feminist Criticism." *Diacritics* 12.2 (Summer 1982): 42–47.

Kaplan, Carla. *The Erotics of Talk: Women's Writing and Feminist Paradigms*. New York: Oxford UP, 1996.

Kaplan, Cora. "*The Thorn Birds*: Fiction, Fantasy, Femininity." *Formations of Fantasy*. Ed. Victor Burgin, James Donald and Cora Kaplan. London: Methuen, 1986. 142–66.

Katzman, Jason. "From Outcast to Cliché: How Film Shaped, Warped and Developed the Image of the Vietnam Veteran, 1967–90." *Journal of American Culture* 16.1 (Spring 1993): 7–24.

218

Kinsale, Laura. "The Androgynous Reader: Point of View in the Romance." *Dangerous Men and Adventurous Women: Romance Writers on the Appeal of the Romance.* Ed. Jayne Ann Krentz. Philadelphia: U of Pennsylvania P, 1992. 31–44.

Kitses, Jim. *Horizons West.* Bloomington: Indiana UP, 1970.

Klawans, Stuart. "*The Piano.*" *The Nation* 6 December 1993: 704–6.

Klein, Joe. "Deadly Metaphors." *New York* 9 September 1991: 26–29.

Kolodny, Annette. *The Land before Her: Fantasy and Experience of the American Frontiers, 1630–1860.* Chapel Hill: University of North Carolina Press, 1984.

Kroll, Jack. "A Woman for All Seasons." *Newsweek* 1 June 1992: 74.

———. "Fire in the City of Angels." *Newsweek* 28 June 1993: 62–63.

Kronke, David. "*The Ballad of Little Jo.*" *Hollywood Reporter,* 18 August 93: 7+.

Lacoue-Labarthe, Philippe. *Typography: Mimesis, Philosophy, Politics.* Cambridge: Harvard UP, 1989.

Lahr, John. "Under the Skin." *New Yorker* 28 June 1993: 90–94.

Lane, Anthony. "Sheet Music." *New Yorker* 29 November 1993: 148–51.

Laplanche, Jean, and Jean-Bertrand Pontalis. "Fantasy and the Origins of Sexuality." *Formations of Fantasy.* Ed. Victor Burgin, James Donald, and Cora Kaplan. London: Methuen, 1986. 5–34.

Levy, Emmanuel. "*The Ballad of Little Jo.*" *Daily Variety* 17 August 1993: 2+.

Limerick, Patricia Nelson. *The Legacy of Conquest: The Unbroken Past of the American West.* New York: Norton, 1987.

Logan, Andy. "Around City Hall." *New Yorker* 23 September 1991: 102–8.

Lott, Eric. *Love and Theft: Blackface Minstrelsy and the American Working Class.* New York: Oxford UP, 1993.

Lowell, Elizabeth. *Only Love.* New York: Avon, 1995.

Lyotard, Jean-François. *The Postmodern Condition: A Report on Knowledge.* Trans. Geoff Bennington and Brian Massumi. Minneapolis: U of Minnesota P, 1984.

MacKinnon, Catharine. *Feminism Unmodified: Discourses on Life and Law.* Cambridge: Harvard UP, 1987.

Mailer, Norman. "The White Negro." *Advertisements for Myself.* New York: Putnam, 1959. 311–31.

Maltin, Leonard. *Movie and Video Guide 1997.* New York: Signet, 1997. 1053.

Marshall, Paule. *Brown Girl, Brownstones.* New York: Feminist Press, 1981.

Martin, Andrew. *Reception of War: Vietnam in American Culture.* Norman, OK: U of Oklahoma P, 1993.

Martin, Biddy. *Femininity Played Straight: The Significance of Being Lesbian.* New York: Routledge, 1996.

Martin, Biddy, and Chandra Mohanty. "Feminist Politics: What's Home Got to Do with It?" *Feminist Studies/Critical Studies*. Bloomington: Indiana UP, 1986. 191–212.

Martin, Nancy. *Fortune's Cookie*. New York: Silhouette, 1993.

Mayne, Judith. *Cinema and Spectatorship*. New York: Routledge, 1993.

McCunn, Ruthanne Lum. *Thousand Pieces of Gold*. Boston: Beacon, 1988.

Mercer, Kobena. "Black Hair/Style Politics." *New Formations* 3 (Winter 1987): 33–55.

————. "Skin Head Sex Thing: Racial Difference and the Homoerotic Imaginary." *How Do I Look? Queer Film and Video*. Ed. Bad Object Choices. Seattle: Bay Press, 1991. 169–210.

Michie, Helena. *Sororophobia: Differences among Women in Literature and Culture*. New York: Oxford UP, 1992.

Miller, Nancy K. "Emphasis Added: Plots and Plausibilities in Women's Fiction." *PMLA* 96.1 (1981): 36–48.

————. *Getting Personal: Feminist Occasions and Other Autobiographical Acts*. New York: Routledge, 1991.

————. "The Text's Heroine: A Feminist Critic and Her Fictions." *diacritics* 12.2 (Summer 1982): 48–53.

Modleski, Tania. *Feminism without Women: Culture and Criticism in a "Postfeminist" Age*. New York: Routledge, 1991.

————. *Loving with a Vengeance: Mass-Produced Fantasies for Women*. New York: Methuen, 1984.

————. "Our Heroes Have Sometimes Been Cowgirls—an Interview with Maggie Greenwald." *Film Quarterly* 49.2 (Winter 1995–96): 2–11.

Moore, Suzanne. "Getting a Bit of the Other: The Pimps of Postmodernism." *Male Order: Unwrapping Masculinity*. Ed. Rowena Chapman and Jonathan Rutherford. London: Laurence and Wishart, 1988. 165–92.

Moraga, Cherrie, and Gloria Anzaldua. *This Bridge Called My Back: Writings by Radical Women of Color*. Watertown, MA: Persephone, 1981.

Morris, Meaghan. "Banality in Cultural Studies." *Discourse* 10.2 (Spring-Summer 1988): 3–29.

Morrison, Toni, ed. *Race-ing Justice, En-gendering Power: Essays on Anita Hill, Clarence Thomas, and the Construction of Social Reality*. New York: Pantheon, 1992.

Mulvey, Laura. "Afterthoughts on 'Visual Pleasure and Narrative Cinema' Inspired by *Duel in the Sun*." *Feminism and Film Theory*. Ed. Constance Penley. New York: Routledge, 1988. 69–79.

————. "Visual Pleasure and Narrative Cinema." *Movies and Methods*. Vol. 2. Ed. Bill Nichols. Berkeley: U of California P, 1985. 303–15.

Mussell, Kay. "Where's Love Gone? Transformations in the Romance Genre." *Paradoxa* 3.1–2 (1997): 3–15.

Myres, Sandra L. *Westering Women and the Frontier Experience 1800–1915*. Albuquerque: U of New Mexico P, 1982.

Noel, Peter. "Crown Heights Burning: Rage, Race, and the Politics of Resistance." *Village Voice* 3 September 1991: 37–41.

Owens, Craig. *Beyond Recognition: Representation, Power and Culture*. Ed. Scott Bryson, Barbara Kruger, Lynne Tillman, and Jane Weinstock. Berkeley and Los Angeles: U of California P, 1992.

Pellegrini, Ann. *Performance Anxieties: Staging Psychoanalysis, Staging Race* New York: Routledge, 1997.

Penley, Constance. "Time Travel, the Primal Scene, and the Critical Dystopia." *Fantasy and the Cinema*. Ed. James Donald. London: The British Film Institute, 1989. 192–212.

Pettit, Sarah. "The Lesbian Vanishes: Sandra Bernhard and Her Big Joke on the Sisterhood." *Outweek* 81 (January 16, 1991): 36–42.

Phillips, Susan Elizabeth. *It Had to Be You*. New York: Avon, 1994.

————. *Nobody's Baby but Mine*. New York: Avon, 1997.

Prendergast, Christopher. *The Order of Mimesis: Balzac, Stendhal, Nerval, Flaubert*. Cambridge: Cambridge UP, 1986.

Probyn, Elspeth. *Sexing the Self: Gendered Positions in Cultural Studies*. London: Routledge, 1993.

Radway, Janice. *Reading the Romance*. Chapel Hill: U of North Carolina P, 1994.

Rainer, Peter. "*Ballad of Little Jo*: A Revisionist Western." *Los Angeles Times* 10 September 1993: F8.

Reitinger, Douglas W. "Paint It Black: Rock Music and Vietnam War Films." *Journal of American Culture* 15.3 (Fall 1992): 53–59.

Resnik, Judith, and Carolyn Heilbrun. "Convergences: Law, Literature, and Feminism." *Yale Law Journal* 99.8 (1990): 1913–56.

Rich, Adrienne. *Of Woman Born: Motherhood as Experience and Institution*. New York: Norton, 1995.

Rich, B. Ruby. "At Home on the Range." *Sight and Sound* 3 November 1993: 18.

Rich, Frank. "Diversities of America in One-Person Shows." *New York Times* 15 May 1992: C1+.

Richards, David. "And Now, a Word from Off Broadway." *New York Times* 17 May 1992: H5+.

221

Richards, Sandra L. "Caught in the Act of Social Definition: *On the Road* with Anna Deavere Smith." *Acting Out: Feminist Performances.* Ed. Lynda Hart and Peggy Phelan: Ann Arbor: Michigan UP, 1993. 35–54.

Robinson, Suzanne. *Lady Dangerous.* New York: Bantam, 1994.

Rodowick, D. N. "The Difficulty of Difference." *Wide Angle* 5.1 (1982): 4–15.

Rogin, Michael. "Blackface, White Noise: The Jewish Jazz Singer Finds His Voice." *Critical Inquiry* 18.3 (Spring 1992): 417–53.

Rose, Jacqueline. *Sexuality in the Field of Vision.* London: Verso, 1986.

Ross, Andrew. "The Private Parts of Justice." *Race-ing Justice, En-gendering Power: Essays on Anita Hill, Clarence Thomas, and the Construction of Social Reality.* New York: Pantheon, 1992. 40–60.

Rothstein, Edward. "A Piano as Salvation, Temptation, and Star." *New York Times* 4 January 1994: C15+.

Rubin, Gayle. "Thinking Sex: Notes for a Radical Theory of the Politics of Sexuality." *Pleasure and Danger: Exploring Female Sexuality.* Ed. Carole S. Vance. Boston: Routledge and Kegan Paul, 1984. 267–319.

———. "The Traffic in Women: Notes Toward a Political Economy of Sex." *Toward an Anthropology of Women.* Ed. Rayna Reiter. New York: Monthly Review Press, 1975. 157–210.

Russo, Mary. *The Female Grotesque: Risk, Excess and Modernity.* New York: Routledge, 1994.

Schiesari, Juliana. *The Gendering of Melancholia: Feminism, Psychoanalysis, and the Symbolics of Loss in Renaissance Literature.* Ithaca: Cornell UP, 1992.

Sedgwick, Eve Kosofsky. *Epistemology of the Closet.* Berkeley: U of California P, 1990.

———. "Gosh, Boy George, You Must Be Awfully Secure in Your Maculinity!" *Constructing Masculinities.* Ed. Maurice Berger, Brian Wallis, and Simon Watson. New York: Routledge, 1995. 11–20.

Senelick, Laurence, ed. *Gender in Performance: The Presentation of Difference in the Performing Arts.* Hanover, N.H., and London: UP of New England, 1992.

Sheinbaum, Stanley K. "One-Woman Show Has Message for All of Us." *Los Angeles Times* 5 July 1993: F3.

Shirley, Don. "Tonys Cheer Taper, What's It Mean?" *Los Angeles Times* 18 May 1994: F1+.

Silverman, Kaja. *Male Subjectivity at the Margins.* New York: Routledge, 1992.

Slotkin, Richard. *Gunfighter Nation: The Myth of the Frontier in Twentieth-Century America.* New York: Harper, 1992.

Smith, Anna Deavere. *Fires in the Mirror.* New York: Doubleday,1993.

————. *Twilight: Los Angeles, 1992*. New York: Doubleday, 1994.

Smith, Henry Nash. *Virgin Land: The American West as Symbol and Myth*. Cambridge: Harvard UP, 1950.

Smith, Jennifer Crusie. "Romancing Reality: The Power of Romance to Reinforce and Re-vision the Real." *Paradoxa* 3.1–2 (1997): 81–93.

Smith, Valerie. "Black Feminist Theory and the Representation of the 'Other.'" *Changing Our Own Words: Essays in Criticism, Theory, and Writing by Black Women*. Ed. Cheryl A. Wall. New Brunswick: Rutgers UP, 1987. 38–57.

Snitow, Ann Barr. "Mass-Market Romances: Pornography for Women Is Different." *Radical History Review* 19 (1979). 141–61.

Snoe, Eboni. *The Passion Ruby*. New York: Kensington Publishing-Pinnacle, 1995.

Spivak, Gayatri Chakravorty. "Acting Bits/Identity Talk." *Critical Inquiry* 18.4 (Summer 1992): 770–803.

Stansell, Christine. "White Feminists and Black Realities: The Politics of Authenticity." *Race-ing Justice, En-gendering Power: Essays on Anita Hill, Clarence Thomas, and the Construction of Social Reality*. New York: Pantheon, 1992. 251–68.

Stovall, Thomas G. Letter to the Editor. *People* 2 December 1991: 5.

Thomas, Virginia Lamp. Interview. "Breaking Silence." *People* 11 November 1991: 108–16.

Tompkins, Jane. "Sentimental Power: *Uncle Tom's Cabin* and the Politics of Literary History." *The New Feminist Criticism*. Ed. Elaine Showalter. New York: Pantheon, 1984. 81–104.

————. *West of Everything; The Inner Life of the Westerns*. New York: Oxford UP, 1992.

Walker, Alice. Letter to the Editor. *People* 2 December 1991: 5.

Walton, Jean. "Sandra Bernhard: Lesbian Postmodern or Modern Postlesbian?" *The Lesbian Postmodern*. Ed. Laura Doane. New York: Columbia UP, 1994. 244–61.

Warner, William Beatty. *Reading Clarissa: The Struggles of Interpretation*. New Haven: Yale UP, 1979.

Washington, Mary Helen. Afterword. *Brown Girl, Brownstones*. By Paule Marshall. New York: The Feminist Press, 1981. 311–24.

West, Cornell. *Race Matters*. Boston: Beacon, 1993.

White, Richard. "Little Jo." *Gateway Heritage* 14.3 (1993–94): 63–64.

————. "Race Relations in the American West." *American Quarterly* 38.3 (1986): 397–416.

———. *The Roots of Dependency: Subsistence, Environment, and Social Change among the Choctaws, Pawnees, and Navajos.* Lincoln: U of Nebraska P, 1983.

Whitman, Christina Brooks. "Feminist Jurisprudence." *Feminist Studies* 17.3 (1991): 493–508.

Williams, Patricia J. *The Alchemy of Race and Rights.* Cambridge: Harvard UP, 1991.

Williams, Tony. "Narrative Patterns and Mythic Trajectories in Mid-1980s Vietnam Movies." *Inventing Vietnam: The War in Film and Television.* Ed. Michael Anderegg. Philadelphia: Temple UP, 1991. 114–39.

Wood, Daniel B. "Many Voices in One Mouth." *Christian Science Monitor* 8 July 1993: 12.

Woolf, Virginia. *A Room of One's Own.* New York: Harcourt, 1957.

Wright, Damon. "A Seance with History". *New York Times* 10 May 1992: H14.

Wright, Richard. *Native Son.* New York: Harper, 1969.

Yellin, Jean Fagin. Introduction to Harriet A. Jacobs. *Incidents in the Life of a Slave Girl.* Cambridge: Harvard UP, 1987. xviii–xix.

Zeitlin, Froma I. "Playing the Other: Theater, Theatricality and the Feminine in Ancient Greek Drama," *Representations* 2 (1985): 63–94.

INDEX OF FILMS

INDEX

Abortion rights, 62, 66n, 201n. 1
(intro.); and feminism, 14
Adair, Gilbert, 127
Adorno, T. W., 57, 68, 204n. 4
Affirmative action, 26; and Blacks and
Jews, 115–116; and feminism, 20;
and feminist legal scholars, 25–26
African American audience: and *Without You I'm Nothing*, 84–85, 88, 94
African American culture: white appropriation of, 81, 85, 96, 207n. 6
African American romance novelists,
59. *See also* Jenkins, Beverly
African American ("multicultural") romances, 58; African American identity in, 59
African Americans: and feminism, 99;
and mainstream culture, 85; and
popular culture, 150. *See also* Smith,
Anna Deavere
Allison, Dorothy, 180
Amis, Suzy: in *The Ballad of Little Jo*,
154, 156, 158, 169, 170
Annie Oakley, 209n. 8
Anti-war activity, 130, 137; and feminism, 131–132
Anzaldua, Gloria, 6
Apocalypse Now, 128
Apter, Emily, 40
Arnold, Tom, 97, 99
Aufderheide, Pat, 130
Austen, Jane, 53
Auster, Albert, 128
Authenticity, 17, 42, 97; challenges

to, 118–119; and ethnicity, 114; and
race, 20–21; and the Western, 151
Autobiography, 24, 88, 179, 203n. 4.
See also Personal criticism

"Bad object," 183
Ballad of Josie, The, 160
Ballad of Little Jo, The (Greenwald),
10, Ch. 8, 210n. 12. *See also* Authenticity; Cross-dressing; Fantasy;
Greenwald, Maggie; Identity; Masquerade; Oppression, shared experience of; Race; Racial stereotypes;
Racism; Rape; Spectator; Transvestism; Western(s); Women
Barr, Geraldine, 99; *My Sister Roseanne*,
97–98
Barr, Roseanne. *See* Roseanne (Barr)
Bates, Milton J., 145
Beatty, Warren, 84, 89
Beauvoir, Simone de, 68, 190, 192,
199
Benjamin, Walter, 68
Berg, Rick, 131
Berlant, Lauren, 91, 95
Berlin, Irving, 206n. 5
Bernhard, Sandra, 11, Ch. 5, 205n. 3,
206n. 5, 206n. 8. *See also* African
American audience; Authenticity;
Blackface; Black women; Fantasy;
Identity; Madonna; Masquerade;
Mimicry; Minstrelsy; Parody; Queer
theory; *Without You I'm Nothing*
Bestiality, in *The Piano*, 40

226

ABOUT THE AUTHOR

TANIA MODLESKI is Florence R. Scott Professor of English at the University of Southern California. She is the author of *Loving with a Vengeance*, *The Women who Knew Too Much*, and *Feminism without Women*.